Happiness Is A Choice
for Teens

**PAUL MEIER, M.D., JAN MEIER,
AND THEIR CHILDREN**

A
JANET
THOMA
BOOK

THOMAS NELSON PUBLISHERS
Nashville • Atlanta • London • Vancouver
Printed in the United States of America

Printed in the United States of America.

dedication

I studied adolescent psychiatry in medical school as well as during my psychiatry residency at Duke University, and I'm thankful for my education. But I learned a lot more about helping teens to get the most out of life by 1) having been a teenager once myself; 2) raising six children through their teen years with my wife wife, Jan; and 3) by personally treating hundreds of teens, some for a period of several years, in my own psychiatric practice.

Now I am the medical director of more than a hundred New Life Clinics internationally and have the responsibility of overseeing the care of more than 1,000 teenagers each week through the several hundred therapists who work at our adolescent hospital units, day hospital units, and outpatient clinics.

And so my family and I want to dedicate this book to all teenagers—past, present, and future—who have the courage to seek out help during those tough times in life.

—Paul Meier, M.D.
Dallas, Texas

contents

Chapter 1   Inner Reflections   1
Chapter 2   Who, Me? Depressed? Naaa!   7
Chapter 3   Brain Juice!   17
Chapter 4   Good Grief, Charlie Brown!   35
Chapter 5   The Problem of Projection   44
Chapter 6   The Roots of the Problem   56
Chapter 7   Why Not End It All?   68
Chapter 8   Obsessed   79
Chapter 9   Control   91
Chapter 10   Histrionics   104
Chapter 11   Paranoia and Other Traits   112
Chapter 12   Stressors and Stressees   118
Chapter 13   Other Stressor-Depressors   128
Chapter 14   Guilt and Shame   140
Chapter 15   Pregnancy   150
Chapter 16   Guideline One: Make Time for Work and Play   167
Chapter 17   Guideline Two: Develop Family Relationships   181
Chapter 18   Guideline Three: Build Friendships   193
Chapter 19   Guideline Four: Do Something Nice Frequently   200
Chapter 20   Guideline Five: Commit Yourself Daily
               to Glorifying Christ   207
Chapter 21   Guideline Six: Spend Time Daily in the Word   211
Chapter 22   Guideline Seven: Get Rid of Grudges Daily   219
Chapter 23   High Anxiety   231
Chapter 24   What About Medication and Hospitalization?   241
Chapter 25   Stuff to Bank On   251
Chapter 26   Triumphing in a Haywire World   259
Chapter 27   A Final Word   274
               Study Guide   279
Appendix   Personality Traits of Depressed Persons   315
               Notes   323
               About the Authors   329

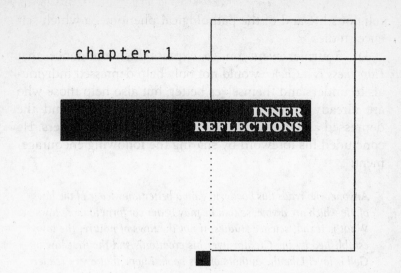

chapter 1

INNER REFLECTIONS

On June 23, 1978, a very wise, loving, grandfatherly psychiatrist from Geneva, Switzerland, wrote the foreword to our book, *Happiness Is a Choice*.[1] I was thrilled that he did so, because I had read all of his books, books that have helped millions throughout Europe and America.

Unfortunately for us and fortunately for the citizens of heaven, Dr. Paul Tournier died of old age a few years back. I'm sure he's partying right now with the millions he helped bring there.

Back in the 1970s—when Tournier was going strong—spirituality was a taboo subject among people who considered themselves intellectuals, like scientists, physicians, and especially psychiatrists. Those same proud scientists now admit the overwhelming scientific research that proves the value of true spirituality for our mental health and even our physical well-being.[2]

Paul Tournier had the guts way back in the seventies to say that the "relationships between spiritual life and psychological health are subtle and delicate. They must be envisioned in their complexity. We must take account of the importance both of religious life and of the pathological phenomena which science studies."[3]

Dr. Tournier went on to express his confidence that *Happiness Is a Choice* would not only help depressed individuals to understand themselves better, but also help those who are already healthy and happy to better understand the depressed and then reach out in love to help their peers. He concluded his foreword by sharing the following encouragement:

> *Anyone who reads this book will gain a better knowledge of the laws of life which are divine, so that he may better conform to those laws. What is it that science studies, if not the laws of nature, the laws established by the Creator over his creation? And the first law of God is love! Like the authors of this book, I hope that every reader finds in these pages an opportunity to approach both God and good health.*[4]

Geneva, June 23, 1978
Paul Tournier

Happiness Is a Choice, which was revised in 1994, has gone on since 1978 to help hundreds of thousands of readers, and continues to help thousands of new readers, even now.

But since I co-authored that book back in the seventies, my wife and I have successfully nurtured six children who have all grown up, gone to college, and left us with a peaceful empty nest. My wife, Jan, is a marriage and family therapist, and my oldest daughter, Cheryl, is currently a graduate student in psychology at Rosemeade, in La Mirada, California. She has already published a helpful book for teens entitled *I Know Just How You Feel*.[5]

And so, with all of this childrearing experience behind us, including the many inadvertent mistakes we've all made along the way, and with the varied growing-up experiences our children have had, *Happiness Is a Choice for Teens* has been born as a family project. Two of our daughters-in-law have even helped. We've decided to be vulnerable, discuss many of our own personal struggles to obtain joyful meaning in life, and still include the valuable scientific and spiritual principles from the original version that have helped so many.

Our youngest daughter went through a clinical depression at the age of fourteen, largely due to accidental mistakes I was making at the time in spite of all my medical, psychiatric, and theological education and what I thought were my best efforts to be a great dad. She and I both share in this book what went wrong and *what went right* to lead her to successful recovery.

If you think this book will help your parents or your counselors to understand you better, then go ahead and let them read it too. But it was written for you—the teenagers of this world—by a large number of young persons in their teens and twenties (our children and daughters-in-law), by a therapist/mom in her fifties (Jan), and by a psychiatrist/dad in his fifties (myself).

· THE TERRIFYING LEAP

The teen years, for most human beings, are the hardest of life. At twelve you're still considered a child. You are highly dependent on your parents, even thinking that they are brilliantly correct about most things in life (which, in reality, they may or may not be). By sixteen, just four short years later, you have grown into a young adult capable of reproduction. You have undergone a miraculous and amazing transformation physically, hormonally, psychologically, and spiritually.

At sixteen you're pretty sure you know everything and your parents know absolutely nothing. You've probably developed a keen insight into all of their conscious and unconscious faults, but you don't yet have enough insight into your own. By now your folks have keen insights into most or all of your conscious and unconscious shortcomings but not enough insight into their own personal faults and dynamics. So you go through the usual stages of self-righteous rejection of each other that everyone calls "teenage rebellion."

Some kids never go through even the slightest hint of rebellion. Those are the ones we psychiatrists worry about the most, because they are more likely to commit suicide as a result of stuffing their anger. Stuffing anger—that is, refusing to let it erupt when it has to—causes the most important chemical in the brain, serotonin, to get low, and low serotonin, we now know, causes the vast majority of clinical depressions. This vital brain chemical will be discussed in simple terms several times throughout this book because it is so important.

Suicide is the second leading cause of death in teens, next to accidents. And some accidents, we know, are also covered up suicides.

················· **IMPROVING THE RAW DEALS**
■

We all start out thinking life will be easy, and why not? Mom is always there for us, giving us hugs, milk, fellowship, and the comforts of life. Fifty percent of our basic personalities, including our attitude about life itself, are formed by our third birthday. Eighty-five percent of our personalities and attitudes are formed by our sixth birthday. But no matter how old we are, thank God, we can—with His help—change.

You see, three things determine how we turn out: *Genes, our environment*, and *choices we make*. Luckily, with proper guidance and Heavenly help, our choices can, over a period of time, pretty much make up for the raw deals we may have gotten from our genes or environment.

Personalities are kind of like antique furniture. Antique furniture is actually more valuable if it has scuff marks on it from ages of wear and tear. Some antique store owners have been known to rough up their pieces with chains to make them look more mature and valuable. And sometimes the most wonderful adults we know came from very rough backgrounds but made excellent choices to correct for defects in their genes or early childhood environment.

4

The teen years are especially difficult because that is the stage of life in which most individuals wake up to the reality that *life is tough*. When wise teenagers discover that the rest of their lives will require a great deal of hard work physically, emotionally, and spiritually in order to survive, they grieve their losses. They've lost their youthful, naive perspective and their extreme childish dependence on parents to take care of them and make the hard decisions for them.

Wise teenagers then take a deep and reflective journey within themselves and, with the help and wisdom of the God who created them in His image in the first place, make responsible decisions and conquer life. Oh sure, they make wrong decisions as well as right decisions. We all do. But they learn maturity from the wrong ones and grow more and more confident as they find themselves making right ones.

Unfortunately, "broad is the way that leads to destruction," and "narrow . . . is the way which leads to life."[6] Far too many kids take that broad road—heavy alcohol use, drugs, sex, unwholesome relationships with peers, and law-breaking. They find themselves using other people for selfish desires even though it lowers their own self-esteem and ultimately wrecks friendships. They fearfully yield to peer pressures, thinking they're holding onto their friends, and find instead spiritual and emotional loneliness, depression, and possibly even death. They fall into the painful pit of "nobodyness."

Equally unfortunate, too few kids choose the narrow road when they come to that necessary fork—that fork in the road that forces each individual to make a choice to run away from responsibility and toward escapism or to accept and learn to conquer personal responsibility with the help of God who designed us. This is the narrow road.

We've treated thousands of teenagers over the years in the Minirth Meier New Life Clinics scattered all over America and Canada. So I fully realize that most kids aren't purposely choosing misery for themselves. But most of them found it anyway, and quite accidentally.

You see, the world lies. The world tells you that the broad road will give you happiness. It never delivers. Never. The narrow path, on the other hand, requires hard work, tough choices, and sometimes finding new friends and new work. But faithfulness to the narrow path brings fulfillment, peace, and abundant joy.

The loving psychiatrist, Dr. Paul Tournier, took the narrow path. He died at a ripe old age with peace in his heart and a smile on his face, having made a contribution to society, and looking forward to eternity in Heaven.

Which road will you take? Don't decide yet! Read this book first, cover to cover and you will realize the truth: that *Happiness Is a Choice for Teens.*

Dallas, October 1996
Paul Meier, M.D.

6

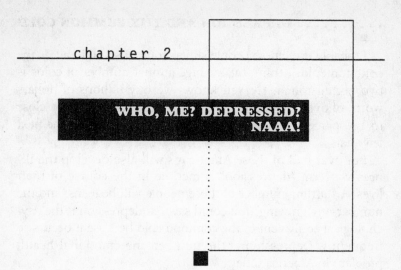

chapter 2

WHO, ME? DEPRESSED? NAAA!

When Kathy's parents divorced and her mom remarried ("How could she?" Kathy roared. "He's a world-class jerk with the IQ of pond scum!"), Kathy, a high school junior, sank into a depression like you wouldn't believe. Her grades went down the tubes, she quit laughing, and she didn't seem to mind snapping at her best friends.

Everyone understood what was wrong, especially when her new stepfather kicked her out of the house for being "spoiled and insolent." His words. Even when she kept shoving them away, her friends hovered around her, on the lookout for the first hint of suicidal tendencies.

And then one day, their classmate Carlton drove off the road into a pine tree—hit it square. He was going nearly sixty when he left the asphalt and he must have kept the gas pedal floored to the very end, because his rear wheels dug in up to the axles. Carlton had always been a quiet kid, moody sometimes, with so-so grades and the kind of flat, whiny personality girls weren't interested in dating.

With the support of her friends and teachers, Kathy eventually made it out to the other side of her illness. No one had ever even realized that Carlton had a problem.

.... DEPRESSION AND THE COMMON COLD
■

Probably the illness people suffer from most, all in all, is the common cold. I think the average annual number of colds is two per customer. Heaven knows we buy billions of dollars worth of over-the-counter cold remedies each year. Very close to 100 percent of Americans will catch a cold within the next few years.

But over half of those Americans will also develop the illness we term "depression" sometime in the course of their lives. A startling number of those people will be teens, and the numbers are growing. You could say that depression is the psychological equivalent of the common cold because it occurs so frequently. Depression is the number one emotional health problem in America today.

But there are differences between a cold and depression. If you catch cold, it's because a virus invaded your body against your will. Nobody says it's your fault you have that sneezing, runny nose, itchy throat, and all the rest. People will probably avoid you for a while, as well they should because you're spewing germs all over the place. But there is no stigma attached to catching a cold.

Unfortunately, there's a whole boatload of stigma and misunderstanding in store for the person who becomes depressed. For hundreds of years there's been a strong social aversion about emotional problems and mental health in general. "Nice" people didn't talk about problems, and certainly not in public. In well-to-do families, people with emotional problems or mental problems were closeted away until they either got better or died. Less wealthy families saw their hurting friends and relatives carted off to insane asylums. That kind of unhealthy attitude is starting to lose ground; we talk about such things openly now, at least in most circles (and on TV talk shows all the time) but the stigma is still too much with us.

Even though it's out in the open however, and, pardon the pun, depressingly common, people simply don't know how to

8

relate to the depressed person. They don't know how to respond. They feel helpless and often back away, pretty much abandoning the hurting friend or relative at the time when that person needs support most.

Also, there's this undercurrent of feeling that depression is somehow the person's fault, and even if it's not, the person still should be able to fix it somehow; if the person stays depressed, that person has only himself/herself to blame.

Would we tell anyone, "You're a social outcast because you dared to catch a cold. If you would just imagine yourself healthy, all those ugly, nasty symptoms would go away!"

Well, that doesn't work for depression, either.

Besides, colds are almost never fatal. Depression too often is. And it kills teens more frequently than it does adults. Teens have a higher suicide rate per capita than do adults. Suicide is the second leading cause of death in teens after accidents, and, as we've said before, we're pretty certain that some accidents, such as Carlton's, are really suicides.

Teens don't have good defenses yet against the pain of depression. You haven't lived long enough. If I as a fifty year old find myself in crisis, I think about what I did the last twenty-seven times I had a crisis. I know from experience that one way or the other, this crisis will pass. When a teenager slams into a crisis situation, you have almost no extensive life experience with which to weigh it. You can't be blamed for thinking life is over, because you can't see past your immediate circumstance.

The culture you're growing up in doesn't help a bit. How many pop songs on the Top Forty wail, "Can't live without you!" and that kind of stuff? Teens feel misery and elation more strongly than do older people, perhaps because it's all still so new. We believe one reason teens commit suicide may be that tendency to view things in the extreme. Great is absolutely-two-hundred-percent great and terrible is a-thousand-times-worse-than-terrible. Adults laugh at teens who over-dramatize. But it's not funny.

Also, depression severely magnifies crises. See the bind?
But how do you know someone is depressed?

· · · · · · · · · · · · · · · · · · SYMPTOMS OF DEPRESSION
■

For years and years, psychologists and psychiatrists who studied depression carefully catalogued lists of signs and symptoms. These were the telltale clues that would reveal to them that their patient was depressed. Teens and small children didn't display those symptoms, so the psychiatrists and psychologists cheerfully announced, "Children don't get depressed, and teens very rarely do."

Oh, how wrong we were!

Recent statistics suggest that up to a third of pre-teens experience depression, and it's epidemic among teens. If as many kids got measles as become depressed, they'd close the schools. The difficulty is, children and teens don't show the same signs and symptoms that adults do. The problem is there, all right, but it shows itself differently.

In fact, small kids especially show all kinds of behaviors and attitudes you don't see in adults. Teens, still having a foot in both worlds, display a mix of kid behaviors and adult signs. Here are some signs of depression that may show up in you or your friends. I'm using "she" instead of "he or she" simply for convenience. Guys show them too.

Sad Affect (Mood)

Moodiness. Okay, so all teens are moodier than they used to be when they were children. We're talking major moodiness here, and it shows on the outside. The person—let's say in this case it's a girl—looks sad. Downcast expression. She droops. Because people tend to gravitate to cheerful, joking people this sad affect—the cheerlessness—tends to turn people away whether they realize it or not. If the girl used to wear makeup, she may quit doing so or use it carelessly. Guys may quit shaving.

10

These hurting people just plain don't look good, and you get the impression that they don't care beans about their appearance. That's not true at all. The truth is, they lack the energy and impetus to keep up appearances. Their hangdog look may in fact reflect physical ills.

Physical Symptoms

Body, mind, and spirit are closely interlinked. When the mind is tortured by depression, the body suffers too.

Insomnia. Our girl is probably going to have noticeable sleep problems. Insomnia is not only difficulty getting to sleep at night, it also can take the form of waking in the middle of the night, unable to get back to sleep easily. It can be awakening too early. It can be fitful sleep. She may sleep much too much—many hours a day—or perhaps get far too little rest. In short, her sleep patterns become messed up.

Appetite. Teen girls (and we'll explore this in detail later) obsess on weight and appearance. It's part of growing up. Guys do also but to a much lesser extent. Our depressive teen will probably really have appetite problems. She'll eat too little and lose weight or eat too much and balloon. She can't get the balance right. Her out-of-control appetite (either direction) scares her.

Physiological problems. She may suffer from diarrhea or constipation, headaches, maybe heart flutters. A variety of random symptoms may convince her that she is seriously ill. There's a deep, dark little reason for this. It's socially much more acceptable to have a physical ailment than an emotional one. She *wants* to have a physical reason for the way she feels. It's safer; then she doesn't have to admit to herself or anyone else that she has psychological problems.

Her menstrual cycle, probably not well established yet anyway (cycles usually stabilize with full adulthood), may become highly irregular, coming every couple weeks or ceasing for months at a time. If she happens to be sexually active, you can see the anxiety that can cause.

Anxiety or Agitation

Indeed, anxiety is a big problem with folks who are depressed. She's irritable. There are times when she can't sit still. And yet, she doesn't really get anything significant done. When she is active, it's not a productive activity. Anxiety is caused by a fear of finding out the truth about our own thoughts, feelings, or motives.

Anxiety taken to the extreme manifests itself as panic attacks. Adults have trouble coping with panic attacks; they truly terrify younger people. The term "panic attack" refers to a temporary episode of severe anxiety that may include one or more of the following symptoms: shakiness, stronger and faster heartbeat, hot flashes, sweating, dizziness, fainting spells, tingling sensations, numbness in some areas of the body, chest pains, difficulty breathing, feeling "unreal" or like you are outside your body but observing it somehow, fear of death or of having a dreaded disease, or fear that you are "going crazy." Many teens or adults who have their first panic attack rush to the nearest emergency room thinking they are having a heart attack.

Painful Thinking

Our depressed teen girl sprawls in a lunchroom chair and moans, "I'm fat. I'm never going to get a date. I'm stupid. I'm never going to pass algebra. I feel miserable. I'm never going to feel good again. Never."

Her friends, if they bother to hang around at all to listen to this litany of woe, argue with her. "You're not stupid. Stop talking that way." And of course, if they should happen to get so fed up with the constant moaning that they agree with her just to shut her up ("Okay, so you're fat and stupid"), her depression *really* dives into the toilet.

People who suffer painful injuries—a skiing accident, a car wreck—claim physical pain is easier to take than emotional pain. You know the physical pain is going to ease up eventually. You think the emotional pain will never go away.

12

Painful thinking comes in so many different flavors. These are some of them.

Plain old sadness. The blues. Moping. More crying than usual. A lot of teens, guys especially, try to medicate out of this sadness with drugs or booze.

Introspection. Introspection means looking within. Our depressed teen is constantly turning her thoughts inward on the self. She's always analyzing her own inner shortcomings, her faulty motivations, the lousy things she does and thinks. They may not actually be lousy; she may really be one smart cookie. But her introspection will almost certainly be 100 percent negative.

Teens tend to be extremely self-centered anyway. It's not a fault; it's just the way you are at this age. In fact, you have to be, because this is the time of life, this switch from childhood to adulthood, when you have to figure out who you really are inside. Depression magnifies this natural tendency and warps it into extreme self-pity.

Self-concept. Since depressed people almost never think good things about themselves during these introspective periods, their overall picture of themselves, their self-concept, is not only negative but exaggerated. Frankly, teens (girls especially) are extraordinarily good at this. To our depressive teen, her faults loom far larger in her mind than they really are. She blames herself for everything she sees wrong in her life (and probably in the rest of the world as well). Or, she might go to the other extreme and blame someone else. In any case, the attitude is inappropriately black-and-white and very, very negative. When she talks to herself, it's usually derogatory. "You dumb jerk! Why can't you do anything right?"

Teens are extremely sensitive to rejection. They feel unloved very easily. This too intensifies in a depressed teen. To the non-depressed teen, life can be cruel. To the depressive one, life is hellacious.

Hopelessness. Our girl is totally convinced she's going to be this way forever. Although 75 percent of all depressive people

13

feel like that, it's especially bad for teens. Teens haven't had enough life experience yet to realize that nothing lasts forever.

Painful thinking, the feeling of futility in particular, weighs so heavily that our girl is going to find her motivation sliding away. She loses interest in activities, in school, in being with friends. She can't muster the energy and enthusiasm to keep her grades up. She prefers solitude, so she can pity herself to her heart's content. She closes in upon herself.

Delusional Thinking

In really severe cases of deep depression, when painful thinking gets way out of hand, it can deteriorate into delusional thinking. People who are delusional have lost touch with reality. That is, what they believe does not match up with the way things really are.

They may hear voices no one else hears or see hallucinations everyone else knows are not there. They may think others are out to get them—persecution feelings. They might get grandiose ideas about who they are or what they can do.

This is serious business, because breaking away from reality is nothing less than psychosis. When psychotics go over the top, hospitalization and a tough drug regimen are necessary to bring them back. Some psychotics require lifelong medication to prevent relapse.

···············THE SPECIAL CASE OF TEENS

All this insomnia, anxiety, and everything sometimes translates out much differently for teens than it does for adults. Basically, in a clinical setting when I look for depression in a teen, I look for behavior that's not the normal thing for that person.

For example, anxiety and agitation may manifest itself as fistfights in a kid who rarely gets in trouble and normally never hits others. Poor motivation almost always shows up as a rapid deterioration in grades. The person may show these signs that are atypical (not usual):

■ More active and feisty, sometimes alternating with periods of lethargy
■ Aggressive and oppositional behavior; that is, getting in everybody's face a lot
■ Sexual acting out
■ Running away
■ Alcohol and/or drug use
■ Oversleeping (hypersomnia) and other forms of sleep disorders
■ Withdrawal and deteriorating personal relationships, especially with other teens
■ Other problems worsen, such as eating disorders, getting into abusive relationships (not all abuse is physical. It can also be verbal, emotional, or psychological.)
■ Nightmares

These are not the only symptoms. Rather than go on and on for pages, I will put a more detailed listing of symptoms into the Appendix at the back of this book. If you think depression may be a problem for you or someone you care about, the extended list in the appendix may clarify things.

· · · · · · · · · · · · · · · · · · · **SO HOW ARE YOU DOING?**
■

Did any of these signs and symptoms ring a bell? Do they seem to describe you? If, as you go through this chapter, you can nod and say, "Yeah, that's me" to more than four or five of them, you may have a problem with depression. If that is so, I have one little piece of good news for you:

The common cold is not curable. Depression is.

But what causes these signs and symptoms?

Years ago, I read a story about a test pilot. One day, he took an experimental plane up and started putting it through its paces. But something suddenly went haywire and he had to eject. He parachuted safely to the ground. Now came the tough part, the paperwork. He sat down with his big long forms and filled in the top few lines. Next there was this huge white space taking up most of the page, where he was supposed to describe what he thought had gone wrong. His analysis: "Engine quit."

His terse little response described *the* cause, all right. But of course, what the aeronautical engineers reading his report wanted to know was, what caused the cause?

It's the same with depression. There are a variety of causes, and we'll discuss them. But first, let's examine *the* cause, the ultimate, underlying reason for depression. Brain juice.

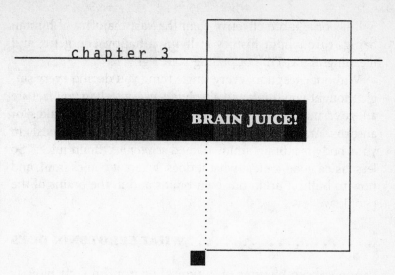

chapter 3

BRAIN JUICE!

Picture yourself in a little red Miata, tooling down the pike to pick up your date. Sun's shining, the top's down, the breeze is riffling your hair. Oh yeah. This is living!

The engine sputters and skips a beat. Another. These are dependable cars; what could be going wrong? Then you glance at the gas gauge, and your hopes trickle away with the last of your fuel. Your zippy little sports car, with which you were going to truly impress your date, coughs its last and rolls to a silent stop on the expressway shoulder. You, my friend, are fresh outta luck. Hope you've got your walking shoes on.

Just as you can't drive a car that's out of gas, in the same way, you can't run your own brain or your own life without "brain juice"—the chemicals on which all of your thinking and motor neurons run. You can have the best car in the world, but without gas, you aren't going to go anywhere. You can have the strongest, the most beautiful body in the world, but without sufficient serotonin, life is going to be ugly indeed for you and those around you.

When you finish reading this chapter on "brain juice," you'll understand something that very few people know about. You will become more effective than the vast majority of human beings throughout history at living a happy, energetic, and meaningful life. I'm not pulling your leg!

Without exception, every single thing you do and every single thought you think and absolutely every feeling you feel are all governed by chemicals that the body either makes or absorbs. And the most important of these many chemicals in your body is a brain amine named *serotonin*. "Brain juice." So let's take a good look at what it does, where it comes from, and how to build it up in our own brains and in the brains of the people we love.

· WHAT SEROTONIN DOES
■

You've seen pictures of "a typical neuron" in your biology text. It's a nucleated cell with lots of thread-like arms called axons extending in all directions. It looks kind of like a many-legged spider you just stepped on. In real life, incidentally, it's not flat; the axons really do go in all directions. Your brain is made up of billions of these neurons with hundreds of axons, all packed together.

Your brain creates a thought or a process (such as walking up stairs) by connecting up various neurons by their axon tips and sending a tiny, tiny electrical impulse through. But none of the tips touch each other. The connections are all made with microscopic droplets of electrolytic brain juice—serotonin and a certain few other chemicals.

I'll bet you're starting to see the importance of serotonin already. No juice, no connection, no thought or action. The amount of serotonin available for your brain determines your energy level, your degree of motivation, your sex drive, your ability to memorize, and your ability to concentrate on school-work or sports or whatever you are trying to concentrate on. The serotonin level also directly controls how happy you feel.

Should the amount of available serotonin decrease, you will become increasingly lethargic, irritable, depressed, possibly suicidal, hopeless, obsessed with loneliness and guilt, critical of self and others, and withdrawn from people. You will find yourself being more aware of emotional pain, especially when you first wake up in the morning. You'll tend to wake up fairly often in the middle of the night and require an hour or longer to fall back asleep.

Some people with low serotonin sleep too much, but most don't sleep enough, and lack of sleep lowers the brain's serotonin level even more. Without enough serotonin, most people dream less, and dreams are necessary to mental health. Among other things, they're the way the brain processes the day's events and problems.[1]

Without enough serotonin, students find that good school performance becomes practically impossible, and a person's grades can go downhill pretty fast. When serotonin is low, most individuals will suffer diminished appetite and lose weight even without trying. This is especially dangerous for teens, because the early-to-mid-teens are when the body is shifting from child to sexually mature adult, requiring a lot of wholesome food (4,000 calories a day for boys, a little less for girls!). About 20 percent of affected teens will experience increased appetite and their weight will balloon rapidly.

In a word, persons with a low-serotonin problem are unhappy and depressed. Unhappiness and depression are *not* something these folks can simply talk their way out of. When your brain chemicals are out of balance, no amount of happy talk in the world is going to fix things. You have to restore the balance.

So now I hope you can clearly see that serotonin is by far the most important chemical in your body. It is, indeed, the "juice" your brain and muscles run on just like a car runs on gasoline. So how do you gas up?

· · · · · · · · · · · · · WHERE SEROTONIN COMES FROM

We can't get serotonin by eating some. As soon as the chemical reaches the stomach, it's instantly digested into other chemicals. So there's no such thing as serotonin-filled capsules, although I'm sure someone will make a lot of money by inventing some very soon—probably in the next few years. After all, insulin too is quickly and easily destroyed by digestion, but they've managed to circumvent that difficulty and come up with an oral insulin for mild diabetics.

Our bodies *build* serotonin, manufacturing all the serotonin we use *in vivo*—that is, within our living system. And we build it out of a natural chemical in our foods called *tryptophan*. Tryptophan is found in meats and dairy products. It's especially high in turkey meat. Although most vegetables, including legumes, offer no significant tryptophan, rice, corn, and chocolate contain small amounts. That's why a diet of legumes plus rice (such as beans and rice, called Hoppin' John in some areas) or legumes plus corn (beans and tortillas) offers a fairly balanced diet.

Vegetarians who forgo meats need to drink lots of milk and eat lots of dairy products to make up for the lack of tryptophan in their diets, or they will find themselves getting depressed and non-functional—at the extreme, even suicidal.

If all you lived on was meat, however, you would still get depressed due to serotonin depletion, because serotonin manufacture requires that you eat the meats or dairy products along *with* carbohydrates and Vitamin B_6. The full complex of foods is necessary for adequate serotonin production.

Come to think of it, it would really be good for your happiness and drive to eat one banana or more every day. Have you ever seen a depressed monkey? Why are they always having so much fun hanging around with each other and swinging joyfully from limb to limb? It's because they have lots of serotonin in their brains, and you can too! I'm being a little bit facetious, but bananas do provide excellent nutrition for serotonin production, because they contain lots of tryptophan *and* Vitamin B_6.

"This brain juice isn't bad stuff. What," you may be asking, "can I do to build up serotonin in order to reach my maximum potential?"

There are ways, and I have personally taught them to several of the professional sports teams in Dallas, including many of the Dallas Cowboys and Texas Rangers. The methods really work.

· BUILDING MORE JUICE
■

Basically, there are two general means: One is to improve the production of the chemical, and the other is to prevent its depletion.

First, to improve production, we must eat a balanced diet, with a mixture of proteins, carbs, and B$_6$, and get adequate rest. That's easy to say but hard to do, particularly for teens. Serotonin ("Brain Juice") is made out of tryptophan in our diets, and tryptophan is highest in bananas, turkey and other meats, and dairy products (milk, cheeses, yogurt, cottage cheese, etc.). Eating these "brain foods" will help build up your serotonin.

Alcohol and drugs like marijuana actually *lower* serotonin levels in your brain. Lack of sleep also lowers the serotonin, so please get plenty of sleep. Go to bed early enough so you wake up naturally and feel refreshed before your alarm clock even starts ringing. This is difficult, I know. School, dating, sports, extracurricular stuff, driver training, maybe part-time work to earn auto insurance money—it all comes at once, crowding out sleep time and the time necessary to sit down and eat good meals.

The English coined a good phrase for this dilemma: penny wise and pound foolish. The penny was the smallest coin of the realm, and the pound is the equivalent of several American dollars. In other words, it may cost you heavily to save a few cents. That's true with eating and sleeping. You cut a little out of sleep time because you have to study. You grab potato chips on the go or you'll be late to basketball practice. You're saving the penny of time, but you're paying for it with reduced ability, reduced energy, and reduced mental "sharpness."

How can you resolve the dilemma when there are only twenty-four hours in a day and you've got eighteen of them booked already? I don't know. Every teen is unique; every schedule is unique; every person's needs and desires are unique. The resolution of your dilemma will be uniquely yours. I can only tell you this: You will reap surprisingly valuable benefits if you find some way to get enough sleep and eat well.

But you know what? You can eat turkey, bread, and bananas until you turn blue in the face and still have a low serotonin level if you are holding grudges.

. . . . **GRUDGES?**

Yes! You heard me right! Grudges: bitterness, guilt, shame, vengeful motives, stuffed anger. When God assembled the first humans, He built into us this feature that whenever we hold significant grudges, our serotonin level goes down. And I see it all the time in practice. *All* the time.

Over 90 percent of the thousands of depressions we treat at Minirth-Meier New Life Clinics all over North America are caused by holding grudges. Nine in ten. What a horrible loss! What terrible waste! No grudge is worth all that. For when we entertain our little grudges, whether they be petty or major, available serotonin is reduced and depression results.

There are other effects as well. While serotonin is dumping from our brains, we tend to get headaches—sometimes even migraines. Serotonin in the blood stream attaches to special receptors in our blood vessels. This causes our blood vessels to either dilate or constrict, and that in turn creates headaches.

What's the difference between a migraine and the everyday tension—stress—headaches that teens so frequently get? Anyone who has suffered a migraine will tell you, there is no comparison. On a scale of one to ten, migraines are twenties. Although you don't necessarily outgrow your tendency to have migraines, people under thirty or so seem to get more, proportionately, than do most population sub-groups.

There is a wonderful new medicine out there that stops the worst of these headaches dead in their tracks. It's called Imitrex. The only problems are that it is somewhat dangerous for people with heart trouble or blood pressure problems. But when it works, it works great—by simply blocking the serotonin receptors in our blood vessels. No vessel dilation, no headache. So when you get really mad at yourself, or at God, or at other humans, you'll still dump serotonin and become clinically depressed; but you won't get the headache along with it because the Imitrex blocks your blood vessels' serotonin receptors.

Now don't get me wrong! It doesn't hurt you to get angry. Anger is a normal human emotion, even a necessary response. Jesus Himself got furious enough to chase the crooked money-changers[2] out of the temple with a whip. But when we get angry—and we will to some extent or another almost every day of our lives—we must learn to control it (not stuff it away and ignore it; control it!), express it tactfully, turn vengeance over to God, and forgive.

This isn't just pretty theory. It's practical. We cure thousands of patients' depressions each week by helping them learn how to get in touch with their anger (that is, recognize that it exists, understand why it's there, and see that it's affecting them), verbalize it (talk about it out in the open; the opposite of stuffing it), and pray about it. They ask God to get even with the jerks in their lives who have hurt them, rather than seeking vengeance themselves. And then the greatest step, forgive. You may even pray for God to change the jerks who have hurt you—which He won't do, of course, unless they cooperate with the process.

True forgiveness from the heart enables our bodies to start building our serotonin levels back up in our brains. But as long as we hold on to our grudges and our bitterness, our brains will keep dumping serotonin no matter how many bananas we eat.

In the Torah, which is the first five books of the Old Testament, God inspired Moses to teach this principle to the Jews. Moses said, "Don't hold grudges. On the other hand, it's wrong not to correct someone who needs correcting. Stop being angry and don't try to take revenge. I am the LORD, and I command you to love others as much as you love yourself."[3]

The Apostle Paul expressed the exact same principle in the New Testament: "Don't get angry so that you sin. Don't go to bed angry and don't give the devil a chance."[4] In this passage, Paul teaches us that we can get angry sometimes without sinning, but we must control our anger, "speaking the truth in love." Then we ought to forgive by bedtime, or else we give demons a foothold in our lives by hanging onto our bitterness and vengeful motives. Paul didn't know about serotonin, but he knew the effect—depleting our serotonin level brings depression and poor functioning upon ourselves.

In short, how well we learn to handle the normal but dangerous emotion of anger determines how well we control our own brain physiology.

The same apostle also wrote the following excellent advice, nearly two thousand years ago, to his friends in Rome: "Dear friends, God is good. So I beg you to offer your bodies to him as a living sacrifice, pure and pleasing. That's the most sensible way to serve God. Don't be like the people of this world, but let God change the way you think. Then you will know how to do everything that is good and pleasing to him."[5]

Then, in the same chapter of his advice to his friends in Rome, Paul teaches them and us something that goes exactly contrary to human nature: "Ask God to bless everyone who mistreats you. Ask him to bless them and not to curse them. When others are happy, be happy with them, and when they are sad, be sad. Be friendly with everyone. Don't be proud and feel that you are smarter than others. Make friends with ordinary people. Don't mistreat someone who has mistreated you. But try to earn the respect of others, and do your best to live at peace with everyone. Dear friends, don't try to get even. Let God take revenge. In the Scriptures, the Lord says, 'I am the one to take revenge and pay them back.' The Scriptures also say, 'If your enemies are hungry, give them something to eat. And if they are thirsty, give them something to drink. This will be the same as piling burning coals on their heads.' Don't let evil defeat you, but defeat evil with good."[6]

Hard, hard advice, but doesn't it reap the benefits!

These verses don't mean you should be a masochist and look around for ways to get abused by people. You should use your common sense and protect yourself from abuse, even if it's by your own parents in your own home. But biblical pacifism means you control your anger, verbalize it (remember what Moses said), forgive, turn vengeance over to God, pray for the jerks in your life to be converted to God themselves, then protect yourself from future abuse and disputes as much as you can. Jesus said it beautifully: "Therefore be wise as serpents and harmless as doves."[7]

Following this advice will allow you to better build up serotonin and thus enjoy more success in life than can most of the rest of the people in this world. Think of all the poor souls who devote much of their lives to bitterness, vengeance, proving their own significance, and other stupid "rat race" mentality activities.

If you need another argument for putting away grudges, consider this one. So long as you hold a grudge against a person (let's call that person "X"), you aren't functioning at your peak, and X is therefore still hurting you. Whatever the original infraction X did, you're letting X cause still more ill effects. That's the last thing you want. "Living well is the best revenge," said someone of just this situation. When you forgive X's original act, you thrive in spite of X. You blossom, and phooey on X. As good as grudges seem to feel, overcoming is a much, much better feeling.

Face it though! When people are critical of us, lie and gossip about us, or yell at us, it is very difficult *not* to hold grudges. Two problems tend to occur when you are yelled at and shot down all the time. One is, your serotonin level suffers. The other is, you feel like dirt. "I'm no good. I'm nobody. I can't do a diddling thing right" and so on. These feelings are the natural reaction to anyone yelling at you—others, your parents, and also yourself.

How many times have you made a mistake or messed something up and said to yourself, "You stupid idiot!" That produces the same effect as someone else chewing you out. You feel insignificant. Let me tell you something I know for a fact: You *are* significant, no matter how your parents or anyone else treats you, because *God says you are!* He's the one who designed you in your mother's womb. He gave you specific strengths and weaknesses on purpose. He was thinking about you when you fell asleep last night. He was still thinking about you specifically when you woke up this morning. He loves you. He leads you in mysterious ways, with one arm leading you through life (like reading this book, for example), and with the other arm hugging you.[8]

So you don't have to feel like a nobody. Those feelings are lies straight from the pit! It's worth repeating: You are significant. God says so. So don't waste your valuable life trying to prove to others that you are significant. You don't have to. Dedicate your life instead to the Kingdom Team—to serve God by benefiting mankind in whatever ways you can. The rat race is stupid and it doesn't work anyway.

Quick definition here: The rat race is any means people use to try to prove they are a somebody. They might try to use sex, power (gaining a position where they can tell other people what to do), money (which includes owning expensive toys, a "my speedboat is fancier than your speedboat" frame of mind), or popularity ("If only I can be elected Queen of the May, I'll feel like I'm somebody."). Understand, I'm not saying there's anything wrong with being elected to the student council, or being chosen Garlic Princess or Daffodil Princess (yes, there are both titles) or whatever. Such positions can be excellent opportunities to serve the community, an industry, or whatever. It's when you tie these positions to your sense of worth or significance—when your motives are self-serving—that you run into trouble.

I've found this progression of attitudes to be true in my life, in the lives of my children, and in the lives of those persons I serve professionally: When you're thirteen years old, you worry about what everyone else thinks about you. By the time you reach twenty-three years of age, you mature and make up your mind that you're going to do what is right and quit worrying about what people think about you. Then, when you turn thirty-three, you finally find out that nobody was thinking about you in the first place! So you might as well grow up now and get yourself past that thirteen-year-old stage. Live to please God, not man; that particular mindset will do as much as anything to help the old serotonin level stay up there.

Now before we finish this chapter, there are a few more things about serotonin you really need to know.

•••••••••••••••• STUFF OTHER THAN GRUDGES
■

You already know that 90 percent (or more!) of all depressions are caused by holding significant grudges toward God, self, and/or others. Forgiveness is the main cure for the serotonin depletion that automatically comes whenever you hold significant grudges.

But 5 to 10 percent of depressions come from other sources. As you think about your own situation and how you can achieve happiness, you must consider these other possible causes of depression also.

Genetic Tendencies

Everyone agreed the identical Moore twins were gorgeous—pretty and dark-haired. Marie excelled in music, Margaret in math. They shared being queen of the junior prom, the only time in the school's history that two girls were queen at once. Their senior year, Margaret won a full math scholarship to the state university. Marie attempted suicide.

They were genetically identical. What happened?

Five years before Marie and Margaret were born, their aunt was hospitalized for severe depression. She never really recovered. Their mom plunged into a terrible postpartum depression when they were born and spent two years on strong antidepressant medication.

When Marie's doctor put together a detailed medical history, she found that the twins' extended families had far more than a normal incidence of depression. In short, the twins had been born with a tendency to become depressed. It was in the family, the same as their brown eyes and white teeth. The twins also illustrate the difference between a genetic tendency and a genetically determined trait. Their eye color cannot be changed. They don't have a tendency to dark eyes, they have dark eyes. But a genetic tendency can often be altered. To phrase it another way, a tendency is not cast in cement, the way eye color is. Margaret successfully countered her tendency and escaped depression. Marie did not.

Simple depression is not the only problem for which we sometimes find a genetic predisposition. Various kinds of bipolar disorder seem to be genetically based (people with bipolar disorders can be depressed most of the time, or they can shift from depressed to wild and crazy and back). People with a genetic tendency to illness of some sort may become depressed secondarily because they are growing so weary of fighting the sickness.

For a few people, weather or amount of daylight can have a profound effect and that too seems to follow a genetic predisposition, at least part of the time. In far northern areas, when winter nights are twenty-one hours long or longer, the lack of daylight can decrease serotonin levels. Some people have a genetic predisposition to depression if skies are overcast for too many days in a row, winter or summer, particularly if rain is involved. These tendencies can almost always be overcome one way or another, such as with antidepressant medications or treatment with special lights.

Some Lifestyles and Habits

Although Margaret and Marie were identical, they developed different personalities, which is normal for twins. It's not a conscious thing, but below awareness, twins usually try to avoid competing directly. So as Margaret developed her latent math gifts, Marie used exactly the same gift for grasping numerical relationships in a wholly different direction—music. Unfortunately, her music also set her on a different lifestyle, and that lifestyle (as we'll see later), not like Margaret's at all, added to her depressive tendency.

A number of circumstances or substances actually lower your serotonin level. Anyone with a genetic tendency to depression is going to be particularly hard hit by these. But even if you have no family bent toward depression, you do very well to avoid these things like the plague:

Lack of sleep. Go to bed early enough that your body wakes up naturally *before* your alarm clock goes off. If you get behind a little during the week, you can try to catch up on weekends, but it's far better to go to bed and get up at the same time each day, approximately. Rule of thumb: Most teenagers need about nine hours of sleep a night, for they're using a bundle of energy just shifting from child physiology to adult physiology. Most adults require eight. Most elderly do fine with seven.

Alcohol. Alcohol, nothing more nor less than a drug, acts as a chemical depressant. Drinking alcohol is exactly like taking a pill that encourages depression. But there's more. Not only does it lower serotonin, it also kills brain and liver cells. After about six months of age, you no longer form new thinking types of brain cells. So you have to take good care of the ones you have. I learned in medical school that one shot of whiskey on an empty stomach kills about two thousand brain cells. That is *killed*, as in dead permanently.

Alcohol also "does in" those brain cells that control coordination. The end effect is to reduce your athletic ability and increase your lack of coordination.

Do you want to prove you are a real man by getting stone drunk in front of your peers weekend after weekend? Well, let me tell you something I have seen over and over in my medical practice. All men and women have both male (androgens) and female (estrogens) sex hormones. Our livers metabolize these—that is, break down what isn't needed—and keep them in balance.

You guessed it; alcohol kills liver cells too. Men who get drunk often enough, overloading the liver, will kill off enough liver cells that their livers can't get rid of estrogen anymore. The excess estrogen in those men makes their noses get big and bumpy and causes small blood vessels to break on their noses and faces. In extreme cases, and I've seen quite a few, the sum effect is impotence and breast development in men. These men require breast tissue removal surgery for their condition, termed *gynecomastia*. So if you really want to be a real man with your hormones doing what they're supposed to do, instead of a wimp who yields to peer pressure, don't drink! And if you decide later in life, after your adult body is fully developed, that you want to drink, don't use the strong stuff, don't drink on an empty stomach, and avoid getting drunk. But my advice is not to drink at all. It's really the best way to serve your body and your emotional health.

Marijuana. The active chemicals in marijuana are drugs that lower serotonin and also eventually make you more and more passive. They leave permanent deposits in your brain cells. Because of its adverse effects, don't ever use pot at all, even if it's legal someday. Legal or not, it messes you up.

Most addicting prescription medications. Pain medications, sleep medications, and the majority of minor tranquilizers lower serotonin. For most people, the drugs called beta-blockers are good for helping lower blood pressure, but 20 percent of the people who take beta-blockers become depressed on them.

Hypothyroidism. That's a fancy word meaning the thyroid gland fails to make enough of the hormones it's supposed to be making. Teenagers should get a good, thorough physical exam every year or two, including drawing blood to check various blood cells, enzymes (like liver enzymes), and thyroid hormone levels. Too little of these hormones can lead to severe depression, deep enough to invite suicidal tendencies. People accidentally commit suicide because their thyroids are not performing properly but they never knew it.

Infectious mononucleosis. This and certain other physical illnesses or physical trauma can cause serotonin depletion and lead to depression. If you fall ill and start feeling worse than rotten, suspect lowered serotonin levels.

Too much stress. Very generally speaking, stress is pressure. You just can't get away from stress, particularly in today's environment. Fortunately, some stress is fine. Our bodies are geared to handle stressful situations now and then. But too much will result in too many anger-producing situations and overwhelming pressures. "Burn-out," which you hear a lot about, is just another term for serotonin depletion and early depression.

Inactivity. Here's an interesting tightrope walk to try to keep balanced: Physical activity, especially vigorous physical activity, promotes the kind of brain juices you need. And yet, goofing off does too, on a limited scale. So do you vege out in front of the TV set, or do you go outside and shoot baskets?

People who spend long hours being inactive—working or playing at a computer, for instance, need the activity. And I do mean *need*. People who are active—sports players, for instance—need some off time too.

Nearly all Marie's recitals, rehearsals, and concerts took place in the evening, and consisted basically of simply sitting there, playing one of the three instruments—jazz violin, acoustic guitar, and flute—on which she was really, really

31

good. When she developed insomnia, her doctor prescribed a sleep medication. In addition to the normal stresses of school and home, she was subject to the stressful uncertainty of trying to succeed in a field with an extraordinarily high rate of failure. Very few music students ever make it in a music career. Every now and then, she'd share a joint with her friends, not because she particularly wanted to but because she wanted to be part of the group.

How many factors in Marie's life can you identify that might be contributing to her tendency to depression?

Most of the time you can alter your own lifestyle enough to minimize or eliminate the factors I listed above. If you have any genetic tendency to depression at all, it is imperative that you do so. Remember too that there may be several different causes of depression going on simultaneously. Just because you find one doesn't mean there aren't more.

Depression (serotonin depletion) is 100 percent curable, if the teen gets enough of the right kind of therapy—therapy that includes treating the whole person. Therapy that treats the spiritual, emotional, and physical (including serotonin depletion) aspects of depression.

· · · · · · · · · · · · · · · · · COMBATING THE PROBLEM
■

Basically, we treat depression in one of three ways. Sometimes, if one way doesn't work well, we shift to another. Often we employ two or all three together. The three ways are counsel, counsel plus medication, and hospitalization.

When a teenager—anyone, for that matter—becomes serotonin-depleted and depressed, we recommend that he or she go to weekly sessions with a Christian outpatient counselor, one who understands the principles we discussed above from Moses, Paul, and Jesus. We recommend that teens who are so depressed that they can't function adequately in school or in life go to a day hospital or the psychiatry unit of a hospital also serving inpatients.

In a day hospital situation, the teen lives at home at night and on weekends, but daily attends about eight hours of group and individual counseling and education, five days a week, in the hospital until the depression goes away. If the teen has a suicide plan or is tempted to commit suicide, then we recommend a locked adolescent psychiatry unit until the depression is well controlled.

When do we medicate, if at all? Every situation must be evaluated individually, and few persons are alike in their needs. Sometimes treatment includes drug intervention, and we'll talk about that in a later chapter.

The title of this book, *Happiness Is a Choice for Teens*, does not suggest that most depressed teens really want to be depressed. What it does mean is that any teen with reasonable intelligence can choose otherwise, by learning and doing the things that we cover in the book to eventually recover from his or her depression.

The more abused that teen was in early childhood, the longer it will take to recover. The average length of time for a total recovery varies, but in general, a serious clinical depression takes about a few weeks in a hospital or day hospital (eight hours a day of education and therapy), or six months to several years of outpatient therapy (45 minute sessions once a week until recovery).

And again, genetic disorders are lifelong and require lifelong medication and follow-up visits, but even the genetically depressed can live normal lives, thanks to modern-day, non-addicting antidepressant medications.

This was a long chapter, wasn't it? Now do you see how extremely important it is to understand how to replenish your "brain juice"—alias serotonin? I hope so.

. . . . **NOW WHAT?**
■

What is your plan now for building up your own serotonin level and reaching your maximum potential intellectually, emotionally, spiritually, and physically? You bet you need a plan. A specific goal. Otherwise, you'll slip into lax habits that allow or encourage low serotonin levels. Let me make some suggestions to get you started here.

1. **Get a physical. You may need one for school or sports anyway. Make sure your thyroid and other internal organs are operating up to par.**

2. **Going through the discussion of lifestyle items above, build a list of things you're going to quit doing. Stick to it!**

3. **Again referring to the items above, choose three positive things you can do to improve your brain juice flow. For each of those three, itemize exact steps you can take to achieve the goal.**

For example, let's say you decide you're not getting enough exercise. A positive thing you can write down is "Get more exercise." But how? So also promise yourself (I'm making these up, of course; you find your own specifics), "bike to school at least two days a week," "swim laps on open pool nights," "practice cheers for fifteen minutes a day even though I'm not on the team this year." Whatever.

What fits you? This is *your* list because it's your life. The more you take charge of your own life, the better you're going to feel. Trust me on this.

Start to formulate your own personal plan now. You will continue to find more ways to develop it as you read further about why and how happiness is a choice for teens.

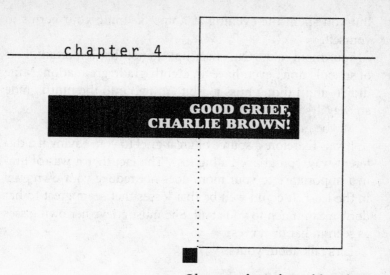

chapter 4

GOOD GRIEF, CHARLIE BROWN!

Okay, so what's the saddest thing that ever happened to you?

You missed a big event because you were sick.

Your dog died.

You didn't make a sports team or cheerleading squad.

Your parents divorced.

A parent re-married, to a real loser.

You've been disabled by disease or accident.

Your grandparent died.

Your One True Love dumped you.

Other.

The list could go on and on. The one thing all these tragedies have in common is that they trigger grief reactions. It doesn't matter how important any of them seems to other people. What matters, and it means everything, is how important the event is to you.

Let's illustrate. You got sick, really sick, right at eighth-grade graduation. You couldn't go. You would have been able to sit next to your best friend. You would have paraded up to the decorated stage to receive a diploma. Just like at the Oscars ceremony, the school band provided the background music.

But you spent the evening at home, keeping your germs to yourself.

Your mom said, "Oh, cheer up! It's not that important. Lots of schools don't even have an eighth-grade graduation. Mine didn't, and I didn't miss it a bit. You go into the ninth grade anyway. It's no big deal."

Maybe not to your mom. It sure was to you.

It was therefore a source of great grief to you. Saying it a different way, you grieved a big loss. The fact that it was of limited importance to your mom does not reduce your own grief in the least. It could well be that losses that seem great to her don't mean much to you at all. She must grieve her own losses as seen in her own eyes.

Let's talk about yours.

. . . . **THE GRIEF REACTION**
■

Grief reactions, which are people's responses to tragedies and losses, are an incredibly important part of happiness for two reasons. For one, how you get through them—in fact, whether you get through them at all—determines whether you will be able to restore your former happiness. Also, depression is a major part of the grief reaction, and if you're depressed already, your emotional life can dissolve into disaster.

There are five stages to grieving, and everyone goes through them. The stages may last only a few moments or they can hang on for months. There is no acceptable time frame for any of them. If a well-meaning friend says, "Oh, snap out of it! You should be over it by now," that may or may not be true. If another friend says, "Boy, you sure got over that in a hurry. Are you certain you're all right?" the statement may also be false.

There are two cautions to observe as you go through these five stages. One is, you don't want to skip past a stage because it's too painful or tedious to handle. The other is, you don't want to get stuck in a stage. Some are easier to get stuck in than others, as we shall see.

Stage 1: Denial

"No! It can't be!"

"Gimme a break! Not really."

"I don't believe this."

"This couldn't be happening to me!"

It's your first reaction when something goes dreadfully wrong. You think it couldn't be the way it is. And this first stage happens to everybody.

For example, I'm thinking now of a baby born with a severe birth defect. Spina bifida, where the spinal column fails to develop properly. The mother, nineteen, immediately told the doctor, "Your diagnosis is wrong. My baby is normal!" But spina bifida is pretty hard to ignore; it's right there on the surface as well as deep within the newborn.

The mother slipped past the denial part within moments as her normal maternal instincts took over. Within hours she had adjusted to the tragedy and was blotting up the nurses' instructions about the special care her baby would need.

Now she had the sad task of telling her own mother that the first grandchild in the family was not "perfect." Her mom's immediate reaction? "It can't be! They're mistaken, Sugar!" Unfortunately, the grandmother was still stuck in that denial stage six months later, insisting the problem was not at all the serious situation the doctors claimed.

Did the young mother skip past denial too quickly? No. Did the grandmother dwell on it too long? Probably. She was facing a long, hard time once she got past the denial into the next stages of grief.

Stage 2: Anger Turned Outward

Says Cavin, a ninth-grader, "When Dad told me he and Mom were splitting, the first thing I wanted to do was knock him into the next zip code."

This intense anger is a normal part of the grief process and happens right after the denial stage. For Cavin, denial lasted almost no time at all (which is perfectly okay). But his anger burned hot for weeks.

Whether we admit it to ourselves or not, when bad things happen we feel angry, with ourselves, with others, and also with God. After all, God is all-powerful and therefore could have stuck His divine finger into the mess and kept the tragedy from happening—or at least made it less terrible than it turned out to be. He didn't, and we get mad at Him for that.

Teens almost always get mad at their parents for the same reason. Even when teens know better in their heads, their hearts hope that their parents are all-powerful, able to save them from anything. The parents should have seen this catastrophe coming and taken steps to prevent it. Sound logical? Of course not. But we're dealing with the heart here, and the heart ignores logic. These are the thoughts our hearts have, and they are normal.

It is also normal to get intensely angry with other people or with the self. It's even normal to feel extremely angry with a beloved person (a grandparent, a friend, whomever) who dies. You didn't want that person to die and are furious that the person did so. Whether the person wanted to die or not doesn't matter. Granny may have succumbed to old age; a friend may have died through no fault of her own. Again, the heart is firmly at the steering wheel, doing its own crazy thing, and you just have to work past it. Logic helps, but logic alone won't turn these feelings off. So don't be afraid of them. They're part of the process. Time helps. Time heals.

The best illustration I can think of is Brent Verkler, my nephew. His parents divorced when he was young. Preschool. He lived with his mom and stepdad. But when he was nine, his mother died. He was sent to live with his birth father in Kansas City. They didn't get along.

Says Brent, "It sure wasn't Dad's fault. At that time, I wouldn't have gotten along with anybody."

Soon after, I took Elizabeth, Brent, and his brother Brian on a vacation to Hawaii. We really did the islands! We even rented a Ferrari to tool around in. Everywhere we went and everything we did, Brent snarled, "This sucks." Nothing pleased him.

Brent deeply regrets now that he was such a jerk. Even yet, he mentions it every now and then. But he wasn't. Not really. He was consumed by anger, and why not? Think of all the tragedy in his life that he had to grieve through, and he was still just a kid!

Unfortunately, many adults do not realize that anger is an important part of the full process, and they get mad at you for expressing your anger. Not just you; they react angrily to anyone who does. There is nothing you can do about their attitudes or actions. Try to explain to them that anger is part of the grief process. But if they won't listen or don't believe you, just hang in with it. This stage doesn't last forever and soon you'll be out the other side.

People do sometimes get stuck in this stage, though. The anger seethes for months and months. In some persons, outward-directed anger may also be a sign or symptom of the next stage as well.

Stage 3: Anger Turned Inward

Guess what anger turned inward is? Right. Depression. In this case, the depressive tendencies of the third stage of the grieving process are framed as strong inner feelings of guilt.

You feel guilty because you didn't do something to prevent the catastrophe. It doesn't matter, since this isn't logic, that you could have done nothing whatsoever. The tragedy would have unfolded with or without you. The guilt will come anyway. It's normal.

Some situations can generate terrible guilt. The Oklahoma City bombing provides a tragic example. Those who came out of the building alive experienced "survivor's guilt," feeling guilty because they are alive while other, possibly "worthier," people died. Many heroes emerged among the workers and medical people who attended survivors, dug out victims, retrieved bodies. As the drama of the aftermath unfolded, thousands in the city and elsewhere felt guilty about not being heroes, about not going down to the site to give their time, or money, or blood, or whatever else they felt strongly about. They felt guilt about continuing with their ordinary activities.

You feel guilty about being angry toward God, your own parents, a deceased person, or whomever else you were furious with. Your logical mind chides your heart that these feelings are stupid, and your heart fills with guilt anyway.

Guilt surfaces in an incredible number of ways at this point in the process.

During this stage of grieving you will feel guilty about things you are not guilty of. Your parents both tell you that you had nothing to do with their decision to separate but you feel immense guilt anyhow. Surely you did something to contribute to their decision, or else there must have been something you could have done to prevent the split. That's called false guilt.

You may actually have true guilt as well. Perhaps a moment of carelessness on your part contributed to the tragedy. Maybe you were driving the vehicle that wrecked, killing your friend. Or you knew the driver had been drinking but you did nothing to prevent that person from getting behind the wheel. This kind of guilt, for which there is some justification, weighs terribly. Terribly! And because you are grieving, both false guilt and actual guilt loom much, much bigger than they really are.

Teens and younger children often express these strong guilt feelings with what adults call "acting out." That's polite talk for blowing up and misbehaving. The actions that look like the teen or youngster is expressing anger-turned-outward are actually uncorking this guilt stage.

If these powerful feelings of guilt fail to subside after a month or so, you may want to talk them over with a trusted friend. Or, you may wish to seek counsel with someone familiar with the grieving process to get past this third stage and on to the fourth. True guilt or false, you are only human and we all make mistakes. A professional counselor can help us to not only obtain God's forgiveness, which is free for the asking, but to forgive ourselves, which is often a long, drawn-out process.

Stage 4: Genuine Grief

Here's the stage most people think of when they hear the word "grief." This is the sadness, the weeping, the cleansing. The true mourning.

Unfortunately, people have no patience with you when you're in the anger stage. It frightens them. They don't understand the guilt feelings of the third stage because those feelings are illogical. But this one they understand. Here, at last, is where the grieving person gets some sympathy.

Finally!

You can get hung up in this stage also. You'll be in royal company if you do. Queen Victoria married her beloved Prince Albert when she was twenty-one and lost him when she was forty-two. She slipped into a depressed state of grieving from which she never really emerged, although she lived almost forty years more. Royal company or no, you don't want to waste a lifetime of happiness, missing out on the best things life offers, the way she did.

So weep and cry all you have to. Belly out on your bed, the door closed, and let it roll. You've experienced great loss. That loss would have ground you down, but now it won't because you're cleansing yourself of its power over you. Never be ashamed of tears. They are the correct response, whether you're a girl or a guy.

And while we're talking about it, is it really macho to keep the tears penned up? Jesus wept in Israel.[1] Joseph wept in Egypt.[2] You're not going to find any manlier men than those two. Do tears in a guy's eyes turn a girl off? Just the opposite. It tells her he cares, and genuinely caring is pretty near the best thing a guy can do for a girl. Girls know that.

Stage 5: Resolution

Resolution is something like the period at the end of a sentence. It lets you know it's over. After the denial, the anger, the guilt, the grieving, resolution slips quickly and quietly into your heart. In essence, you have resigned yourself to reality. This is the way life is from now on, and you go with it.

Resolution does not mean you forget. There are losses you never want to forget, especially the losses of people or dreams. You may always feel the loss you've grieved, particularly if it is the death of a loved one or a marriage, and that's perfectly all right. Some empty spots don't fill again. But they don't have to keep hurting anymore, either.

In some cultures, it's taboo to mention the name of a dead person out loud. In mainstream America it's not only okay, it's encouraged. When you talk about the loss, sharing it with others (don't get carried away with all this, or you'll turn people off!), that person is remembered in the best possible light. That's almost always a good thing.

One other point about resolution: Don't be afraid to talk about deceased persons with the friends and relatives of those persons. Bereaved people usually like to talk about the dead loved one; it is a form of having that person—more properly the memory of that person—close at hand. When you recall things about the deceased, the living person knows in a concrete way that the dead have not been dismissed or forgotten. If for some reason the person does not want to talk about the deceased, he or she will say so. So don't be afraid to bring up fond memories you may have, or to ask questions.

.... ALL THAT OTHER BAGGAGE

Folks with strong grief reactions are also often depressed. Grieving reduces serotonin temporarily. Whether intense or mild, though, the depression passes as the grief process is completed and serotonin levels build again. Well, it's supposed to. If the grieving person is depressed to start with, the grief process may take much longer or may get hung up in a stage. It's a problem to look for if you're having trouble reaching resolution.

But grieving is not the only factor that influences depression. Let me tell you about an incident in our own family that illustrates another very important thing you have to know about interpersonal relationships, whether they're smooth and healthy or bumpy and difficult. Projection. It's not just for movie theaters anymore.

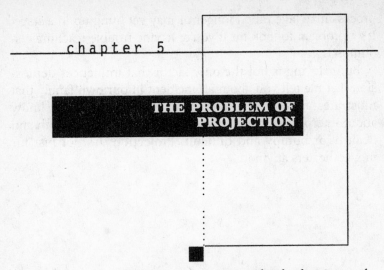

chapter 5

THE PROBLEM OF PROJECTION

In 1991, Elizabeth Meier, the youngest of the Meier clan, turned fourteen. What a year that turned out to be!

Now Elizabeth has always been a very creative, inventively expressive sort of person. From birth on, she mixed relatively compliant behavior with occasional visits to the principal's office, mostly to discuss her unusual attention-seeking stunts.

One time in elementary school, for example, she hid under a pile of pillows in a bathtub that was in the classroom. Her wise teacher finally figured out where Elizabeth was and asked her to come out.

Pillow-muffled, Elizabeth replied, "I can't."

"Oh? Why not?"

"The pillows are too heavy."

She got the attention she was seeking, but she also won a trip to the principal's office.

· · · · · · · · · · · · · · · · · · TROUBLES AND DREAMS

All in all, she always seemed relatively happy until she turned fourteen. Then she suddenly started becoming sad a lot. She grew increasingly irritable. At times she slept too little and at other times too much. She'd appear too fatigued some of the time and too agitated at other times. She withdrew, distancing herself not only from us but also from most of her peers as well. She became more openly defiant, too, insisting she was always right and we her parents were wrong.

As her father, I was supposed to figure out what was troubling her, right? So I jumped right into a big vat of denial and wrote it all off as a "normal rebellious stage." Her mom, who is more honest with herself and quite astute, doubted my analysis. But I reassured her that our emerging teenager would soon outgrow this behavior.

I failed to recognize that Elizabeth was displaying the classic signs of a clinical depression, even when her grades at school started taking a nosedive. School performance is usually even better than psychological testing for determining the mental health of a teenager, with this exception: the compliant straight-A student may well be the most vulnerable to suicide if that student is also a perfectionist who feels that no matter what he or she does, it's not quite good enough.

In Elizabeth's case, I found it easy to deny her obvious depression. After all, all of our kids were sweet from birth to age two, then obnoxiously rebellious from two to three, then sweet again from three to about thirteen or fourteen, then relatively obnoxious again for a year or two, then sweet again—at least most of the time. It all seemed like clockwork—right out of my psychiatry textbooks.

Then Elizabeth ran away from home and stayed gone for several weeks. Disappeared. Poof. It finally dawned on me that my own daughter was clinically depressed.

I cannot describe the pain we felt. Pure, terrifying anguish! Rage. Fear. Guilt both true and false.

We hired a private detective to try to find her. No luck. Until a kid gets a driver's license, it's next to impossible to find a lost teen who wants to stay that way. She left a note, but she never called us.

I found out later that on what had become her journey of personal discovery, she went places where she could visit people who live simple lives and do not measure wealth in money. She visited the Amish, for example, in Pennsylvania. Did I mention, we were living in California at the time? She ended up seeking out pastoral counseling on her own at a country Baptist church in Kentucky.

Now I had grown up quite poor financially. My dad was a carpenter in Saginaw, Michigan. So when I became a successful psychiatrist, entrepreneur, and author with millions of copies in print, I wanted my children to have all the finer things in life that I couldn't afford when I was growing up. And now my daughter, blessed with plenty of finances, was seeking out simplicity.

She coerced her pastoral counselor in Kentucky to refrain from calling us at first; she claimed she would run away from his church again if he did. But after a few sessions, this godly man felt that God had revealed to him the root problem that was causing Elizabeth's depression, and he obtained her permission to call us to let us know she was safe and sound.

Praise God! We were shouting for joy, so relieved to hear the news. We begged that she fly home immediately so we could get her the best psychiatric care in California.

The counselor replied, "No. She's not ready to come home yet. We would like you and your wife to fly out here on Friday night so the two of you can meet with Elizabeth and me at 9 A.M. Saturday morning. I believe we can point out some things you have been doing wrong. Then, hopefully, she'll go back with you. But she may need to stay awhile here with us or perhaps go somewhere else for awhile. Will you come, Dr. Meier?"

I told him I would love to come.

I lied.

I was humiliated. I was insulted. I worried that the counselor might have his own little cult of some kind, even though he seemed very warm and practical.

Hey, I am Paul Meier, co-founder of the largest chain of psychiatry clinics in the world, author of over forty self-help books and two successful novels. I wrote the books on child-rearing, literally. I'm a great father. I'm a Duke-educated psychiatrist. I have a degree from Dallas Theological Seminary. I even have an extra graduate degree in cardiovascular physiology from Michigan State University. I'm the one who meets with hundreds of sets of parents to tell them what *they* are doing wrong. I don't need to fly all the way to the backwoods of Kentucky so some young no-degree advisor with one tenth of my training can tell me I'm doing something wrong.

After all, there's three things that determine how any teenager turns out, including my daughter—*genes*, early childhood *environment* (especially the first six years), and his or her own personal *choices*. Elizabeth obviously inherited excellent genes, and how could any child have better surroundings than the nearly perfect home environment I created for her? Obviously, she has only her poor choices to blame for her depression.

But I'd better jump through the hoops now and fly to Kentucky to deliver her from a potential cult counselor, and persuade Elizabeth to come home. What would my readers think if they found out *my* daughter got depressed and ran away?

I hate to admit it even now, but those were the kinds of arrogant and narcissistic thoughts that were going through my head that week, even on Friday night when Jan and I arrived in Kentucky. We planned to get a good night's sleep before our 9 A.M. session with Elizabeth and her pastoral counselor the next morning.

I fell asleep fine at about 11:00 P.M. Friday night, but I woke up at about 2:00 or 3:00 A.M. with an extremely intense, vivid dream. I knew for certain that God Himself was speaking to me in that dream. I'd had a few dreams like that in my lifetime. For instance, when I was growing up, I was planning to be a carpenter like my Dad. That was until I had an intense dream at age sixteen in which I felt certain that God was calling me to become a physician. That dream changed my whole life.

My dream that night in Kentucky was another of those, and I was filled with the fear of God. In the dream, God told me that I was denying my own faults and projecting them onto my daughter Elizabeth. He told me to read Matthew 7:3-5 and I would understand.

I then woke up. I slipped to the other side of our hotel room and turned on the light, trying to avoid waking Jan (and she never woke up until the next morning). I found a Gideon Bible in the drawer under the telephone book and looked up those verses:

"Why do you look at the speck of sawdust in your (daughter's) eye and pay no attention to the plank in your own eye? How can you say to your (daughter), 'Let me take the speck out of your eye,' when all the time there is a plank in your own eye? You hypocrite, first take the plank out of your own eye, and then you will see clearly to remove the speck from your (daughter's) eye."[1]

I read that passage over and over until I realized for the first time what I had done wrong with Elizabeth. And I wept.

.... HOW PROJECTION WORKS IN REAL LIFE

You see, all humans have sinful and selfish motives mixed in with our good ones. About 80 percent of our thoughts, feelings, and motives are unconscious—that is, outside our conscious awareness. That's why we humans feel so uncomfortable around certain people—they have similar unconscious faults to our own, so they threaten to make us aware of our similar faults. We feel anxious around those people and reject them or are critical of them because of that threat, never realizing that we are really rejecting ourselves.

I remember learning this principle in a psychiatry course back in medical school. At the time I took the class, there was a fellow medical student whom I absolutely hated to be around. I'll call him "Sam." If I was eating lunch in the school cafeteria with my friends and "Sam" came to eat with us, I would feel nauseated just to have to be around him.

So when I learned that this is called projection and it dawned on me that I probably hated to be around Sam because Sam had faults similar to my shortcomings though I was unaware of mine, I made a list of things I didn't like about Sam.

He got straight A's and was arrogant. Sam thought he was the world's leading authority on everything from politics to medicine to doughnuts. And he talked too much and he ate too much. He was also somewhat of a flirt and had a few other faults I couldn't stand. As I looked over my list, I found myself saying, "Meier, you idiot, you're looking in a mirror!"

So I went to Sam, showed him my list, and told him why I hadn't liked him these past four years.

He stared at the list a minute. Then he laughed and said, "Meier, those are the exact same reasons I've hated to be around you!"

We apologized to each other for our hypocrisy and would you believe it? We became good friends. We even shared a rinky-dink little office together for three months and got along just fine, now that we had humbled ourselves and admitted our own faults.

In most families, the father projects the most onto the oldest boy, and the mother projects like this onto the oldest girl. The oldest boy walks like dad and talks like dad and copies dad's faults, including the faults dad doesn't even know he has. So dad tends to be most critical and hypocritical and conditionally loving with his oldest boy, who then grows up feeling like no matter what he does, he's not quite good enough.

The same thing happens with mothers and oldest daughters. That's why the oldest boy and oldest girl in most families are more perfectionistic—to try to win the approval of the conditionally loving parent of the same sex. They get better grades, get more college training, and get better jobs than their sibs, but they enjoy it less, with a higher degree of depression, anxiety, and workaholism.

Fifteen out of the first sixteen American astronauts were firstborn sons. Why? Was it a coincidence? Of course not! Only firstborn sons were perfectionistic enough to get the grades and have the discipline required to make it to the moon and back. About 80 percent of medical students who graduate are firstborn sons and daughters (or the oldest of their sex in their respective families).

I learned this well in psychiatry, so I vowed to myself before I ever had children that I would not do this projection stuff to my oldest son. So when I caught myself projecting onto my oldest son, Daniel, like getting mad at him for being too lazy to go out and get the newspaper for me, I apologized to him and we discussed it openly with each other. Now Daniel is in his twenties and works with teenage drug addicts and alcoholics at a youth home, and he and I still have an easy time sharing our sinful, selfish thoughts with each other and love each other as unconditionally as we possibly can.

But since I didn't project much with my oldest son, I started doing it automatically with my next son, Mark. Again, when my wife and friends pointed out to me that I was being overly critical of Mark, I admitted to myself that the problem was projection. I tried to quit doing it and apologized to him whenever I accidentally did it again. He and I also have a very loving, open relationship.

Certainly, Mark would do things wrong as a teenager sometimes, as all teenagers do. But he would come confess them to me the next day so we could chat about his behavior and discuss its natural consequences. It has been a delightful friendship and continues to be, even though Mark is a married adult now.

So I thought I had that nasty "projection problem" licked. I didn't keep looking for it anymore. That was my big mistake. Because out of my six children, Elizabeth is the most like me.

She's really artsy craftsy; so am I. She's the creative type, and so am I. I can hear a song on the radio for the very first time and sit at the piano and play it with both hands by ear. But I can't read sheet music without lots of practice. She's the same way.

Okay, and I get lost all the time.

I'll be working on a novel as I'm driving along, and forget where I'm supposed to be going. Suddenly I realize I'm in the next city. So I have to go to a gas station to get directions to drive back to where I originally intended to go. Despite that, Elizabeth made it clear from California to Pennsylvania unaided, and she's no great shakes at getting somewhere either.

So here I was, projecting onto Elizabeth, being overly critical of her for reminding me of myself. But I never knew I was doing that until God spoke to me in that intense dream in the hotel room in Kentucky.

It went both ways. Elizabeth projected onto me too. Eighty percent of her own faults exist below the conscious level, so she conditionally loved me and projected onto me and was overly critical of me for reminding her of herself.

The projection problem is one of the biggest causes of teenage rebellion and teenage depression and even teen suicides, and very few of us humans ever even know that we are doing it.

.... **WHAT CAME OF IT**

When God showed me the problem, I wept bitterly. I apologized to God for doing so and promised to actively seek out and snuff out my overbearing tendency to project. I went back to sleep, then. When we awoke the next morning, I did not tell Jan about my intense dream.

At that counseling session the next morning, we met the pastoral counselor for the first time. I was surprised to find that he was an old college acquaintance of mine, a couple of years younger than I, though I never got to know him in college. A gentle, personable man, he greeted us warmly. He was one of those people who just naturally gives you the distinct impression that he's on your side.

Jan and I sat down beside my daughter, relieved and grateful after her absence to be able to do that again. It's such a simple thing, to sit beside another, and so emotionally powerful.

The counselor opened up his Bible. "Paul, I think I've figured out what you've been doing that brought us all to this, and I hope you won't be offended if I show you."

To my utter and complete shock, he read Matthew 7:3-5, the exact passage that God had revealed to me in my dream six hours earlier.

Now you have to realize that there are thousands of passages in the Bible—thousands!—so when he read the very same one God had shown me the night before, you're looking at either an extreme coincidence, like being struck by lightning just as you've won a state lottery, or a divine act of God.

I am convinced, of course, that this was of God. I began weeping out loud.

The counselor stopped. "Paul? Why are you weeping?"

"Because God already showed me that very same verse last night in a dream."

Thanks to God's direct intervention, the counseling session ended on an extremely positive note. I wish all could be so successful. I apologized to Elizabeth and explained everything I was feeling. She and Jan laid out their feelings. We hugged each other as if we were old, dear friends meeting after a long absence—which, in a very real sense, was absolutely true. We worked things out and Elizabeth returned home.

A few months later, she chose on her own to live for awhile at a youth home, Heartlight Ministries in Hallsville, Texas. There she could experience the more simple life she yearned for. Too, they insisted upon lots of firm rules to live by. The tighter structure was new for her, for she and her siblings had only three inviolable rules when they lived as teenagers in our home: no drugs, no sex, and let us know where you are.

She lived at Heartlight for a year and thrived on it. We have referred many teens to the ministry before and since Elizabeth went there. We'll get into this matter of home environment in greater detail later. This experience with Elizabeth, Jan, and me, though, illustrates an important point worth making now. Because every parent and couple are unique, they provide a home uniquely theirs. We as parents can't do anything else. But our children are also unique, each one his or her own person. Usually, the child fits comfortably into the environment; sometimes the child doesn't. Elizabeth hungered for more structure and austerity than our home provided. Fortunately she found a satisfactory alternative that answered her hunger.

She came back to our home a year later more mature and quite happy with life, and she and I have been good friends ever since. She is still a delightfully eccentric, free spirit. The different living arrangement did not squelch her personality in any way; it allowed her to flower. She is in college now, studying to become a weaver, a potter, a writer, or some other type of creative person someday, and already she is far more creative than I've ever been. In fact, she wrote more of this chapter than Jan or I did.

· **WHAT ABOUT YOU?**

But it's time to think about you, the reader. May I suggest you ask yourself these questions and think about the answers.

First, to assess what you're really like, try looking at your day-to-day public and private behavior from a point of view outside yourself. Pretend you have a TV documentary on your life, and you're a remote viewer watching it. Don't try to explain anything or excuse anything. Just check out what you usually do in a day and how you do it. Now:

1. Who projects onto you? Hints: Who that is close to you as an authority figure is most constantly critical of you? Who among your friends is carping at you all the time?

2. List what you see as that person's faults. Is there any clear

relationship between the shortcomings you see in that person and the topics that person complains about when he or she chews on you?

3. Whom do you project onto? Who really turns you off? Whom can't you stand?

4. List their faults. Check back on your TV docudrama; do you ever find yourself doing those same kinds of things? Perhaps you don't actually do those things, but do you share similar attitudes?

Remember that projection is a problem; it can really louse up relationships; but it is *not* a fault as such. It's unintentional and *everyone does it*. Don't kick yourself if you do it. Just look out for it and try to reduce it and correct for it.

Let's tackle relationships with parents and other authority figures first (by the word *parents*, I may be talking about a single parent, grandparents, stepparents, or someone else in your particular case; whoever is primarily responsible for you).

THESE ARE BIGGIES;
. . . . CONSIDER THEM CAREFULLY:

5. Do you think explaining the "projection problem" to that person will help overcome your difficulty or just make it worse? In other words, is that person teachable?

6. Do you think counseling (for both of you!) would help?

7. Are you willing to confront and *forgive* the projectionist?

8. Can you protect yourself from future verbal abuse by the projectionist? Are you willing to?

When we, the Meiers, say that happiness is a choice, we're not suggesting that you simply sit down one day and choose to be happy and that's that—all bluebirds and butterflies from then on. Choosing happiness means making a lot of little choices that will, acting together, result in happiness and freedom from debilitating depression.

The steps above are necessary and responsible actions for overcoming or preventing depression. You see, the pressures projection can cause can affect you physiologically. Serotonin again.

Now that you're aware of some of the mechanics of depression, let's look at the roots.

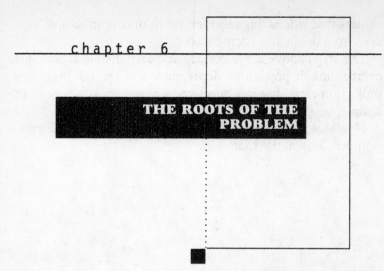

chapter 6

THE ROOTS OF THE PROBLEM

Her name was Melba, and she was born about seventy years ago. Deceived by a young man who promised to marry her but skipped town instead, she ended up alone and pregnant. In those days, unmarried girls who became pregnant were pretty much cast out of society without any choices. If the young man was around, he married the girl. No ifs, ands, or buts. Abortion was unheard of. The stigma of out-of-wedlock motherhood clung to both mother and child their whole lives long. The only single mothers with any respect whatever were widows.

Melba faced added heartache. People of her cultural background were particularly unforgiving toward unwed mothers. Single mothers simply did not raise babies, and that was that. Too, she was expecting twins and her people clung to the Old World belief that twins were touched with evil. Since Melba's man had fled, and with him any hopes of marriage, her twins were taken from her as soon as they were born and parceled out to adoptive parents in different states.

Melba's plight was by no means unique. Every now and then, twins were separated that way. Also, a mother who could not handle two babies sometimes had to give up one. Twins of mothers who died in childbirth usually went to two different adoptive homes. By whatever reason, these children would grow up usually never even knowing that their carbon copy siblings existed.

It still happens. In fact, very recently, I read an article on the sports page about two running backs on the same football team of an Alabama college. They were so much alike that they checked it out and discovered that they were in fact twins who had been separated at birth.[1]

We psychiatrists and psychologists get lots of interesting information by studying twins. And identical twins like Melba's, separated near birth and raised independently, provide especially fascinating data. Assuming that genes, environment (surroundings and upbringing), and personal choices determine the course of our lives, we ask, just how much influence on a person's life do genes have? Exactly how much power does our environment exert as opposed to genes? How well can we escape the fate of genes and environment, making smart choices as we go? By learning answers to those questions, we can make better choices and offset genetic and environmental shortcomings far better.

When studying identical twins raised separately, we can assume that there are no genetic differences. Any significant differences would be caused, then, by the environment—where and how they grew up. There are, as you know, two kinds of twins. Fraternal twins come from two different eggs fertilized at about the same time. Therefore, their gene make-up differs; they are simply siblings with the same birthday, and each has his or her own placenta, or birth sac. (There are cases on record where mothers have given birth to fraternal twins of different races!) Identical twins, however, arise from but one fertilized egg, which accidentally divides into two individuals during its early development. Both share the same placenta, and their genes are virtually identical. Therefore, any differences between the two people, you should think, would come not from the genes but from their environments—the way they were raised.

······················ **GENETIC INFLUENCES**

Researchers, specifically looking for twins like Melba's, found her birthing records and managed to track down both her sons (she died a few years before). Now fifty-five years old, they lived in Indianapolis and Columbus respectively. They looked almost identical and weighed within five pounds of each other. They cut their hair similarly. Both, good craftsmen, had built picket fences around their properties. Their IQs, as measured on standard tests, were only a few points apart. Both had married girls named Anne and both had divorced once.

In many other ways, they were unalike, or no more similar than you would expect non-twin brothers to be. But simply noting where the differences and similarities lay is of limited value by itself. For example, they each stood a 50 percent chance of divorce whether they were related or not. Anne is not an uncommon name in their generation. The researchers, though, sought out, measured, and interviewed hundreds of such twins raised separately. The larger your sample population (number of participants), the better your numbers crunch. When many sets of twins do the same things in the same ways far more frequently than random chance and the general population would allow for, you start to see the role genetics plays.

As regards depression and other forms of unhappiness, researchers found that there is a strong genetic component. That is, if one twin suffers depression, the other probably will. This is important information. When depression runs in families, it could simply be that children learn the behavior from their parents as a way of coping with misfortune (this learning doesn't have to be conscious. They can blot it up below conscious level). And sometimes that happens.

But if learned behavior were the only reason depression tends to run in families, twins raised separately would pick up the coping mechanism of their adoptive parents and correlate not with their lost twins but their present families. When the statistics are analyzed and as many factors as possible considered, the answers start to fall into place. See how the researchers go about it?

(Incidentally, since you ask, no. Melba's two sons didn't know about each other. When they found out, each wanted eagerly to meet his twin, so it was arranged. Maybe you can picture the tears and joy when they came face to face for the first time since the womb.)

We can learn a lot about tendencies by analyzing public records and medical reports. These sources tell us things about major population groups—races, cultures, and sub-cultures (if your family is Polish-American, that's your culture. If your parents are upper middle class, that's a subculture). Certain races, cultures, and subcultures, for instance, have a lot more drunk-driving convictions than do others. Immediately, we ask, "What are the biases that could skew this statistic?" If it were drunk-driving arrests, you could possibly say, "Well, that's because law enforcement officers don't like this group and make more arrests." But convictions are usually based on blood alcohol level, and that's black-and-white. So we try to use common sense and good care when picking apart bare numbers.

Some races and cultures have, statistically, a much higher incidence of depression than do others. Does that mean that if you're in that group, you're doomed? Of course not. See how many people in that grouping do *not* get depressed! But it tells you to keep a closer eye out for signs and symptoms of depression. It also tells you that others beat the odds by making good choices, and so can you.

Maybe because people seem to love spouting statistics, newspapers often report on statistical studies identifying genetic tendencies. It's information that's fun to know, and possibly useful. Just remember that statistics by themselves say anything the compilers want them to say. You have to think and analyze, even if it's statistics about twins and other siblings.

But what about twins raised together? They tell us a great deal about human behavior also. Same genes, same parents, same environment, same school experiences, same just-about-everything. They should be peas in a pod, right? Interestingly, they tend to take different paths. From them, and in other ways, we learn much about family dynamics—the way family members interact and change each other.

We see that there seems to be an innate need in children to avoid competing head-to-head with brothers and sisters. Rather, each child must find a niche that's his or hers alone. This comes through clearly in twin and triplet studies. When siblings grow up, even if they happen to be genetically identical, they nearly always choose different paths in their likes, dislikes, and talents.

If one's the scientist, the others are the dancer or avid reader or auto mechanic. It's as if each child in the family claims a certain territory in which to specialize or excel, so the other kids claim different fields, and this is good. It's the way it should be.

. . . . **ENVIRONMENT**
■

So are some people naturally gifted as dancers or mathematicians or mechanics? Yes. And some of that natural giftedness is genetic; for example, kids with Attention Deficit Syndrome often have a special flair for things mechanical or mathematical. Do you see what that means for you? Many of the gifts you personally have chosen to develop have to do with what kinds of gifts your older siblings have already adopted.

And *that* means that when you say, for instance, "Math is too hard for me!", you're probably wrong. It might just not be a "natural" gift you adopted early on. Far more than you can imagine, wonderful gifts lie within you, waiting for you to find and develop them. Most of us have many *potential* talents and gifts.

One of the reasons I went into this particular kind of study in such detail is to show you that psychology and psychiatry are not flimsy, guess-and-golly attempts to make kids (and adults) conform to some sort of behavior standard. Many, many people in medicine and psychology work hard—and become very inventive at times, as they devise experiments and studies—in order to find answers to the questions at the beginning of this chapter. Then we who work directly with patients use their findings to help people get past the problems hindering happiness.

It's not just professionals who use the information. When you read a book like this, you do too. Now you know that unless you're an only child, you and your siblings may have been playing a game of don't-compete-directly all your lives and never even realized it. People sometimes complain that they had bad parents, or spoiled brothers and sisters. But *all* your family surroundings, good, bad, and indifferent, shaped your behavior, your preferences, and the way you feel.

And knowing *that* is the first step to making smart choices that will minimize your short suits and make your long suits even stronger.

Let's stop a bit here and look at your family statistics.

. . . . AND NOW ABOUT YOU

My Genetic Tendencies

Let's start with your race, which is genetically determined. In other words, it's it, that's that, and you can't change it.

Think of some of the false stereotypes you've heard regarding your race. That is, statements "everybody knows" that are not true in the least. Some examples; Blacks are all great athletes; Whites are arrogant; Indians don't feel pain. . . . These false labels affect you more than you know, especially if you're in a slump anyway.

Now give yourself at least three specific reasons each why these labels you thought of are false and do not apply to you personally. Although you cannot change your race by thinking thoughts or making choices, you can adjust to some degree for the cruelties of others. This item is ammunition to help you spiff yourself up in the future when you're down.

This next point, diseases and abuses, is worth asking around to find out about. Talk to your parents, your relatives, friends (especially older friends) that have known your family awhile. Find out all you can about your family's uniqueness.

Some families try to hide everything that's not "nice" or impressive. So when someone clams up, saying, "That's family stuff and none of your business," you respond (politely, of course!), "It is my business to learn as much as possible about my genetic history, because that knowledge can help me."

Some things to ask about in particular:

- Any diagnosed depression? (You're looking for a tendency, or trend, toward it.) How about a family history of Attention Deficit Disorder (ADD), bipolar disorder, or alcoholism, all three of which may be related to each other?
- Might anyone, particularly in your close family, be subject to undiagnosed depression? List the major symptoms and see if the description fits any relatives.
- Anyone at all commit suicide? Go back a couple generations if you can.
- Has anyone been diagnosed as schizophrenic? Schizophrenia (believing delusions and usually hearing audible voices that aren't there) is also a genetic disorder that may only show up every two or three generations. Proper medication can often help correct this disorder.
- Has anyone been diagnosed as having a "nervous break-

down"? In the past, doctors sometimes labeled severe depressions as nervous breakdowns. I suppose, in a way, they were. The term was also applied to some other conditions, such as psychotic breaks with reality.

- How about drug addiction? Any known addicts (they may be recovering, as in a twelve-step program, but afflicted, all the same)?
- Anyone who "liked the booze" or was down at the bar a lot, but no one will come right out and say the word "alcoholic"?
- What other substance abuse has surfaced in your family?
- Anyone convicted of a drug- or alcohol-related offense?

Based upon what you find, build a genetic profile of yourself. Remember at all times that these possible tendencies *never* indicate that you're going to fall prey to whatever the predisposition is. It means only that you may be more vulnerable than are most. Knowing the truth and making wise choices helps *you*, rather than your genes, to determine the path of your future.

Factors Shaping My Environment

Now let's tackle details of your surroundings. These include your family, friends and school people, neighbors, other people you bump into on a daily basis, and your cultural background.

You didn't ask to be born into the cultural milieu that is yours any more than you chose your family. But it's all part of you, and you don't want to change it. You do, however, want to know how it affects you.

Cultural factors include the region of the country (or world!) where you grew up, whether it was urban or rural, your parents' nationality and national heritage (Irish, West African, Eastern European . . .), economic level—wealthy, poor, in-between, and your immediate family. We'll include your religion in this also, the faith you were raised in.

Remember as you examine your life with your family, school, and friends, that at this point you are not going to confront anyone, chide anyone, or praise anyone, for that matter. This is strictly a researcher's investigation and analysis, and you are the researcher. If you're going to figure out the best choices for you, you have to know what's pulling your strings, what has shaped you, and in what ways. That's what we're doing now.

Regarding culture:

- Again, what are the derogatory terms you've heard about your culture (All Baptists are . . . All Poles are . . . All Italians . . . All Southerners . . . You've heard a million of them)?
- Now again, list a whole raft of reasons why these derogatory terms and stereotypes do not apply to you personally.
- What aspects of your parents' culture embarrass you (Some examples: Your deeply religious mom crosses herself when she says grace in restaurants; your father speaks with an Oklahoma accent; your older brother's too Italian for his own good . . .)?
- Can you list good things your cultural background has instilled in you? Be as silly and as profound as you wish (Examples: respect, ethnic pride, an appreciation for chicken soup . . .).
- What are the shortcomings (I won't call them bad things)? Again, you can get quite a list by being both silly and deep (Examples: My people don't celebrate Christmas the way I wish we would; I feel like a freak, not being able to celebrate the way my friends do. People look at you funny if you speak Yiddish in public.).
- In what ways has your faith shaped you? What do you

think you would be like if you didn't hold to the beliefs you do?

Regarding school:

- Describe the group of friends you're close to.
- What clique or cliques do you wish you belonged to? Do they snub you?
- Does your academic work fit okay—that is, not too hard, not too easy?
- Which teachers like you and which are out to get you? Recalling what you know about projection, how does projection enter in—in both directions?
- What are you scared of most at school?
- What do you hate most about school? Okay, okay, make another long list. But you also have to make a list reflecting this next item:
- What do you like about school?

Regarding home:

- Any alcohol or drug use in your home? To what extent? Consider prescription drugs in this analysis, because they so frequently alter behavior for better or worse.
- Are you still with both original parents in an intact home?
- How do your parents (including stepparents) handle anger? Not getting angry at all is a significant sign also.
- When you get yelled at, what's usually the beef? What do they yell at you about? Who does the yelling—one or both parents, a sibling? You?
- How often do you fight with other family members (this includes yelling, confronting, arguing, objecting, complaining, and plain old, dirty, mutual-accusation fighting)?
- Do your parents or another family member ever get

physical with you—slapping, hitting, poking, touching in ways that make you uncomfortable, tousling your hair? Does the other parent protect you from this abuse?

- Again consider whether depression is present in your immediate family. This is not a consideration of genetics but of the daily impact on your home. If your parent is severely depressed, for instance, you don't get the attention and care you need. If a sibling is depressed, that kid is going to be really hard to live with.

Think about your brothers and sisters (and stepsiblings) a moment, including yourself:

- What is each one's favorite activity and interest? What are the similarities and differences in these interests?
- Which one is pushiest? Bossiest?
- Which one is the shrinking violet, the one who gives in or backs off?
- Which one is the family scapegoat or black sheep?
- Which one irritates you most (Remember the chapter on projection? It's probably at work here.)?
- Which one do you most hope will be your best friend when you're fifty?

Since you're a researcher, you're expected to draw up a report of your findings. Piece of cake. Just step back, so to speak, and observe your family in broad overview. If you were a stranger looking at this family, would you be impressed or dismayed? Are ethnicity, culture, religion, and extended family (aunts and uncles, in-laws) big players, or is your family pretty much alone?

Now here's the hot ticket: How do you think all this has affected you? Does it make you more or less argumentative, fearful, bold, worried . . . the list goes on.

················ **THE ROOTS OF UNHAPPINESS**

Most people never stop to think how their genes and their surroundings affect them. So their genetic tendencies and their environment just go on and on, putting the pressure on them, sometimes threatening their happiness and sometimes protecting it, and they don't have a clue what's happening. I hope that you now have some idea of the forces at work in your life. For until you've identified them, you won't have much luck dealing with their negative sides.

But there are, remember, three shaping factors, and the third is the choices you make. The worst choice is suicide, because it cancels out everything. It's the most pressing negative effect on teens that there is. I'd like to look at that in detail first.

Then let's look at the specific factors that can damage your happiness and bring on depression when you least expect it. We've already considered grudges. But what causes the grudges? And why do those factors affect you and not others?

You're going to be getting pretty deep within yourself. But that's good—in fact, necessary—if you want to make happiness one of your life's choices.

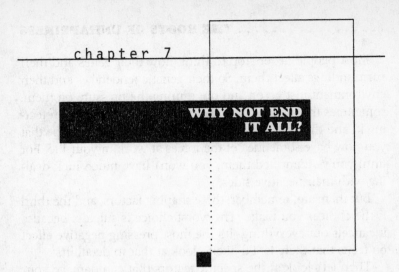

chapter 7

WHY NOT END IT ALL?

Remember Carlton back in Chapter 2? He drove his car into a tree. On purpose, knowing he would die. In my medical journals and in practice, I occasionally run across a teen who did something like that and did not die. More than once, the person (usually a boy) has ended up a paraplegic (lower half paralyzed) or quadriplegic (the whole body paralyzed) to the end of his/her days.

We'll never find out what went on in Carlton's head because he never talked to anyone about his feelings. But I know for a fact that suicidal thoughts are common in teens.

A Centers for Disease Control article I read not long ago said that the suicide rate among people ages ten to fourteen rose 75 percent between 1979 and 1988—only nine years. Not only that, the rate at which depression occurs in teens has gone up 300 percent in the last forty years because of more broken families and other cultural factors.

In short, statistics suggest that you are at risk simply because you are a teenager living in a sick society. And that is terribly, terribly sad.

· · · · · · · · · · · · · · ·**AM I POTENTIALLY SUICIDAL?**
■

So now Carlton is another statistic. You know, the strange thing is, Carlton may not have considered himself as a potential suicide. When you reach the degree of hopelessness he reached, your thinking gets pretty weird. He may have decided this was a perfectly logical way out of his hopelessness, and calling it "suicide" didn't even occur to him.

Whether you call a person suicidal or not doesn't matter. What matters is how that person feels, and what that person is thinking. When I say "person," I'm referring to you as well.

These are the more obvious signs psychiatrists and psychologists use to assess suicidal tendencies in people. As you go down through them, weigh them in two ways: 1) Do I feel this way? and 2) Do I have a good friend who shows these signs?

The Riskiest Factors

■ You constantly read about death and dying. It fascinates you.

■ You don't give a rip about the future. Anticipating adulthood and preparing for the future couldn't interest you less. *Now* is where it's at, and now is bleak.

■ You think about dying, or killing yourself somehow. "I wish I could die today." These thoughts might take the form of fantasies you can't control.

■ You develop a working plan for suicide.

■ You feel terribly, horribly, desperately hopeless. There's no way out, it couldn't get any worse, and it's never going to get any better.

■ Something or other has made you feel extremely anxious. This anxiety grips you and you can't ease it.

■ Your parents divorced.

If I had to finger one main reason for the dramatic rise in teen depression and suicide in the last forty years, it would have to be the breakup of a family. For a number of reasons,

69

we live in a society where nearly half, and in some groups more than half, of kids grow up dealing with divorced parents or the death of a parent. We're just beginning to realize how traumatic this is for kids. All kids.

Children who grow up in a broken home have a much higher incidence of every kind of emotional disorder. Not only that, if a child grows up in a home divided by divorce, his or her own chances of getting a divorce jump by over 90 percent! In fact, losing a parent to death is apparently not as bad as losing one to divorce.

Other Risk Factors

- Your family, or a family situation, has been violent. Teens from homes where violence is the way to resolve a problem or conflict—a swat alongside the head, even in some cases the use of firearms—have a higher chance of committing suicide.[1]
- You really do feel like killing your parents or stepparent. You become so enraged sometimes, you're afraid you might do it.
- You feel so overwhelmingly guilty about something that your death seems like a good atonement.

You don't have to exhibit all or even several of these signs in order to qualify. Just one might do it.

· · · · · · · · · · · · · **WHAT YOUR SHRINK WOULD SAY**
■

Let's say you see these signs in someone, or in yourself. What do you do about it?

Above all, talk about it. But not with just anybody. Choose someone you trust, someone who cares about you and is concerned about your well-being. Someone who will understand. Then let him know about your doubts and feelings. The more you talk about it out in the open with a friend who cares, the easier your burden will become. If you are the one with the signs of suicidal tendencies, you'll be less likely to act on your feelings. If you are seeing them in a friend, confiding your fears and worries will help you immensely and might also help your friend, as others join you to reach out.

Had Carlton revealed his feelings to a trusted confidante, he'd probably be alive today, ramming around on a motorcycle or graduating from college, or going wherever his dreams would take him. Life is not meant to be lived alone.

What about professional help? If I, a psychiatrist, were to evaluate you (or a friend), one of the first questions I would ask is, "How would you commit suicide if you were going to do it?"

If a method comes immediately to your mind, that suggests to me that this isn't the first time you've considered it. Whether consciously or not, you've been harboring these thoughts, and the thoughts indicate that you are seriously depressed, mired in desperation, or feeling overwhelmed by hopelessness. In any case, happiness is eluding you and you need help.

If you've entertained any temptation to actually haul off and do it, we prefer placing you in a hospital unit that can handle you and your problem until you yourself manage to get a grip on it. If you report suicidal thoughts, but there's no way you'd actually do it (still, you're afraid you might get up the guts to do it sometime) quick, competent counsel is a must and a day hospital isn't a bad idea. If you aren't actually suicidal, but you feel so lousy and depressed that you wish you could die, out-patient counsel is the treatment of choice.

A day hospital, incidentally, works this way: You drop out of regular school for a couple weeks and go instead to the hospital. There, under the care and supervision of a psychiatrist and counselors, you get eight hours daily of therapy, plus you keep your schoolwork up. You go home at night and on weekends. In a regular psychiatric hospital, ward, or other facility, you're essentially locked up and you don't leave.

Do we recommend medication? Sometimes. Relieving the depression, the hopelessness, the desperation is priority number one. Once those feelings are under control, we can work more efficiently on the root problems that led you to this state. Antidepressant medication combined with immediate, thorough counseling is the fastest way to ease depression and, above all, suicidal inclinations.

But they're only a temporary solution. They pave the way for effective psychotherapy, because you aren't going to progress as well or as fast in therapy if you're feeling bottom-of-the-well lousy. Were we to offer drugs without appropriate therapy, as soon as you ended the drug regimen, the old problems—issues which caused your depression in the first place—would drag your serotonin level down again and before long you'd be back in the pits. The therapy and a drug regimen, then, work hand in hand; neither is as effective without the other. There are however a few exceptions.

Occasionally, we'll come across a person with a strong genetic tendency to depression—in other words, perpetually low brain juice levels—who can feel suicidal even when everything is going great. That person is a possible candidate for a lifelong drug regimen to keep those brain juices up at an acceptable level.

Now although therapies are tailored carefully to the person receiving them, there are a few things you'll hear from just about every counselor and psychiatrist you talk to.

Depression and feelings resembling depression are 100 percent curable. It's a glad message. No matter how rotten you feel now, no matter how black everything looks, it won't stay this way forever. One way or another, even with a genetic predisposition, you can get out of the morass you're in. And suicide is never one of the ways.

As you become aware of the truth, through this or another book, by means of therapy, or in some other way, the hopelessness will lift. Then you work through the conflict properly and come out the other end stronger than you were when you went into it.

There is no such thing as incurable depression.

You're not alone by a long shot. Welcome to the human race. If you're a depressed teen, you've just joined the rest of humanity.

It happens to nearly everybody. Grief reactions not included (*everyone* suffers through grief from time to time, of course), almost everyone has periods of feeling sad and depressed. Probably close to half of all Americans will suffer a severe bout of depression at some time in life, whether it be officially diagnosed or not. Many never are, at least at the time they're happening.

Being depressed is not a sign of weakness. As a rule, teens tend to think it is. No wonder. This is the age when machismo and desirability count for everything. Hanging around with a whiny, sad, depressed crank is hardly desirable. Dissolving in tears or asking for help doesn't exactly define machismo. So teens do their level best to fake their peers and parents into thinking everything is okay. We see it all the time in clinical practice.

Here's the scenario that so often happens. The worried parent drags the teenager into my office for counsel. "I just don't know what's wrong. She won't talk to me."

And you can tell from the girl's body language that she's not about to talk to anyone else, either.

The mother and I chat awhile. It's obvious from the mother's conversation that whether she really wants to communicate with her daughter or not, it's not happening. Momma's frustrated.

So then the daughter and I talk awhile. Within the hour, she's weeping and pouring her heart out about the misery in her life. I'd like to say it's because I'm such a great psychiatrist, but I can't. Sure, I know a few tricks for opening people up, but that's not the reason at all.

The reason is, that girl knows instinctively that if she doesn't

73

unload her heavy burden of guilt, grudges, and depression, including suicidal thoughts, they're probably going to kill her. She also knows that talking about it helps (girls seem to know this; guys sometimes don't). It's good old survival kicking in.

Too, she knows that her depression is in full control of her life, and she can't stand it. It's hard to lose control, but losing control to an illness like depression is hardest of all. Because I'm a virtual stranger who's not going to be spreading rumors around her school, I'm a pretty safe bet for her to unload on.

And that's a key to coping with suicidal thoughts. Talk about them.

· WHAT YOU CAN DO
■

Let's change history here to provide an illustration. Let's say that you are a neighbor of Carlton, the kid no one knew was suicidal until it was too late. When you're out on your patio you can sometimes hear Carlton's stepfather really blistering him, being nasty and verbally abusive, for no good reason you can tell. You don't know why Carlton hasn't bopped the guy by now. You do know Carlton is secretive and incommunicative, has no close friends, and just plain looks sad all the time.

Having read about the symptoms of depression and suicidal tendencies, you see Carlton in a new light. Repulsive as he may be socially, here is one tormented kid. In fact, he is a possibility for suicide, particularly if he feels strongly about doing in his stepfather. What can you do?

Talk.

There are three people you should talk to.

1. **Try to talk to Carlton. We've learned that one of the things that can abort suicidal thoughts is to get the person talking about what his or her death would mean.[2] People who kill themselves are usually trying to express something that, obviously, cannot be reduced to words. They hope to get back at people they love and hate, hope**

to be remembered, hope to make a powerful statement of some sort. Talking to Carlton could defuse his intentions and save his life.

2. Also talk to appropriate adults about your concerns for Carlton. Talk to a school counselor, Carlton's home room teacher, the principal, a social worker or other person with authority in a situation like this. Let others know. Maybe your fears are groundless. But maybe not. . . . And if they have a basis. . . .

3. Talk to a trusted friend. When I say "trusted," I mean someone who's not going to blab, especially to Carlton. Someone who cares about you. Your concern for Carlton is a heavier load than you realize. This one is for you. You need support also, and friends can help here.

A word of caution: Always remember that it is not *your* job to keep Carlton alive (even some professional therapists slip into that trap and picture themselves as preventing a client's suicide. It doesn't work that way). That is strictly Carlton's responsibility. However, talking to Carlton, to a school counselor, or to a close friend are all wise and loving choices. They *could* end up helping Carlton to make wiser choices himself. But the ultimate success or failure of your efforts rests squarely upon Carlton.

But what if you yourself are potentially suicidal? What do you do?

Talk.

Go ahead and pick one or two of your closest friends or relatives, people whom you trust to accept you as you are, and let them know how you feel. Let them share the sadness.

It works both ways, of course. You can help by listening to people you love when they're going through sorrow. When Saint Paul was writing down his listing of the best way to live, which includes, "Let love be genuine,"[3] he says, "Rejoice with those who rejoice, and weep with those who weep."[4] Paul and his Master, Jesus, both experienced times of crying and of rejoicing. And neither person was ever once phony about either feeling.

But don't stop with a close friend. Talk to a professional, just as you would beg Carlton to do. And talk to people at school who are in a position to help you. Then, and this is most important of all, *let* them help you.

It's one thing to appeal for help; it's another to accept it. It's scary, to let someone into your life so closely. But it's well worth the chance.

For some, it's especially hard. We all depended upon our mothers for survival at birth. We didn't have any choice! So if our parents hurt us too much when we were babies, it will be particularly scary to depend on any authority figure, even a Christian therapist, to help you now. In fact, depending on an antidepressant medication to assist your recovery might be frightening.

I might also add one more item. As you think about life and see nothing but hopelessness, it sometimes helps to dwell on positive thoughts. Now don't get me wrong. I don't want to say, "Just think positive thoughts and it'll all turn out great." Hardly. Trying to keep a positive outlook simply doesn't work if you're deeply depressed and potentially suicidal. But it does indeed help in mild situations where conditions aren't too terribly bleak. And even the most painful of situations can have positive outcomes if wise choices are made along the way.

. . . . SUICIDE SURVIVORS

Now there's a contradiction in terms if ever there was one. "Suicide survivor." If suicide is death, how can there be a survivor?

Actually, *suicide survivor* refers to the persons left behind when someone commits suicide. The family, friends, teachers, church associates, and others. Carlton didn't have any friends in the sense we usually mean, but his death hit a lot of people hard. You can't sit next to a guy every day in class and casually blow off his unexpected death. If you *can* blow it off, I pity you.

Here for the survivors are some points I've learned from my years of clinical practice. They are also documented in the work of other psychologists and psychiatrists.[5]

The people who feel guiltiest for not doing enough to help the victim are always the people who actually did the most. The more you invest yourself in that person who later commits suicide, the more blame you lay on yourself when it happens. That's the way people are. It's the way you are. So when guilt and blame overwhelm you, keep this truth in mind. You're feeling terrible because you did a lot. Your guilt is false!

People inevitably feel guilty about conflicts with the victim. Depressed persons are difficult people to live with, and potential suicides even more so. Interpersonal relationships go right down the toilet. Then after the victim is gone, the survivors feel terrible about not being nicer, or kinder, or more tolerant or whatever. It's almost always a false guilt.

But let's say there's an element of truth to this feeling. You really did treat the victim like dirt and that may be one reason the person took his or her life. Still, and I cannot emphasize this too much: *It was the victim's choice to check out. No matter what the factors, it was not your choice. It was the victim's.* Ultimately, every person takes responsibility for his or her own actions. This is one situation in which the victim must be allowed responsibility for a terrible act.

How do you handle your guilt, especially if it's not all false? Ask forgiveness from others. Ask forgiveness from God. Know that regardless whether others forgive you, God does, and freely. You *are* forgiven! Then get on with life.

You're going to feel deserted, shamed, and angry. Suicide is the most intense of affronts to the survivors. It says, if nothing else, "You aren't important enough to me that I'd want to hang on."

Accept that these kinds of feelings are natural and expected. Talk about them. Are you angry toward the victim? You ought to be! In addition to ending his or her own life, he or she messed yours up royally. Changed you forever, and probably not for the better. So go ahead and be angry. Talk it out. Work it out. Eventually, you'll be able to step past it. But don't think you're bad, or unworthy, or undeserving if you think such thoughts. They are natural.

...... THINGS THAT MAKE A BAD THING WORSE
■

This was a pretty morbid chapter. But when you hide suicide in the closet or under the rug or behind the door, you make things worse for everyone. We know that talking about it openly removes a lot of its appeal. I hope you'll never need the information here.

Let's look now at some other ways depression gets a toehold in your life and robs you of happiness.

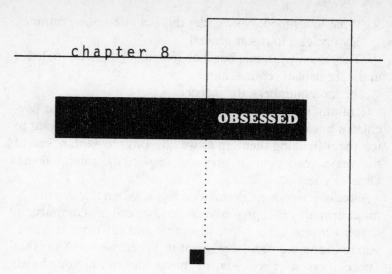

chapter 8

OBSESSED

Rita H. is the best on her cheer-leading squad. At the games, she's featured in the elaborate routines because she's both pretty and very good. In private, the other team members laugh at her because:

Rita H. makes straight A's. She gets the best marks in all her courses, and teachers embarrass her terribly by reading her "wonderfully insightful" essays aloud in class.

Rita H. is active in her church's ministries. She helps out by making salads and washing dishes on Senior Meals days, she's a leader in the youth group, and she shares responsibilities with her mom on the altar guild.

What hurts as much as anything is:

Her little brother refuses to walk to school with her because he doesn't want to be seen in public with a female nerd.

Rita is a compassionate, brilliant young woman. . . . And a prime candidate for a major depression. We'll tell you why later on in this chapter.

THE OBSESSION SPECTRUM

Everybody loves ranking systems.

"On a scale of one to ten, how did you like the movie?"

"What lousy food! No wonder this is a one-star restaurant."

"My uncle's a four-star general."

"They're only juniors, but they scored 5.4, 5.5, 5.1, 5.3, 5.4 in the ice dancing competition!"

The more numbers, the merrier.

Ranking systems are seldom used in psychology and psychiatry, but let's have a little fun with them anyway. I want to use them (making them up as we go along) to explore one of the major causes of depression, especially among teens. Obsessiveness.

Obsessiveness is single-minded focus. When that one-track-mind mentality is expressed as action, we call it a compulsion. If you get into a hot Nintendo game and can't put it down, you're becoming obsessive about it. When you can't get that Special Person or rock star or movie idol out of your head, you're obsessing on him or her. When all you can think about is sex, or grades, or being popular, or keeping your hands clean, or making sure your car looks exactly right all the time, you're being obsessive.

Psychologically, we measure obsession by three rulers:

1. **How much time is it consuming?**
2. **Is it interfering with normal daily living?**
3. **Is it damaging or potentially dangerous?**

Obsessiveness spans a spectrum of many degrees, from one, hardly any noticeable tendency at all, to ten, pathological. Obsessiveness to some degree within that spectrum is a part of just about everyone's personality. Because we are each unique, what is normal for one person may be overboard for another, but we can still make some generalizations.

Laid-Back Louie

Louie would rank one on a scale of one to ten. He doesn't really give much of a rip about anything. He goes with the flow, as they say. Because Louie does not naturally care deeply, he doesn't get hurt deeply or let down often. Unless he has a genetic tendency toward depression, he's probably going to be one of those lucky people who escapes ever being clinically depressed.

Ordinary Jane

"Ordinary Jane" sounds like a bore, if you only go with the nickname. Actually, she's ordinary only because she'd rank maybe a five on the scale. Average. Like most people. She cares about things. If you need a youth group leader, she's a good pick because she's responsible, but don't expect 110 percent from her.

She likes to do well. She's conscientious about schoolwork and extra-curricular activities, but if something doesn't get done, it doesn't get done. There are only twenty-four hours in a day, and when they're filled up, that's it.

She's fun to be around because there's nothing high pressure about her. She doesn't insist on her way when everyone else wants something different, like where to get pizza.

Rip-Roaring Rita

Rita H., on the other hand, the girl I described at the beginning of this chapter, is what some people call a type A personality. Overachiever. Has to be perfect in everything. On the obsessiveness scale, she'd rate a seven or eight.

Now there isn't a thing wrong with trying to do your best, and certainly some people's best is better than other people's. Getting A's is admirable. I wish more kids would strive for good grades. It's great to have the talent and appearance to do well as a cheerleader or anything else. Her charitable attitude and participation in church activities is wonderful.

But for all these superlatives, she's not a happy person. When you're in high school, being laughed at or rejected hurts terribly. It's not her fault; in fact, she should be praised. In the face of painful ridicule, she's being the person she wants to be

81

and was made by God to be. But that doesn't make the hurt any less.

This is the time in Rita's life when it's important to be a part of what we call the peer group—other kids—as a stepping stone to separating out from childlike closeness with the family. When Rita was a child, her family was nearly her whole world. In another couple years she'll be building her own world and probably her own family. Making that separation, that shift, takes a lot of energy and causes a lot of stress.

Add to that the enormous energy her lifestyle requires, and the stress of not fitting perfectly; perfectionists want to be perfect in every detail, you know, and that includes fitting into the group, and sometimes you simply cannot achieve two opposing goals at the same time—in this case, academic excellence and popularity.

Anger? Grudges? Rita has plenty! Believe it or not, perfectionists are almost always angry with themselves for not doing even better. They fault themselves on the slightest mistakes. Rita does that. She is angry with her brother for his rejection and everyone else at school also, for not accepting her as she is. She's angry at the teachers for singling her out. She's even angry with her parents for not somehow shielding and protecting her.

None of this is really rational. The parents can't help, and the teachers don't see what they're doing (although her brother probably does! Shame on him). If you ask Rita about her anger she might not even realize it's there. But anger is not a product of the reasoning mind. It's a gut emotion. It generates grudges against the people who should be supporting her and are not, and perhaps it even generates a grudge against God. After all, she's working so hard, and it feels to her that He's virtually ignoring her efforts. Rita stands a very high chance of going down in flames with a major depression.

Rita's ranking is extremely common. Over 90 percent of medical doctors and maybe three-fourths of church ministers rank like Rita. These are the go-getters, the dedicated public servants, the conscientious workaholics who hone duty to a fine edge. We see it a lot in musicians, lawyers, dentists, cops, even missionaries. Not coincidentally, the highest suicide rate occurs in dentists, doctors, cops, and musicians.

Sick Sol

Poor old Sol is beyond grudge. On our scale of one to ten, he's the ten—the personality so obsessive-compulsive that he's destroying himself. He becomes fixated on one thing—the obsession—and then acts compulsively and repetitively. His brain shifts into a rapid cycling that also happens to deplete serotonin drastically.

Obsessive-compulsives. In psychiatry we refer to them simply as O-Cs. Something in their minds has gotten stuck. People who have grown up with tapes and CDs don't know what a broken record is. The 78, 45, and 33 RPM records and albums were grooved; a stiletto needle rode the grooves and picked up the sound vibrations stamped in them. If even the tiniest nick or scratch defaced the surface, the needle would jump back into the preceding groove when it reached the nick, over and over and over. And of course, it would almost instantly wear the nick in such a way that forever after it jumped the groove when it hit that spot. You'd have, "Happy birthday to y— happy birthday to y—happy birthday to y—happy . . ." and on and on and on.

In O-Cs, very roughly speaking, the same sort of thing happens. Rapid cycling. Repetitive thoughts and acts. Our Sick Sol would wash his hands sixty or seventy times a day. The skin on his hands became so tortured that it turned white and started sloughing, and he didn't even notice. He just kept washing them.

A girl will spend three and four hours a day putting her room in order. But it's already in order, right? Right, to you and me. To her, it must be constantly and meticulously cleaned, constantly and meticulously arranged just so. She will refuse to have her friends in because they just mess things up. She won't go to their place, either, because she doesn't have time. She has to clean her room.

A tense thirteen year old will draw the same formula one racing car over and over and over and over and . . .

Stuck.

The best, most practical way these O-Cs can escape their destructive rut is through temporary medication. We have to break the rapid cycling first. Otherwise, they're so distracted by their obsessions and compulsive action that they can't concentrate. Then therapy will resolve the deep issues that brought the problem on to start with, if there are some. Deeper issues cause O-C in some people, whereas it may be inherited in others. Either way, medication and therapy can enable them to live a more normal life.

. . . . **THE SHADOW BEHIND OBSESSION**

Sol and his fellow extreme O-Cs—the ten rankings—are the exception. They're not common and their problems are usually easy to spot. His obsession-compulsion occurs, it's recognized as being potentially destructive, and it's taken care of.

All those sevens and eights out there, though, have an even more serious difficulty. Their obsessions are often socially approved. Rita H.'s sure are. Nobody's going to step in to cure Rita of getting all A's. Indeed, nobody wants her to slack off. What is Rita to do to eliminate or at least greatly reduce the potential for trouble that her lifestyle holds? How can she choose happiness when she cannot have it if she would remain true to herself and be the person she is?

To help Rita resolve her dilemma (yes, it can be done!), we first have to figure out the mechanics behind her obsessions. There can be a dark side to achievement. Finding it helps us deal with the depression that so often comes with achievement.

To see this dark side, let's make up a pretend example, an adult male we'll call Super Duper Pastor. He heads up a growing church and he's making a difference in his community by doing "the Lord's work" (his words). He married his cute wife right after seminary and they have three kids. Call him Supe for short.

Supe spends many hours a week counseling members of his congregation and preparing Sunday's sermon. He never fails to visit anyone who's sick or in the hospital, and of course, he handles a lot of weddings, funerals, baptisms, and the like. He's putting eighty, ninety hours a week into "the Lord's work." What's wrong with this picture?

Supe is actually being selfish. And running scared.

If he were listening to his Bible as well as preaching it, he would hear it say that a minister of the Lord has to be a good family man first.[1] He's neglecting what ought to be his first priority. He's a conscientious believer. How'd he miss that?

Deep down inside, Supe fears he's a nobody. A loser. A zero. He no doubt got that as he was growing up. What matters, though, is now. And now, he's trying desperately to prove he actually is somebody. He doesn't realize this. It's going on down in the dark closets of his mind that he never looks into.

He's trying to prove himself in two ways. One, he's doing his best to please everybody—the overseers in his church organization and above all, his congregation. People don't love a nobody. If his congregation really likes him, he must be somebody.

Two, he's proving he's somebody by doing more and more great works. Nobodies don't accomplish the wonderful feats of devotion he accomplishes. Nobodies don't do "the Lord's work" this marvelously. Look at all he does! He must be somebody.

Here's the problem. In a couple years, this dedicated servant of God is going to either blow up or fade out. The anger inside will build past containment. Anger? You bet! He'll be angry at God for expecting so much of him and not rewarding all his efforts more. He'll be angry with his congregation for having come to expect 200 percent of him twenty-four hours a day. And even when he gives 200 percent, some of the members will end up dissatisfied with him. People are just that way.

He'll be angry with his family for expecting of him what actually is rightfully theirs—his attention and time. His children are probably going to rebel against all this and there's another source of fury.

And he'll be angry with himself. Remember how perfectionists have to be perfect? He's not. Can't be. But he expects of himself perfection in his counseling and work relationships, family headship, everything. That anger and the grudges it spawns will do him in, one way or another.

His original problem, of course, is that sinking feeling that he's a nobody. That leads to obsessive, compulsive behavior, and that in turn leads to anger and extreme depression, and . . .

What a sad, sad waste of life and of joy! He's lost his happiness, he's drained it from his family, and not even his congregation is all that tickled with him.

Were he to come to us because of his disabling depression, the signs we would notice first is that he is rigid in his beliefs and in his disciplining (of kids, wife, himself, everyone). He can't bend. And of course he'll have plenty of solid reasons why he can never bend. He'll be over-inhibited, unable to loosen up, unable to really enjoy himself or the people around him. His "I must do my duty" cup runneth over. He can't relax easily or stay relaxed for any length of time.

Our therapy would involve, essentially, opening up those dark closets inside, revealing those messages within himself that keep telling him, "You're a nobody, pal. No matter what you do or how much you do it, you're zip."

. . . . THE MAKING OF AN OBSESSIVE-COMPULSIVE
■

So how do you make an obsessive person? Easy, if you're a parent. Just:

1. Tell your kids what they're doing wrong every time they make the least little mistake.

2. Always expect more of your kids than they can deliver. They should be potty trained by eighteen months (paddle them if they make a boo-boo), and by age three they should be able to tell Miss Manners a thing or two about dining etiquette.

3. Don't bother to listen to your kids. They're immature and all they do is prattle anyway, even the teenagers. Their opinion doesn't count.

4. Make sure your kids know they have to work their way into heaven by being moral and doing good deeds. Jesus doesn't forgive errors and neither do you.

5. They have to earn your love as well. As long as they're good and don't irritate you, they're lovable. Use your affection as a bribe and, if necessary, a club to get them to behave exactly the way you want them to.

6. Be critical of everybody's religious convictions except your own, and especially be critical of your children's. What do they know, anyway?

7. Laugh at your kids and shame them when they goof up, even when it's an embarrassing or harmless goof.

8. Never praise. You certainly wouldn't want your kids to be proud of anything. Pride is a sin.

9. Rules are rules and are never ever to be broken. Period. Punish any infractions whatever. God might be in the mercy business, but you are not.

10. Ignore your own sexual aspect and severely shame your children the moment any suggestions of sexuality show up. Squash all questions and leave them unanswered. React harshly to any mention or activity regarding sex organs or secondary sex characteristics (such as breasts on girls). Your children are not sexual beings and any hint that they are is dirty.

If you're a schoolmate of the person in question (we'll call that person a her so we can avoid having to say "he or she" all the time; remember that it works equally on guys), it's almost as easy to make an obsessive-compulsive.

1. Laugh at her. You need a good laugh once in awhile. Belittle her. Especially, make fun of her appearance.

2. Snub her whenever she doesn't do exactly what you want her to. Her opinion doesn't count unless it agrees with yours.

3. If people you want to impress ignore her, you should also. It's probably the only way you can get on their good side. If they turn against her, join them and turn against her too.

4. Don't let her be herself. Insist that she be the way you want her to be. Make sure she knows that you're not going to be her friend unless she toes *your* mark. After all, you know best what kind of people you want to be seen with.

5. Be jealous. *Really* jealous. If she makes better grades, goes out with a cute guy, or is approved of by others and you're not, get back at her somehow, by all means.

. . . . **AND NOW, ABOUT YOU**

Any of that stuff above sound familiar? Think about your parents, your friends, your teachers. The rules above are designed to make a person feel like a nobody. Has anyone you know been following them?

You know why many people want you to feel like a nobody? This is a biggie: It's because they feel lousy about themselves! That's right! Deep down, they're afraid they are nobodies (just like Supe did), so they hope that by tearing you down a little they build themselves up a little by comparison. If you're an even worse nobody than they, they come out looking better. Sort of.

When you know the rules for making someone feel like a nobody, you can do two things with your knowledge. One is to avoid doing those things to other people. The rules hurt terribly when they're applied. Don't do it! The other thing is to remember that when people do that to you, they are actually saying something profound about themselves. And what they're saying about themselves isn't the least bit pretty.

Now I agree it's a hard thing to remember when someone is in the act of putting you down, ridiculing you, yelling at you. You probably won't remember that at the time. But afterwards, when their cutting words are still grinding on you, pick the situation apart. Think about it. Is this person saying something true about you, or is the person jealous and angry and scared? If that's the case, you have a big step up on that person; you see what's really happening. It's not you at all. It's the other person.

How might Rita H. handle her life? We would suggest a couple things.

One is, *be yourself*. If the A's and the cheerleading and the social work are what she wants to do, she should be doing them.

Two is, *know why you are yourself*. Study the two sets of rules above. She should think, "Do they apply to me?" If so, they may be shaping her below conscious level. Bringing those shaping forces to light won't wreck her seven or eight ranking, but it will make her more satisfied with herself. She'll know why she is as she is. That is immensely comforting.

A possible third thing would be to *speak up*. She might go to her teachers privately and ask them not to single her out. Explain that it doesn't do any good and only increases her own unhappiness by turning her classmates off. The teachers might go right on doing what they've always done, but at least now they won't be acting out of ignorance. If you need something, you have to ask. Others cannot guess.

A very important fourth thing is *make sure her motives are right*. Is she trying to please God? That's great! But if she's trying to please Him so that He'll love her, that's not so great. We would tell her over and over, "God loves you. Period. You don't have to earn it! Do good deeds for Him because He already loves you and you want to; you can't buy that love. You don't have to. It's there."

There are many other ways in which doubts and insecurities can fester into full-blown depression. One of them is control. Let's look at that next.

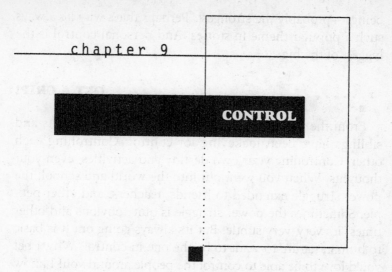

chapter 9

CONTROL

Star Trek in one form or another has been around longer than you have. Do you realize how old that makes *me* feel?—because I remember the original on TV when it was a first-run series. Almost always, the plot would hinge around survival and control, usually both together.

In one episode, a funnel-shaped doomsday machine—sort of a giant hollow sponge—cruises mindlessly around in space consuming whole populated planets. And starships, of course. The survival of the *Enterprise* and Earth depend upon Captain Kirk figuring out how to control the uncontrollable mechanical monster and put it out of commission.

In the episode *City on the Edge of Forever* by Harlan Ellison, Kirk and Spock exercise the ultimate control—changing history by controlling time itself. That's the one where they follow Dr. McCoy down to Earth in the late 1930s and ultimately keep Hitler from winning World War II. In this one, personal control features prominently. In order to save the world, Captain Kirk must deliberately allow the death of a woman he has grown to love.

Control is one of the strongest issues known to human

beings—probably the strongest. Perhaps that's why it's always such a popular theme in stories. And personal control is the biggest of the big.

· **GET A GRIP!**

■

From the time you were born, you and your parents and siblings have been jockeying for control. Controlling each other. Controlling your own destiny and activities, even your thoughts. When you went out into the world and school, the power struggle extended to friends, teachers, and other people. Sometimes the power struggle is quite obvious and other times, it's very, very subtle. But it's always going on. It is basic to human nature to want to be the one in control. Why, I bet you'd love to be able to control the people around you! I know I sure would.

Not so surprisingly, a large part of maturity is simply learning when to control and when to let go. And like so many attributes of human beings, control taken to extreme not only brings misery to the self and everyone else around, but very often also leads to severe depression.

Does this person sound like someone in your life (we'll call this one "he" to avoid the he-or-she clumsiness; remember though that women can have the problem just as much)?

His rules are rigid. No exceptions, no bending. A 10:00 P.M. curfew does not mean 10:01.

What? You didn't finish your green beans? Well, you're going to sit right there until you do. You may be fifteen years old, you may have soccer practice in seven minutes, but by golly, you'll eat those beans. That kind of rigidity.

He has to approve of your friends. If he doesn't, you're not allowed to associate with them. And his standards are extreme. They have to look like he wants them to look and behave the way he wants them to.

He has to approve of what you wear. The problem is, he doesn't want you wearing what all your other friends are wearing; he wants you to wear what he wore twenty years ago. "Give me a break," you moan. Moaning, of course, avails nothing. You end up sneaking clothes to school in your gym bag, just so you won't look like a dork.

You have to do what he thinks you should do. If you participate in sports, they have to be sports he likes rather than what you like. An exception here is a sport that he may not like but it is strongly approved in your community; he'll look good if you play. If you take up an instrument in the band, it has to be an instrument he likes. ("The glockenspiel! I'm not paying for any glockenspiel lessons. If you want to play, play a *real* instrument. A trumpet or something.")

Needless to say, you have to attend his church. No matter that your best friends go to a different one, even if it holds to exactly the same tenets as his. And whatever you do, don't change denominations, at least not in his lifetime—that is, unless he does, of course. Then you're expected to.

You must operate only in his time frame. If he wants his dinner at six, you have to be at the table at six; you'll just have to try to work your schedule around his preferences. Even though you're in high school or soon to enter, your schedule has to revolve around his.

The future is everything. He wants you to prepare for the future of his choice—college, a trade, homemaking, whatever. And always, *now* doesn't count. Today is only preparation time for tomorrow. But tomorrow never comes.

I remember one young woman who struggled at loggerheads with her controlling father. She very frugally saved money for over a year in order to buy the bicycle she wanted. He approved of saving money toward a goal; he himself was always saving for the future. So far, so good. But then she actually bought the bike as she had intended, and he instantly and strongly disapproved. Saving he could see; spending he could not. He badmouthed the bike—wrong style, wrong color, wrong price. He tried to make her take it back and very nearly succeeded. The reason he brought her in for counsel was because, for the first time ever, she bucked his total control by refusing to give up the bike of her choice that she had worked so long for. He wanted us to crush this rebellion in her before it got out of hand.

This list sounds like it applies only to parents. Not at all. The controller can be a grandparent (controlling grandparents can be really big on raising other people's children; they don't even have to be related), teacher, adult friend of your parents (when controllers try to control everything, they don't stop at other people's kids!), and even the kids you go to school with. In fact, especially some of your friends your age. Possibly a girlfriend or boyfriend. Bossy people learn these tricks very early.

But those are all surface characteristics—what you see on the outside. If you peel away the surface of a controller, you find some surprises underneath. Deep inside, these in-your-face domineering types feel insecure, powerless, and hopeless. At the deepest level, they are terrified that an uncontrollable world is going to hurt them, to destroy them. They are scared beyond words.

They are terrified of feelings. Feelings trip you up when you're not expecting it. Feelings often hurt. To control feelings, controllers isolate them—that's psychological jargon for first denying and then sealing off feelings—and replace them with facts. Controllers are big on facts. Down inside, they believe that if you know everything about a thing (a subject or person), you can control that thing. It's probably true of computers. It doesn't work on people.

Worst of all, this intellectual approach to everything, replacing feelings with knowledge, keeps the controller from really getting to know God. The controller may know everything in the world *about* God. All the doctrines, the world's religions—but that's not where God lives.

A story from Scripture illustrates this better than I can describe.[1] On the morning we celebrate as Easter, just after Jesus walked out of that sealed tomb, Mary Magdalene was the first on the scene. When she saw the empty tomb, she immediately ran back into town to the home where the disciples were hiding and told them.

Peter and John ran out to the tomb (with Mary right behind! If you're keeping track, that's twice now that she ran the distance). John was afraid to step inside until Peter did. They saw the empty, folded wraps that had once encased Jesus' body. Yep. Mary was right. Intellectually satisfied that the facts were accurate, they went home again to hide some more and worry.

But Mary remained out in the open, at the tomb, weeping. She let her feelings flow. Who was honored to be the very first to encounter the risen Jesus? Not the disciples with all their facts straight. The person with the broken heart.

Controllers are terrified of uncertainty. Uncertainty is—well, it's uncontrollable. Unknowable. Like feelings, it can nail you when you're not looking. The controllers try to erase that uncertainty with facts, yes, but even more so with rigid rules. If you just make enough rules, and then make sure the universe adheres to them, you can eliminate uncertainty. That's the theory. Obviously, it never works that way, but that doesn't stop the controller from trying.

Control is actually a form of obsession and arises from the same root problem as do other obsessions and compulsions—thinking you're a nobody. We tend to call controllers' deep-down fears "insecurity." That is, they are afraid they are not nearly as good as the world believes they are, and they doubt they can do what they think God and humankind expect of them. They have to prove themselves just as does any other obsessed person. Controllers, though, also have to keep a tight grip on everything, lest something get out of hand and trip them up. I mean they have to control *everything*—their family members, their workmates, their schoolmates, their home and other surroundings, and even God! (They try to do that a little bit by praying, but mostly by threatening and bargaining: "If You'll just do this, God, I promise I'll do such-and-so.") Of course, their church has to be run their way and say the things they want said. They have to direct everything they think and do themselves and everything everyone else thinks and does.

Marriage is extremely hard for a controller. There is emotional attachment and this person cannot attach emotionally. Marriage is a lot of give-and-take, and the controller can't do that. In a good marriage, both partners give up some freedom in order to serve each other. The controller can't do that. Everyone pities the person under the controller's iron thumb; really it is the controller who is most to be pitied.

How do you make controllers? The same way you make obsessive-compulsives, since control is just a form of that. Belittle them. Make them feel like nobodies. The more the controller's own childhood felt abusive and out-of-control, the more controlling he becomes as an adult—in order to compensate, you see.

. . . . HANDLING THE PROBLEM OF A CONTROLLER ■

Ah, but how do you control a controller?

There is only one controller in the world you can change, and that is yourself. And this is the important thing: Unless you do control your own tendency to control (that sounds redundant, doesn't it? It's not), happiness may not be a choice.

You see, *controllers are never, ever happy.* They are constantly trying to control things they simply cannot control—God, other people, sometimes even themselves, and certainly most situations. The more the world spins away on its own, the harder they grip trying to control it, the less control they actually have, the more angry and frustrated they become, the more they build up grudges against the uncontrollable things and persons . . . see the vicious cycle at work here?

If one or both of your parents are controllers, you're getting the fallout from that vicious cycle right now. For one thing, if both are controllers, they have some severe conflicts going between each other, monumental power struggles, and you're caught in the middle. In many ways, you're getting hurt worse than they are.

Even more, you're getting big enough and old enough that you have your own plans for life, your own way of looking at things, and your own desires and enthusiasms. As controllers, though, your parents may feel the need to make you think their way, like their likes, and do things their way. But you don't want to. You don't want to be your parents; you want to be you. And *splack!* You're in the middle of another power struggle, this time between you and your parents.

Know what the first step to improving the situation is? You're not going to like it, but trust me; it's the way out. Get out of the power struggle. Back off.

You're going to insist now that that's impossible, and maybe throw a vase at me or something. And I'm going to say, "Wait a minute. Listen to me."

For one thing, it is next to impossible to buck a controller if that person's authority exceeds yours. Your parents' does. Your teacher's does. Your friend's doesn't. Your boyfriend's or girlfriend's probably seems to, but it doesn't. You're spending an awful lot of effort and emotional energy perpetuating a no-win situation. You need every bit of energy just to make that drastic shift from child to adult. You don't want to squander it in a futile war of words and nerves.

Do you recall two of the factors that drive teens to depression and even, at extreme, to suicide? Frustration and desperation. When you're up against a powerful controller, you're getting massive doses of both. *That* you don't need, either.

What happens if you do back off? If you get out of the struggle? Your stress level nose-dives. Immediately, you have to deal with a lot less tension, a lot fewer problems. Stress, remember, taxes your brain juice levels. You can spend your energy on more productive things, like setting up a date with the cutey in algebra.

But the controller's ways are unjust, irritating, and just plain impossible. You can't live that way. How do you deal with the controllers who have more clout than you do?

Learn to honor those who hold legitimate authority and pass on those who do not. I mentioned grandparents, including other people's grandparents, trying to control you. Friends trying to control you. Even the dog snarls at you to make you go away. It will help your grasp of what's happening all around you, and to you, if you divide the world into three types of people.

One type bosses you around without any authority to do so. Example: You're riding your bike, making a right turn in traffic, and a total stranger yells at you to watch what you're doing. And while you're at it, get a haircut. You could thumb your nose at him, but I strongly advise against it. You know, he could be right about watching what you're doing; did you do something potentially dangerous without thinking? If he's right, consider it a lesson and pay more attention next time. If he's not, ignore it. By crabbing at you and making the haircut crack, he proves he's a jerk. That doesn't mean you have to be. It takes a lot of restraint and maturity to let non-authoritative jerks off the hook when they don't deserve it, but it pays well in the end. Less hassle, less trouble, less irritation overall. Besides, you feel good about yourself when you exercise that kind of guts.

The second type have authority to boss you only if you let them. That's people like friends and Loves-of-the-Moment. For illustration, let's say you're a guy totally, awesomely in love with a control freak. You're taking her out for a big date. She tells you what to wear. She insists on picking the restaurant, picking the movie, and picking the pizza joint afterwards. None of her choices are your preference. In fact, you've never been allowed to choose. But you do have one choice, and it's a biggie. You can choose whether to go along with this nonsense. And either choice you make—to let her control or break it off—is the right choice. The important thing, you see, is that you are deliberately choosing to let her keep control, or not. Phrasing it another way, you allow yourself to be under voluntary control, and that's all right—for a very short time, anyway—if you don't mind it that way.

You can't do that with the third type of person, the one with genuine authority. Parents. Teachers. Police officers. Workplace bosses. Managers. Leaders of organizations to which you belong. People who weigh a seventh of a ton and can bench press a Shetland pony.

With them you have to switch to a thinking mode and work out a plan of action. That sounds like a lot of work, but believe me, it costs a whole lot less grief and energy than does a power struggle.

Learn to recognize what is a control issue and what is not. There are control issues, and there are a lot of other edicts and guidelines non-controlling parents (and others) would also set up. For instance: When your parents don't want you out after midnight in certain parts of town, or with certain people, that may not be control even if they are controllers; it might be just plain survival. They know when the fatal accidents occur, where the dangers are. In that case, bucking them would be stupid. You're not stupid.

If it's control for the sake of control (a curfew without any bending whatever, for instance), it might be negotiable. Worth a try, particularly when you point out that in a few years, you're going to be making decisions on your own, and you need practice negotiating.

Remember when you open negotiations, or try to, that as critical as the controller is, that person cannot stand to be on the receiving end of criticism. So if you hope to win concessions, be very careful not to come across as being critical.

Then talk to them. One of the biggest problems I see when

I counsel a teen and the parents is that these people don't talk to each other. All of them say, "Aw, he/she wouldn't listen to me anyway. What's the use?" You have nothing to lose by trying to get them to sit down and talk to you.

How do you tell when a rule or edict is only a control issue and therefore potentially negotiable? Balance those controlling edicts against these criteria:

1. **Is my safety involved here?** There's a lot of danger in the world I haven't lived long enough to find out about yet. My controlling parents may be over-protective, but they know more than I do about danger. Go with the flow and don't try to alter it.
2. **If something goes wrong, can it be reversed?** Dumb haircuts grow back out after a century or two. They're reversible. A tattoo is not. Virginity is not. Always keep this criterion in mind. Can either time or I reverse it? Very important!

Don't let a blind power struggle make you miss out on anything. I mean this: The parent or friend who is a control freak may have a good point in the middle of all the irritating stuff. You might be able to learn something about life and benefit from that good point. But if you make control the issue, you're so busy fighting that you miss it.

I can think of all sorts of for-instances. Here's one. The guy is a college senior now, but when he was a lowly high school freshman, he got so tired of the continual battle with his mom that he deliberately gave in. He wanted his room at home liveable, which meant clothes, books, and magazines on the floor where he could reach them easily (he didn't mind a few dirty dishes down there with them). She wanted the room sterile enough to perform brain surgery in.

It took him four hours the first time he gave in and cleaned up his room to her specifications. Four lousy hours! Then he made himself the challenge to shave the time down. By the time he entered college, he could take that room from unholy grunge to spick-and-span in seventeen minutes flat. Know how he made pocket money? Cleaning other guys' rooms up for them for a fee. And if they wanted it perfect because their parents or somebody were coming to visit, he doubled the fee.

Learn how to work around them. I am not suggesting being sneaky. I'm suggesting thinking. You're going to have to deal with controllers your whole life. You'll need to figure out means and methods sooner or later. Might as well practice.

A friend who is now in her late fifties tells me this one. When she was a high school senior (making almost all A's, incidentally), her control-freak father told her, "I'll pay for your college education, but only if you prepare for a career I approve of." What she really, really wanted to be was a veterinarian. Her parents thought that was terrible. Girls don't do that. Then she figured out that the first two and a half years of pre-veterinary medicine followed the same track as biology and chemistry majors. So she declared a major in chemistry. Possibly envisioning things like Nobel prizes, her dad heartily approved.

Her story ends in a double twist. Her father died of a heart attack before she completed those first two years, and as she got into college level science, her dream shifted from vet med to research chemist. How would she have proceeded had both her father and her dream lived on? I don't know. But she worked the system, and the system worked her, and she's a happy woman, a Ph.D. up to her ears in cancer research. PS: her widowed mom is terribly, terribly proud of her.

Remember that not even diamonds are forever. As bleak as the outlook may seem this moment, you will not be in this situation forever. You will either grow away from it, or grow strong enough to resist it. Life will not stay like this, and you *can* ride it out.

Picture yourself locked in a struggle with a tree. You wrap

your arms around the trunk and pull all you want, but you don't move that tree. A lot of controllers are that immovable. What do you see? A mess of rough bark in front of your face. Now you step back ten feet. You can see nearly all the tree. If there's a weak spot, you'll find it. If the struggle is useless, you can see that too, and make some other plan or just wait out the difficulty. Once you get some distance, you see the rest of the forest, other options, other worlds. But hugged up against that tree gets you nowhere.

. . . . **AND NOW ABOUT YOU**

It could be that you yourself are the controller. If so, you're derailing your choice for happiness. Ask yourself these two questions:

Whom should I legitimately control? For their own sakes, certain individuals ought to be obeying you. People you may supervise at your job. Younger sibs *when you're taking care of them* and other kids you baby-sit. The family dog (if your family has a cat, forget it. Cats obey nobody). Everyone else is pretty much beyond your authority, including friends and your Love-of-the-Moment.

Do you try to boss them anyway?

It may well be that people such as your friends would benefit greatly from your control. You can see pits they're digging themselves into and they can't. But you damage yourself and often them as well in your attempts to control them.

Here's an alternative course.

Warn, certainly. Advise? Abstain from advising if possible (nobody likes being advised and you're irritating people more than helping). Whenever you catch yourself being bossy (or someone else says "You're so bossy!"), haul back. These people are responsible for their own behavior and you can't change it.

You shouldn't have to.

On those occasions when your friends really do need your advice, communicating your ideas in a healthy, effective way can mean the difference between being listened to and being resented. For instance, use "I feel" messages. "I feel sad about your decision. I feel fearful that your choice may end up hurting you in the long run." *Not* "Know what's the matter with you? You're . . ."! You're telling them how you feel about what they are saying or doing without being accusing. Too, when you lay "You should . . ." or "You shouldn't . . ." all over them, you're acting like a parent, not a same-age friend.

Now, and this is the most important, seek out competent professional help to root out the deep-down causes of your need to control. These causes are exactly the same as those that bring on clinical depression. Easing them will ease depression and the tendency to it. Your help may be a school counselor trained in this sort of thing. It may be professional help.

Journaling can help. Write a letter to yourself talking about your fears and insecurities (you're going to destroy it before anyone else sees it). You'll find yourself telling yourself things you never knew before!

If this need to control comes from deep forces, you won't be able to simply catch yourself doing it and quit. But a lot of it may stem simply from the normal desire everyone has to control. That you can curb. But also, you must ease the underlying root problems.

Control and obsession however are not the only way depression can mask itself. Let's look at some other ways.

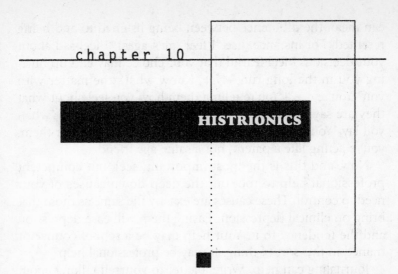

chapter 10

HISTRIONICS

She had straight teeth, clear skin, and more curves than a mountain trail. Her honey hair floated whenever she turned her head. The first day that transfer student Mandy arrived at school in her own convertible, tongues began to wag, and they never slowed down. She was the most gorgeous thing that ever happened to Woodward High School, and Woodward had produced a couple state beauty queens.

Guys talked. You bet. Boys who had never met her boasted of dating her. It got so outrageous, when a guy would say anything suspect, the comeback was, "Yeah, sure, and I bet you dated Mandy, too."

Not all was peachy in Mandy's world. Things tended to upset her easily. She had trouble keeping homework straight and sometimes failed to get it done. She suffered migraines which affected her so severely, people had to carry her around. When she described a horrible auto accident she was involved in, everyone assumed that her convertible was totaled. Turns out it had a crumpled right rear fender. Rumors circulated that she had once attempted suicide over a failed love affair. Every guy in the school hungered to be the love affair that didn't fail.

· · · · · · · · · · · · · · · THE HISTRIONIC PERSONALITY

■

Mandy was a dyed-in-the-wool, picture-perfect histrionic. Histrionic behavior, like obsessive-compulsive behavior, arises from the root causes of depression and strolls hand-in-hand through life with depression. Another word for the personality type is *hysterical*, but we usually don't use it except when talking to other psych professionals, because most people think of hysterical in a different sense—out-of-control laughter, terror, rage, or whatever.

Many of Mandy's histrionic traits are nothing more than desirable traits taken to great extreme.

The Traits of the Histrionic

These characteristics apply to both males and females, though there seem to be slightly more female than male histrionics in our culture. I'll use "she" throughout here, knowing that you're keeping in mind that guys can be this way also.

She looks *good*. Her physical appearance is not only good but she maximizes it with the perfect clothing styles, hair color, and makeup. She is very attractive to the opposite sex and thereby incurs the displeasure of attractive members of her own sex. She's a rival, big time.

Sometimes she is deliberately seductive, but she doesn't have to be. She can be sexy without trying.

She is excitable, theatrical, and usually fun to be with. There's nothing so-so about her. She does everything with a dramatic flair. The clothes she chooses are perfectly matched to her and almost always tasteful, but still she cuts a unique appearance. You can spot her from across the parking lot.

She lives and talks in superlatives. Everything is either the best or the worst. A movie is either must-see or horrible, and her opinion will be based not on the movie itself but how she was feeling when she saw it. To her, either you're a dork or you walk on water. No middle ground.

She functions almost exclusively at an emotional level. The term "airhead" comes to mind because she doesn't try to think clearly. She lets emotion and immediate feelings rule.

Her emotions are labile, which is a polite way of saying they're always on a bungee cord, bobbing from sheer delight to rage, to sorrow, to joy, to surprise—and that's just during a twenty-second TV commercial. Although you always know how she feels at any moment because she makes sure you know, the feelings will change with the moments.

She doesn't do well with planning or details. She misses deadlines. Logic escapes her.

She is exceedingly manipulative. Oh, my! Exceedingly! She knows how to cajole you into doing what she wants. She can threaten like you wouldn't believe. She will pout, throw a fit, be very nice, lie, weep, beg—whatever it takes to keep you in line and do anything she wants. She instinctively knows what tactics work best on which people.

And did I mention instant gratification? When she wants something, it must come to her *now*.

Certainly she gets sick occasionally, just like anyone else. But she has learned to use illness as a powerful manipulating tool. In fact, she will use depression as a tool, either faking it to garner sympathy and cooperation, or actually pushing herself into a depression. We find that very often, her parents encourage this kind of behavior by giving in to her when she gets sick or depressed.

Everything she needs and wants must come in to her from the outside; it almost never arises from within herself.

If anyone is going to use attempted suicide or the appearance of suicidal tendencies to get her own way, this is the person. This is the one instance where the person threatening suicide doesn't really mean it. It's a tool. However, there is no way for an observer to tell whether the suicide threat is a ploy or the real McCoy. So to be safe, we treat every suicide threat as the real thing. After all, 10 percent of those who make a histrionic, manipulative suicide gesture will actually die of suicide some time later, sometimes by a miscalculation.

In fact, that very thing almost happened to Mandy. Distraught because a particular basketball player failed to yield to her charms, she threatened suicide. Instead of giving in, he reported her threat to the school counselor (this guy did the smart thing!). So she overdosed on pills—in the field house. Her plan: The coach and team would come in after classes for practice, find her dying, and call 911, saving her life. Drama! Quite possibly the player would even change his mind and date her. In any case, he would feel terribly, terribly guilty for causing all this, and she would get back at him for spurning her.

But. The coach had to cancel practice that day. The janitor found her almost an hour later, and because of the time lag, they nearly lost her. She was a sick little girl for awhile. Emergency room, tubes stuffed down through her nostrils and all that. Know what really tripped her up? At the hospital, she wailed, "Why didn't they tell me practice was cancelled?"

And you're thinking, "Why in the world would they? She wasn't on the team." But to her, it was a legitimate question. Not only did she not think well or plan well, she was certain the world revolved around her. We call this narcissism (NARsuh-sizzum).

A narcissist is someone who, after talking about nothing but herself for an hour, pauses to say, "I've talked enough about me. Now tell me what you think about me."

She is exceedingly self-centered. Punctuality? That's for others. If she keeps you waiting, so what? Are you inconvenienced? She's worth it.

When she's bored (and that happens regularly), it's up to

you to entertain her. When she needs something, she expects you to deliver for her.

At first, she seems very interested in you. But if you analyze what she says and does as she relates to you, you see that she doesn't care what you think; she cares only what you think about her. She weighs every single relationship in the world against what she likes and what she wants.

She is usually also very big on getting back at people. She probably originated the old saying, "Don't get mad; get even." She'll spite herself just to punish someone she thinks crossed her.

Her religion is, uh, interesting. Assuming she was either raised in the church or converted, she will use the above traits in her relationship with God as well as with the people around her. Need I mention they don't work on God? No matter. She uses them anyway because they come so naturally to her, as much a part of her as the carefully coiffured hair, the perfect dress, and the self-centeredness.

Her religious experience will depend almost totally upon emotional reinforcement rather than the study of God's Word or the messages of good preachers. She really doesn't give a rip about theology. Her religion has to feel good. As a result, her spiritual life bungees just as much as do all the other aspects of her existence. Eventually, other people find her constant ups and downs a little irritating.

She gets angry at God easily and frequently because He doesn't cooperate fully with her plans. She may try to get back at Him. For example, she might take up daily devotions as a way of cajoling or blackmailing God into doing what she wants, then quit them when He fails to come through to her specifications.

Am I being too hard on her? No. However, she does not realize the reasons she is doing all these things. Remember, she doesn't think deeply. She certainly never plumbs the depths of herself.

If she did, she would see the underlying traits, deep down, and they are hardly pleasing. Way down inside, she is as insecure and uncertain as are the obsessive or the controller. She's afraid she doesn't really measure up in any area, and the world is going to find that out. She is running scared and putting on a false front that fools even herself.

Also, as attractive as she makes herself to the opposite sex, she has a love-hate relationship with that whole half of the human race. She loves men (or women, if she is a he, remember) and hates them. She seeks out their company not because she enjoys them but because it is important that she conquer, or master, them. Her seductiveness, then, is not a desire for sex but rather a desire to exercise power over the opposite sex. To control them. To eventually punish them.

In fact, she doesn't particularly enjoy sex. If she is sexually active, she will derive very little pleasure from it. She quickly loses interest in the people with whom she becomes sexually involved. If and when she eventually marries, she'll go to extremes to avoid sex with her mate, but will continue to flirt with other men.

How did she get so messed up that she can't really enjoy life?

The Making of a Histrionic

Let's pretend now that you're a mother or father—a really sick, twisted parent, because you want to deliberately create a histrionic daughter. Here's what you do.

Squelch thinking. Don't let her bother her pretty little head making decisions. Make them for her (or him; it works for males too). Kids learn to think by making decisions and then experiencing their consequences. Before long, the kids figure out what creates a good decision and a bad one. Spare her all that.

Spoil her. Let her have her way when she pouts, cries, or throws a fit. After all, she's going to get enough setbacks in life without you causing them for her now. Your role as a parent is to give her everything she wants, especially when she's dramatic.

Use and teach denial. Make sure she knows that whatever goes wrong or looks bad, it's not her fault. Not yours either. It's someone else's. This practice of denial comes in really handy when life begins to look ugly. And it will.

Give in to bullying. If she runs away or threatens suicide because you refused her something, apologize all over the place. That's your role, you know—giving her anything—and you blew it. It's not her fault she ran away or thought about killing herself.

Emphasize external appearance. Always praise her for her looks. Her character is not worth mentioning. The ability to think isn't important. It's the looks that will get her places. Show her that's all you care about. That way, she'll learn to base her whole self-concept on her exterior physical appearance.

Reward illness. When she's sick and also when she plays sick (you're never certain you can distinguish between them, so don't take chances), for Pete's sake give her what she wants. The poor thing.

Turn her against the opposite sex. It will help to divorce and remarry a couple times yourself, since you're her parent role model. Let her know in no uncertain terms that the opposite sex is scum.

Now that you have one, what are you going to do with her?

Coping with Histrionics

At first glance, it looks as if our Mandy might as well go to Hollywood and become a movie star, because she's doomed to that kind of overblown, self-destructive life. She's never going to be happy, so she might as well make lots of money and buy the kind of unhappiness she wants.

Of course, if her career as a famous actress founders, as 999 out of a 1,000 do, she's got a real problem. Fortunately, no one's problems, Mandy's included, are set in cement. No matter what kind of genes, what kind of childhood, what kind of choices she has made so far, she can alter her course in order to find happiness. With the help of God, perhaps through this book, possibly with the assistance of a therapist, Mandy and other histrionics can overcome almost any genetic or environmental shortcoming and can compensate for past bad choices.

Just as happiness is a choice—with hard work in the right direction—your eventual adult personality is also a choice. God wants all of us—you, me, everyone—to become more and more like Jesus.[1]

· **HOW ABOUT YOU?**
■

Did this chapter describe you? If it did, you are going to have real problems choosing happiness without some major changes. But it can be done. There are seven guidelines we give the people who come to us for help. Of the thousands we have treated, those who stick to the guidelines escape depression and become increasingly satisfied with themselves and with their lives.

And now I'm going to do something I don't like to do—keep you waiting. There are several other aspects of depression and its causes that we should talk about first before we talk about how to stay happy. Among them are paranoia, stress, and guilt. Then we'll get to the guidelines.

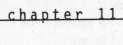

chapter 11

**PARANOIA
AND OTHER TRAITS**

Let's do a cruel experiment. Of course we will do it only in our minds, because performing it for real would be monstrous. Besides, an experiment is supposed to reveal something you don't know; so it's not really an experiment because we already know how it's going to turn out.

We'll use our family pet's litter of puppies, four of them. They're cute little dickenses, warm and soft. The mother is a good dog.

We're going to set out to turn one of those puppies into a regular lovable old dog. The pup will grow up enjoying being petted. It will live to please you, and it will do the stuff family dogs do.

But we're going to turn the second pup into a depressed, passive-aggressive, angry dog.

The third we'll make into a hysterical dog in the psychological sense—histrionic.

And when we're done, the fourth will be paranoid.

· · · · · · · · · · · · · · · · · **PASSIVE-AGGRESSIVE ANGER**
■

Passive is shrinking back. Aggressive is in-your-face. Sounds like a contradiction in terms. Passive-aggressive anger is aggression in that its malice is directed toward someone. But it is passive in the sense that it's not out in the open. If I take a swat at you, that's active aggression. If I stash a toy gun in your overnight bag so that you're detained five hours at the airport, that's passive, but just as harmful.

Passive-aggression is a non-verbal way to express anger, usually toward an authority figure, sometimes toward people you're deeply involved with. We even find people expressing anger at themselves in this way, and they don't realize they're doing it. They sabotage themselves and occasionally spend a lot of their lives getting even with themselves for some fancied reason. This all goes on below conscious level, of course.

Passive-aggressive personalities pout a lot. Incidentally, if a lot of this sounds like our histrionic personality in the previous chapter, you're right. Histrionics are often diagnosed as passive-aggressive.

Passive-aggressives procrastinate, putting things off until the last moment or even until after it's too late. Yes, I know. You do that. So do I. But the passive-aggressive personality does it to extremes in an effort to sabotage someone or something. Often they sabotage themselves. These teens may go to college and complete all the courses right up to graduation. Then they never get their degree because they fail to turn in a five-page paper the end of their senior year. To someone on the outside, it seems insane. To them, below conscious level, it's what they deserve.

They seem to do things in an intentionally inefficient way. For example, someone spilled popcorn all over the inside of the car and you are sent out to vacuum it. You take your sweet time getting out the vacuum cleaner, attaching the appropriate hose and nozzle, finding the heavy-duty extension cord, and uncorking a can of soda. Finally, you vacuum the car interior. You put away the cord and vacuum cleaner. You spot a few kernels you missed, so you get out the vacuum again, suck them up, and put it away. Wait; there's a couple more, down where you can't reach them. Get the vacuum out again. Got

113

the idea? You're stretching a ten-minute job into two hours. Then you also spill the cherry soda on the white carpet.

Or how about this one? When you have to mow the lawn, you leave lots of streaks so that next time, your parents will tell your big brother to do it.

Persistent stubbornness is another hallmark of the passive-aggressive personality. I bet I don't have to define stubbornness, either. Everyone knows it, everyone does it. But this person is calculated and usually constant in it.

In short, these people seem to deliberately block their own progress and the progress of others. We call that *obstructionism*.

It's like the Cairn terrier belonging to the friend of a friend. Cute dog. She'd been well trained, housebroken for years, and she reigned as queen. Until her owners brought their newborn baby home from the hospital and she was dethroned. The terrier left, shall we say, free samples of herself under the baby's crib for three weeks. You're right: It was her non-verbal display of anger at this turn of events. She was getting back at her owners. But it passed quickly.

The passive-aggressive dog will leave samples under the crib for ten years.

To make one, we'll anger our pup repeatedly and then punish him for expressing any anger. We'll always approach the pup in a domineering way, with no affection to speak of. The pup will come to resent authority.

If this were a person rather than a dog, we would give him domineering parents who made all the decisions and didn't let him learn to think. They'd work it so that he remained dependent on them and passive toward them, stuffing anger because of the fear of punishment. They say 80 percent of high school kids try drugs, but only 20 percent become addicted. This guy will probably be one of them. Being a substance abuser is a great way to get back at himself and the parents he love-hates—destructive, yet not openly so. The kid will probably grow up without healthy, interdependent relationships. That causes more and more emotional pain, so he'll become more prone to fill the vacuum with dependencies like tobacco, alcohol, drugs, and sex.

You already have a general idea how to make a histrionic dog, pampering him and giving in immediately to his every wish. Make him the center of the universe and reward him anytime he acts sick or pouty. Groom him a lot and crow over him. Just don't neglect to make him totally dependent on you for love and support.

The paranoid pup is going to be just as easy to engineer.

· · · · · · · · · · · · · · · · **THE PARANOID PERSONALITY**
■

To produce our paranoid dog, we're going to call it to us and then kick it. We'll slap it around, belittle it, holler bad things and yell at it. We'll make promises we don't keep, like holding out a dog treat and then snatching it away. Before you know it, that sweet little puppy will be so full of rage and suspicion that he'll growl at everyone.

If a very nice person, someone who merely wanted to be kind, approaches our paranoid dog, the poor mutt will growl just as if a vicious person were coming near.

A paranoid teenager "pup" will behave in the same way. Yelled at, abused verbally and probably physically throughout his childhood, belittled and hearing promises that would not be kept, he first learned to distrust his parents. From there it was a quick and logical step to distrust any authority figure.

A caring teacher approaches him and he reacts angrily, distrustfully, warily. He assumes that the nice teacher wants to hurt him, psychologically at least. To him, no authority figure is good. No one can be trusted.

The paranoid personality becomes even *more* controlling than the obsessive-compulsive. He also becomes arrogant, condescending, self-righteous, and rigid.

115

···················· DO YOU FEEL THAT WAY?

If you're a paranoid teen because of an abusive past, you have a difficult job ahead. All your experience so far has engraved in your mind that to trust anyone hurts too much. You've been learning nasty lessons since babyhood. Some of those lessons:

- Nobody likes you.
- Everyone is out to get you.
- People like to hurt you.
- You're not worth patooty. No one's going to bother with a nobody like you.

So now you tell me, "This is the way I am. And face it; it's a good defense. When I refuse to let anyone close, no one can hurt me. Believe me, the loneliness is worth it to avoid the pain. Besides, I know for a fact that every single person in the whole world is a [*insert your favorite negative term here. You probably know more names for untrustworthy prime jerks than I do*]."

Then I say to you, "You're forgetting a big statistic. Almost everyone who suffers through an abusive, un-loving childhood picks exactly the same kind of mate and becomes an abusive, un-loving parent. Now you tell me. Do you want to perpetuate this misery into another generation? Is this what you want for your kids?"

"That's why I'm not gonna have kids."

"Want to bet?"

In a sick twist on the term "puppy love," paranoids will almost always choose a mate who will abuse, as a paranoid dog will hang out with dogs that will bite it. It's a way of showing the world, "See? I told you so. I told you they're all rotten."

There is a way out, and it all depends upon you. You have two choices.

You can choose to believe a lie. That lie is that everyone is out to get you and nobody likes you. If you do, you must also choose to dedicate the rest of your life to avoiding intimacy so that no one can hurt you. You get married, but avoid sex because good sex requires love and intimacy. No comfort as you get older, because comfort comes primarily from a close companion. No satisfaction from seeing your kids enjoy a better life than you had, because you're going to condemn them to the same mistakes your parents made.

Or, you can choose to learn the truth and let the truth set you free. The truth is that there are some safe people. This is a "safe people" book. We—the whole Meier clan—have never met you, but we care about you.

"Easy for you to say," you sneer. "It's not that simple. I can't just make some quick decision and overcome a whole lifetime of hearing how rotten and no good I am."

That's exactly right. Happiness is a choice, but it's almost never an easy choice.

You've heard this before: Eighty percent of our so-called "rational" decisions are actually made at gut level—that is, below conscious level. And then our rational minds think up reasons why it's a good decision.

With this book, we want to help you see the power in that other 20 percent. You *can* choose well! But overcoming those disastrous gut decisions takes tremendous effort. Basically, you are telling yourself new things, untested truths that contradict what you've always known. "I am worth something." "I can love and trust some people." That's never easy.

But it can be done.

And when you do it, you can back it up by applying the seven principles we're going to talk about later. You can make your wise choices stick.

Now let's look at another kid with problems, the guy who's life is controlled by Attention Deficit Disorder. His paranoia has more basis than yours. A lot of people really do not like him. And he doesn't help things a bit, because he's accidentally (and sometimes deliberately) making himself unlikable.

See how easy you have it with your paranoia?

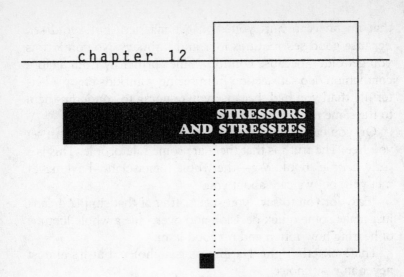

chapter 12

STRESSORS AND STRESSEES

"He's driving me NUTS!" shrieks the fifteen-year-old girl, referring to her twelve-year-old brother.

He comes back instantly with, "That's okay, Miss Dork. You're so weird, nobody's gonna notice anyway."

From the kitchen, their mom hears this and thinks to herself, "He drives me nuts too. All the tranquilizers in the state of Texas couldn't ease the stress in this family!"

The teenaged sister may be going nuts, and the parents might be stressed out, but it's the brother—let's call him Brandon—who's the prime candidate for depression and misery. He's the one stressed to the max because he exhibits many of the signs and symptoms of Attention Deficit Disorder, usually abbreviated as ADD or ADHD (Attention Deficit with Hyperactivity). Well over half of ADD children, boys and girls both, develop significant behavior, attitude, and adjustment problems by the age of thirteen. Major clinical depression may end up as part of the picture their whole lives unless they get proper help.

Some experts claim ADD is the most over-diagnosed disorder in America, and some claim it is way under-diagnosed.

Others say it is often wrongly diagnosed. For our purposes, what diagnostic label you attach doesn't matter. The grouping of signs and symptoms signals trouble later on. That's what we're concerned with here. How extensive is the problem? One in seven kids show some or many of the signs, and they usually don't outgrow it. They tend to carry it into adulthood.

When over 60 percent of ADD kids have significant psychological problems in addition to the ADD, that makes the condition a major cause of trouble and unhappiness. Frankly, this book is not concerned with what adults think about teens. Rather, we're deeply concerned with teens' happiness, and that in large part depends upon what they think about themselves. And these problems prevent happiness. Working past them makes choosing happiness a whole lot easier.

The Signs and Symptoms of ADD

The condition we've named ADD is biochemical. That is, the brain chemistry and nerve connections of some people differ from those of most people. That's it. When I said brain juice is a key factor, believe it. It's the key to ADD as well. Most of the difference in brain chemistry is probably genetic. But the jury's still out on how much the genes influence it. We do know that stressors in kids' lives—divorcing parents, deaths, upsetting events—can bring on or make worse the signs and symptoms sometimes called ADD.

What kinds of signs and symptoms are we talking about that make Brandon and others such stressors and stressees? Again, we'll describe Brandon, keeping in mind that girls are subject also, with differences. For instance, although ADD girls are often less hyperactive than boys, they're frequently more distractible, especially in classroom situations.

He can't concentrate. No matter how hard he tries to apply himself to some task, his mind wanders. It skips from thought to thought like a butterfly flitting across a flowered meadow. He is extremely easily distracted from the task at hand. For instance, he's taking a math test when a trapped fly buzzes up the window pane. Instantly, his attention shifts to the fly, thence to the outside, then to something else. All the other kids finish their math test and he's still on the third problem.

One of the hallmarks of this condition is that the kid spaces out easily.

Conversely, some ADD people, once they really lock onto something interesting, can't break their concentration. Brandon gets going on a Nintendo game, and he can't quit. You have to pull the plug to drag him away from it.

He's frustratingly impulsive. Reckless. Emergency room personnel greet him by his first name. He thinks of something and does it with no thought to consequences. . . . Or to the effect his actions will have on others. Talking to him does no good. Tell him never to run out into the street and a minute later he'll chase a ball out into the street. His mind knows the rule, but the rule just doesn't relate to what he's doing at the moment.

He cannot connect cause and effect well. There are two kinds of thinking, linear and global. Linear is A plus B equals C. Straight-line logic. Global is A plus B equals anything you want them to be, depending on how you arrange them. Most of us learn in linear ways. We do A, B happens, and we derive C lesson from it. You back up over those tire guards at the parking lot exit. Your back tires go plooey. You learn that the sign saying, "Do not back up" really means what it says. Cause and effect. ADD kids have trouble linking up cause and effect, especially identifying the effects their own actions and words cause.

He cannot do more than one thing at a time, and sometimes not that. When Mom says, "Clean your room," most teens have a general idea what's expected and just sort of do it. Such a non-specific command is lost on the ADD kid. There are a number of steps involved in cleaning up a room. You put away the clothes on the floor, stashing some in the closet and tossing the rest in the wash. You pick up stuff, get rid of the dirty dishes, put your books back on the shelf, tack up the poster that's sagging, vacuum, and dust. You tidy up anything else that keeps it from looking pretty good. An ADD room-cleaner-upper has to be told, "Put your clothes in the wash." Then he has to be told, "Gather up those dirty dishes." Then he has to be told . . . But you get the idea. A complex chore must be broken down into small steps. Even then, the teen may be distracted and not complete the task.

He's probably hyperactive. People usually equate ADD with hyperactivity, but constant energetic activity and ADD are two separate things. Some ADD kids are, some aren't. Some non-ADD kids are, some aren't. Brandon was indeed hyperactive, always moving. He couldn't sit still. He physically could not make himself stay quiet.

Because his attention was so easily and constantly distracted, so was his activity. He'd go at something enthusiastically and minutes later be off on something else. Needless to say, he never remembered or paused to pick up after himself when he switched interests. It was this constant buzz, this bouncing-off-the-walls that drove his sister and mom out of their trees.

But most of all, it was his attitude.

The Problems ADD Generates

By the time an ADD kid reaches your age, he (remember that this includes she as well) has honed sarcasm, nastiness, wit, and anger to a fine edge. It's no wonder he's bitter, really. Because of his ADD signs and symptoms, he gets labeled "bad kid," "trouble-maker," "el stupid-o," "weirdo." Heaven knows he's tried to be what the rest of the world thinks he ought to be, but he can't. It's not a matter of will; it's a matter of wiring. There is nothing wrong with him except a difference in bio-chemistry, but the rest of the world doesn't see it that way.

His parents are upset and mad at him for not shaping up. His friends and teachers and everyone else are getting pretty tired of his constant noise and crashing around. By the time he's getting into school, and certainly by the time he enters high school, he believes what everyone says about him. No matter how he tries, no matter what he does right (and he probably does a lot of things right, but no one notices), he gets yelled at for not living up to others' expectations. Always. Constantly.

His self-esteem is so low you'd have to dig to bedrock to find it. He's ashamed of the way he is because no one likes the way he is, and he can't change it. And yet, everyone accuses him of not doing something about it. "If only you would . . ." Everyone insists his behavior is his fault and he's being bad deliberately. Everyone. Why shouldn't he believe it?

It seems that this is the way life is always going to be. He becomes cynical a lot earlier than do his friends. Anger builds up quickly and stays at a high level. He's already been labeled a dunce, and he knows what the inside of the principal's office looks like right down to the color of the paint in the closets. But there's one way he can get the attention every kid needs.

He can get noticed by getting laughed at. Negative attention is better than none. He'll clown. He'll develop a wicked sense of humor that reflects his anger at life. He'll display hostile behavior—fighting, verbally abusing others, defying authority (boy, does he ever!). He's lashing out at life because it frustrates him so.

And in the process he's creating severe, continual stress in others and in himself, everywhere he goes.

You already know the roles anger and grudge-holding play in happiness and lack of it. You can see why this kid has a very high statistical likelihood that he'll suffer major depression.

. . . . SO ARE YOU HYPER? POSSIBLY ADD?

If you have ADD symptoms, it doesn't really matter what the medical people call it. Those traits are causing you trouble. Treatment is available, and yes, it works. The best part of treatment is, it doesn't cancel out the many good things ADD does for you.

Good things? Absolutely. ADD people tend to be intelligent and quick-witted. They're terrible at desk work and routine, but they don't mind living on the ragged edge, entering occupations that just plain scare other people. And they're good at them! ADD people as a rule need slightly less sleep and are active more. In occupations where go-go-go succeeds, they do very well. You find a high proportion of ADD people in jobs such as law enforcement, fire fighting, and even medicine.

For instance, a colleague who is one of the best orthopedic surgeons around has always shown strong ADD traits. He's brilliant, but he doesn't read much. He can't sit still. He's a doer. Notice, he didn't get into brain or eye surgery, skills requiring delicate, patient, close work. An orthopedic surgeon works on the bones. He dives in there with saws, chisels, and hammers. It's very demanding, delicate work, yes, but there's a lot of slam-bang involved, too. It's perfect for him.

Treatment for ADD and ADHD takes three possible routes. One is training. ADD kids are taught how to control their tendencies and reroute them. That is, they learn how to make their shortcomings into strong suits. The other is medication. The third, the one that works best and lasts longest, combines medication with training. The medicine helps you settle down right away and concentrate well enough to make the training sink in. The training then prepares you for a day when you may not need medication. However, many ADD people find they need some form of medication most or all their lives in order to function with peak efficiency and enjoyment.

But one way or another, using whatever works best for you, get treatment. You don't have to fear addiction. Most medicines used for ADD and hyperactivity aren't addictive, and they can be tailored exactly to your needs. Some medicines, such as Ritalin, correct attention problems in 10 minutes and last about half a day. Others, such as Cylert, take 3 weeks to kick in, but they work all day. They are better in the long run, particularly if you have to take them for years.

We also often prescribe an antidepressant such as Effexor, Paxil, or Prozac. The antidepressants work just as well in folks who are not depressed as in those who are. I've had teenage ADD patients go from C averages to A averages after taking an antidepressant daily. They help ADD people control their concentration and activity. True, at times they ease or prevent depression as well. Remember that depression and anger problems loom larger in the lives of ADD people.

But ADD is not by any means the only source of stress in a family.

....................OTHER STRESS SOURCES

When you think of stress, you think of bad things happening to you. Good things cause just about as much stress. The ticket here is not good or bad; it's change. The bigger the change, for better or for worse, the tougher it is on your system.

Some stress is actually good for you. Human beings seem to need some tension in their lives in order to grow and function well. Too much is not good.

Here's a non-scientific little quiz for you. It doesn't prove anything, but it may tell you how much stress is staring you in the face right now. Answer each question with a yes or no. A yes gets three points, no gets none.

_____ **Death.** In the last calendar year, has someone in your immediate family or someone special in your extended family died? This includes stillborn babies and abortions.

_____ **Divorce.** In the last calendar year, has someone very close to you separated-and-things-don't-look-good or divorced (that includes yourself)? If it's your parents, make that "during the last *three* years" and add an extra point.

_____ **Marriage.** Did you marry?

_____ **Change of residence.** Did you either leave home or return home after living independently? Did you and your family move in the past year to a new home or location?

_____ **Illness.** Have you or someone close to you been really, really sick lately?

_____ **Rape.** Have you been the victim of a rape or some form of being fondled or molested in the last year (this applies to guys as well as women)? If it occurred at the hands of a trusted friend or family member, add a point or two.

_____ **Pregnancy and birth.** Are you pregnant or have you given birth in the last calendar year? If you're male, have you caused a pregnancy? An abortion scores twice, counting as a death *as well as* a pregnancy. It takes that big a toll.

_____ **Jail.** Have you or someone very close to you done time this last year, or perhaps are in the slammer now?

These next causes carry less weight, so give them one point for a yes.

_____ **School.** Starting or ending the school year counts. It's the change that counts, not "bad" or "good." If you're on an all-year schedule, the short vacation time probably doesn't rate a point. If you've changed schools, add an extra point.

_____ **Work.** Major changes at work count a point each. New job? Fired? Given more responsibility? Trouble with the boss counts one also.

_____ **Car wreck.** Give yourself a point if either you or someone close to you was involved in an auto accident, even if it was non-injury. If you were driving, add another point.

_____ **Major holidays and vacations.** Awesome though they may be, they're worth a point because they're change.

_____ **Awards.** Have you received a significant award or won something in the last six months? Even awards can be stressful.

_____ **Other.** Now that you have the idea, what big change occurred in your life this past year that isn't covered? Is it worth one point or three?

There are other stressors, but this gives you a good idea. Now add up your points. Again I mention that this isn't scientific or based on some huge study. It's merely an indicator. If you racked up ten or more points in the last six months, it indicates that you are on overload. If you said "yes" to the item about parents' divorce, you may be at a dangerous stress level even if you said "no" to everything else.

What do you do about it? One good thing is to try to avoid further changes for awhile, especially biggies in the three-point category. A lot of them are beyond your control, but at least you know they will affect you more severely now than they might have at some other time.

Another is to simply be aware that these changes are affecting your thoughts, your emotions, and your life. Knowing that the effects of these changes are temporary, you can give yourself a little slack. When you wish you could die, you now know that it's the stress talking, not your logic or even your heart.

A third is to turn to God. If you are a Christian, you can draw enormous strength and solace from God. You already know He cares about you.[1] He probably won't erase the stress effects of change—they are natural, programmed into you, and physiological. But He can ease the results of stress—anxiety and depression. Tell Him what you want and need in prayer. Remember that a shared burden becomes only half of a burden. So share your burdens and hurts with God as well as with a couple really close friends. Also read God's love letter to you, the Bible.

Hear Paul's ode to joy in Philippians. Listen to hurting people in the psalms trust God. Tackle the book of Job. One of Scripture's best lessons is that we are not alone. Whatever our sorrow or stressors, other people knew them also, and the

Bible talks frankly about them without whitewashing facts or characters.

So here you are, with a nice, intact family, a good relationship with God, and great friends. You're doing well at school. Your dog behaves reasonably well. Your little sister's team is winning at soccer. Everything should be peaches; instead, you're in the pits.

Now what?

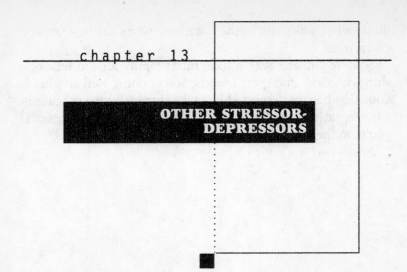

chapter 13

OTHER STRESSOR-DEPRESSORS

When you hear the statement, "Most Americans will suffer a major depression at some time in their lives," your first response is likely to be, "Not me!" In large part, you can make that boast come true. Following the precepts in this book, for instance, will help you avoid landing in the "Most Americans" category. But that doesn't mean you're depression-proof. Here are some ways it might come upon you, when there seems to be very little you can do to prevent it.

The Self-Image Takes a Beating

You try out to be a basketball cheerleader, and you think you're doing pretty well. You have the routines down pat, and you display a certain flair. Enthusiasm. You are not chosen. Later you learn the judges thought you weigh too much and you aren't pretty enough. Depression socks you not when you are passed over but when you find out why. You just took a body blow to your self-image.

A good-looking guy is really, really hung up on this cute girl. She dumps him for a geek. His self-image takes a pounding.

128

Some attribute this saying to literary giant Oscar Wilde, about a hundred years ago: "Being popular is important, otherwise people might not like you." He knew immense popularity for awhile, with three of his plays in production simultaneously. The whole world loved him! A short time later he was jailed for two years because of a homosexual relationship and every shred of popularity disappeared.

Popularity is fickle, particularly in high school. It sometimes seems that popularity has nothing to do with actual character and beauty, and if you see that, you're right! The person who is the hit of the class this year might become as attractive as oral surgery next year. And yet, how you see yourself hinges almost completely on how the rest of the world perceives you. Rotten but true. You are valuable! And yet, when you are snubbed or overlooked, you feel like junk. And when your self-image drops, the chance of depression rises dramatically.

We've found something else about self-image. This happens to pertain to girls. If a girl's father thinks highly of her, she feels good about herself. If he treats her like dirt, the rest of the world can elevate her to royalty; she'll still tend to feel like dirt unless she gets some help.

How is your self-image?

Parents. When I think at length about my relationship with my parents, I [do] [do not] believe:

1. They trust me and feel good about me.
2. They think me valuable enough to really worry about me sometimes.
3. They understand a little bit what my life is like.
4. They congratulate me when I pull something off.
5. They believe I'm doing as well as I can in school.

If three or four of your answers are yes, you have every right to feel good about yourself!

129

School. If teachers and students all voted for the following titles, I would probably make a fairly respectable showing, whether or not I won (M. equals either Miss or Mr.):

1. M. Congeniality.
2. M. Sensible.
3. M. Friend.
4. M. Trustworthy. That includes M. Honesty.
5. M. Good Hearted.

If you would get fairly high marks in three or more of the above polls, you're doing all right!

Myself. I know myself better than anyone else does. When it comes to me dealing with myself (agree or disagree):

1. I tend to be really hard on myself when I mess up.
2. I'm a lot worse than most people think I am.
3. I know I am not in the same league as the most exclusive cliques at school. They're smarter, richer, and better looking.
4. I don't expect to do as well after high school as most of my friends will do.
5. I'm not good enough to earn any significant awards.
6. I wish someone would praise my efforts, but I know it's not going to happen.

If you agreed with three or more of those statements, your worst image enemy may be yourself. Your sense of self could stand some major improvement. Check around for opportunities to learn about managing your self-image. Ask your school counselor or health professional.

Post Traumatic Stress Disorder Nails You

You may have heard of post traumatic stress disorder, usually abbreviated as PTSD. It's emotional problems that come from shocking or horrible experiences months or years after you experienced them. Its effects can be devastating. For instance, 90 percent of Vietnam War veterans have divorced. A greater number of Nam vets have committed suicide than ever died in the war itself. Statistics like these are blamed primarily on PTSD. Divorce? Suicide? We're talking about major depression and desperation, with the fruits coming decades after the conflict itself.

If a major calamity has nailed you recently, depression will probably follow on its heels. It doesn't have to happen to you directly. It could happen to someone close to you. You may witness something horrible happening to a total stranger. Let's make up an example.

You are out driving. You have to stop your car at a railroad crossing gate as it comes down, bell clanging and red lights flashing. The train whistle blasts. You see a kid on a bike on the other side of the tracks coming this way, whipping around the end of the crossing gate. Horrified, you realize that he's going to try to beat the train, and you just know he's not going to make it. He doesn't. Right in front of you, the freight train catches him squarely as he pedals across the tracks.

For weeks afterward, you suffer grotesque nightmares about the blood and mutilation that shattered your own life while you watched, as well as his. You can't eat. You're afraid to sleep. Anxiety grips your throat and tries to strangle you. You can't concentrate; you flunk a test you should have done well on. Your whole existence has unraveled.

You rationalize to yourself, "It's not going to affect me permanently because I didn't know the kid. It didn't really involve me. Besides, I've seen gore almost that bad in the movies. Well, kind of bad."

With support and understanding from others, you work your way past the event. Years later, the nightmares return. Perhaps you get flashbacks of that tragic moment. Panic attacks. Depression grinds you down and you don't realize that its source is that horrible event that by pure happenstance

131

occurred in front of you. You thought you were over it. You're not. That's what post traumatic stress disorder is, and that's what it can do.

If anything of that sort is happening in your life, you should seek out competent professional help. You can work past it, but you need a counselor to lead you.

One other point regarding PTSD. As you grow from child to adult, your life perspectives change. When something horrible happens to you (or in front of you) when you're little, you deal with it with your childlike skills. But as you grow, your understanding about life deepens. You have to re-process the event from the standpoint of your new awareness. Later, you're going to have to do it over again as your understanding deepens further.

Your awareness and understanding of God changes as you grow, also. Let us assume that God is now an integral part of your life.

················· RELIGIOUS CONSIDERATIONS ■

Christians are supposed to glide along hassle-free, right?

Whoever told you that? The Christian life takes a lot of work and some hard decisions in the short term, but all the work you put in will be multiplied as blessing in the long run. That's the key to remember: What does God want in the long term?

When you fail to keep that point of view in mind, you make lousy, rotten decisions that cause problems, emotional misery in particular. What's more, the actual process of making wrong decisions can in itself lead to depression.

Wrong Perspectives

Example: In order to get along with your particular bunch of friends, you have to smoke pot and do an occasional upper. You know who the dealers are and who's buying. It's part of the modern world. In order to fit, you bend. That's the world's perspective, and it's definitely short term; you want to get through school without being roughed up.

What's God's opinion? I think you know already what He wants. But maybe you don't know that He spelled it out. Back in Revelation, the Bible's predictions of the end, the Greek root word *pharmakeia* is usually translated in its various forms as sorcery or sorcerers. A generation ago, no one could envision the widespread drug culture we have today, and figured the Bible must be talking about drugs as used in certain forms of augury—fortune-telling—and witchcraft. The primary meanings however are drug use, drug user, drug dealer.[1] It's right there in black and white for you.

Doing what God wants regarding pot and other drugs may hurt you in some ways in the short term. At the very least, you'll lose some friends—your drug-using friends. But you'll also gain self-confidence, a better self-image, and the approval of the Lord who already saved you from yourself. The long-range effects will be great.

When you get into drugs, even very casually, the short-term effects may seem okay, but you feel rotten about yourself for not living up to what you know is right. Depression results—not to mention that certain drugs create their own chemical depressions.

How do you think drugs work their special effects? Chemical change. And one of the changes that pot makes is a reduction of serotonin levels. Bingo: more depression and passivity. And yet, there's a clique of kids, and you know who they are, who insist that the only sophisticated people are the ones that try stuff.

You're not alone with the peer-pressure dilemma. It's been around as long as peers have. Good old Moses bumped into exactly the same problem four thousand years ago. Raised in the royal court of his world's most powerful nation, he could have lived out his life in cushy comfort and ended up as just another cartouche chiseled in a wall somewhere. But he sided

133

with his blood people the Hebrews, slaves in the land, and ended his days as one of the greatest heroes in all history.[2]

Daniel and his friends, groomed by the Babylonians for public service in the royal court, chose to stick with what they knew was right instead of bending. The long-term benefits far, far outweighed the couple dainties they gave up.[3]

Solomon lived the most luxuriant life imaginable, with an overkill of sex (a thousand wives and concubines; concubines are girls or women who provide sex but do not have the legal rights of wives[4]), food (tables laden daily with all sorts of exotic meats, bread—anything he wanted),[5] power,[6] education.[7] He was blessed beyond measure, *until* he drifted away from God, and it all came tumbling down.[8]

May I suggest you spend twenty minutes tonight thinking about your lifestyle. What aspects of it are you proud of? And do you wish Jesus would leave the room when you are doing certain other things, so He can't see you? Trust me on this; He's watching. And your heart knows that.

Satan's Attacks

You bet he attacks. But how do you tell if it's the evil one (or your own bad feelings about yourself, which, because they defeat you, Satan encourages) as opposed to God trying to tell you something? I suggest a couple guidelines.

1. **If your discouragement and depression are mushy and vague, hard to define, God probably is not delivering a specific message. When He speaks, He speaks. You know perfectly well what He likes or dislikes (whether you like it or not).**

2. **If you feel helpless and desperate, with no way out, that is definitely *not* of God!**

3. **If you feel depressed and worthless, that's not of God either.**

Peter called Satan a roaring lion looking around for someone to grab.[9] If anyone knew what Satan can do, it was good old before-the-cock-crows-three-times Peter.

Do-It-Yourself

Picture yourself as a dedicated Christian working in, say, a church-run day care center. Two others work there also. It's midmorning when an irate mother calls to chew on you because her child came home with poster paint stains on his good clothes. While you're trying to assure her that the paint will wash right out, another mother storms in. She's angry because she thinks you're using a particular educational method you never heard of, and she thinks it's wrong. She wants this other method you've never heard of either used instead. Meanwhile, Jeffy swats Rory with a dump truck and you have to tend to that, and Meghan is up early from her nap and howling, and Kim in her high chair needs her pacifier, and Polly wants another cracker, and . . . Did I mention it's only 10:00 A.M.? You have a long, long day ahead!

But somebody has to do it, and you're certain God identified you as that Somebody.

We find that very often, a major source of depression among Christians comes from their attempts to do everything in their own strength. This doesn't mean much to the person outside of Christ, the person who does not understand the strengths that Jesus and His Holy Spirit can provide. To us who are in the faith, it's the difference between a long history of efficient, cheerful service and inefficient work, depression, and burnout. In this regard also, you can indeed choose happiness!

Inefficiency and burnout go way back. Moses had them. Then his father-in-law, Jethro, said, "Hey! You can't handle it all yourself. There's a better way." Jethro showed him how to use God's strength instead of his own. For Moses, things smoothed out not just at that time but for years thereafter.[10]

In fact, right at the very beginning of the Church, the apostles ran into the problem. They felt called to preach, but they were too busy managing the food and money that were shared in common by the new believers. So they got others to pick up part of the load, and the Word of the Lord was able to spread rapidly.[11]

You in your hypothetical day care situation can also use God's strength to even out your load and make it bearable in the long term. Determine how much you can reasonably do. That, friend, is what you can do. There may be more to be done, but not by you. Therefore, just like Moses and the apostles did, use His servants, whom He will call. Use His guidance by asking for it. Ask Him for His peace and strength; you'll be amazed what comes to you. Most of all, rest in the perfect confidence that He loves *you* without reservation, regardless what or how much you do. If you serve Him, you serve Him out of gratitude for His love which is already being delivered, and not in order to win it.

Wrong Priorities

Let's look at an adult case of wrong priorities. Joe Service really loves to serve the Lord. He makes that his first priority because he says that's what God wants. If there's any time left over, he'll read the Bible or maybe help the wife a little as she struggles to raise their kids. Yes sir, Joe Service is really into serving the Lord!

Know what we discover very, very, *very* often? Joe Service isn't loving to serve the Lord much at all. Below conscious level, he's terribly, terribly anxious to please others so that they'll like him, a very selfish reason to do something. Or he feels so guilty about wrong things he thinks or has done that he's trying to balance them with right things, so to speak. Whatever the reason, one thing's sure: His priorities are all screwed up. And so he works like a madman "serving the Lord" and letting God's *real* will for his life fall by the side. Is that a formula for happiness? Hardly!

What does God's Word really say about priorities?

First, build your relationship with God. That means prayer, Bible study, and close relationships with other Christians. Does

God place that ahead of serving Him? See how Jesus leads the way in that regard.

Luke, a doctor, tells us[12] that as Jesus' fame as a teacher and healer spread, people came flocking to Him. If ever there was a case of serving the Lord, it was Jesus preaching and healing the sick! What a ministry! And yet, says Luke, Jesus walked away from all those people swarming in to be ministered to and went off by Himself to pray. There was "work" to be done preaching and healing, but His fellowship with His Father came first.

Second, take care of your mental health and keep your own strength up. You need nourishment, rest,[13] and recreation. That's right. Recreation. Some goof-off time to recharge your batteries. Not just "it would be nice." Not just "if I had time." You *need!* If you go nuts, you won't be much use to God, family, or friends. So you *have* to take care of yourself.

Jesus Himself did all that, eating with various people, sleeping (even in a boat on rough water![14]), hanging out at people's homes.

The other second-most important thing is your family. If you have family responsibilities, you take care of them first.[15]

Now, finally, there's serving the Lord! With a strong and happy heart! Refreshed and ready to go! Now your service to Him will be of maximum value to Him and to His people who need you.

These are not the priorities that are guaranteed to endear you to humankind. When people want your service for something, they sometimes get a little bent out of shape when you put your own needs or even a family responsibility first. Some church people even preach and teach that any attention you give yourself is sinful. Sure, you can go too far in the wrong direction, being selfish about your own pleasures and shirking service to God's needy. But too many Christians, we find, bend too far toward the legalistic neglect of self. Jesus kept up the pace by keeping Himself up. So should you.

···················· YOUR OWN PHYSIOLOGY
■

It's not just what we've already discussed earlier that can get you down. Sometimes your own physiology can cause depression. Some little chemical balance goes just a wee bit haywire, and boom! You're in the pits. An infection can do it. Genes might be the culprit.

You're not a doctor and you can't go around diagnosing yourself and others. But let me list briefly a couple things to think about if you feel yourself sliding into depression that cannot be explained in some other way. And please note that if some of these chemical imbalances get far enough out of hand, they can cause problems to the point of suicidal tendencies.

Note also that body chemistry and emotional health are deeply intertwined. Does chemical imbalance produce emotional problems, or do the emotional difficulties throw chemical balance off? We know for certain that if you're healthy emotionally, you'll suffer far fewer physical problems than do the emotionally troubled. But at the same time, you could be doing everything right emotionally, physically, and spiritually and still be plagued by an inherited, suicidal, serotonin-depleted depression.

Endocrine problems. Endocrine glands are those glands that produce chemicals and release them right into the blood stream, without sending them out through ducts (as opposed to, for instance, tear glands, which produce tears and send them out through little pipes—ducts—in your eyes).

We've known for some time that too little thyroid activity can cause a common form of depression. However, medication to correct your thyroid imbalances can help in this kind of depression. You see, the thyroid and other glands, such as the pituitary and the hypothalamus, influence each other in complex ways by releasing hormones. Imbalance in one messes them all up, and your emotional health depends upon stable production from these glands. And yes, the glands which control sex drive and reproduction are included in this group. That is probably the reason people who are depressed have less interest in sex than do most.

It may also play a part on a condition we call *postpartum depression*. Postpartum refers to the time in a woman's life right after her baby is born. This kind of depression usually has other causes as well.

To check on these possibilities, your doctor as part of a lab work-up measures various endocrine products which are circulating in the blood.

Electrolyte disturbances. When the brilliant ballerina Gelsey Kirkland nearly killed herself because she was so depressed, the first thing the doctors worked on was her potassium level. It had bottomed out in her. As it rose, so did her spirits. Sodium and potassium are the two major electrolytes which keep all the nerves and muscles in your body happy by controlling the neurotransmitters (brain juice and related juices). Lithium salts used as drugs apparently perform a similar job. Electrolyte levels are easy to check and extremely important to both physical and emotional health. Bulimics (compulsive vomiters) *die* because too much vomiting causes an electrolyte imbalance severe enough to make the heart stop beating.

Viral infections. If you are sick or have been lately, you may have stumbled upon the reason for your depression. Viruses can do that. On the flip side, depression can lower resistance to viral infection so that you get sick more. Even some cancers, we're finding, have viruses involved in their appearance and progress. So depression can make us more likely to develop a cancer.

These are some of the depression- and stress-causers, and they can be controlled in one way or another.

And then there's guilt.

chapter 14

GUILT AND SHAME

Who says professionals in psychotherapy don't have their little battles? We enjoy arguing as much as anyone, and one of the people we argue about is Sigmund Freud, who more or less invented modern psychoanalysis. He coined many terms you may have heard, such as "superego," meaning our conscience, and established the ground rules for psychoanalysis.

Now that we understand psychodynamics better, though, we see that Freud, important as he was in developing the art, was wrong about a lot of things. There's a hot and lively debate in psychiatry now as to just how many of Freud's original theories still hold water.

I'll jump into the fray myself, because I am convinced that at least one of his precepts is dead wrong. He claimed that all guilt is a bad thing; that if people were simply free of guilt, they'd be free of many of the psychological bonds that hobble them. I couldn't disagree more!

The key is that there is false guilt and true guilt. Freud believed all guilt is false because there's no way to say who is "right" and who is "wrong." I agree that false guilt is a bogeyman who robs us of happiness. But I am equally certain that true guilt exists, and it exists to our benefit.

False Guilt and True

We talked about ADD and ADHD teens in a previous chapter. Most of them must deal with emotional problems because the world dumped a big load of guilt on them. "If you would just stop and think, you'd behave better." "You can sit still if you will only try." "It's your fault you're making such lousy grades!" "Quit interrupting! Can't you see I'm talking?" It's always their fault. Shame heaps upon shame. And yet it's not their fault. No matter how hard they try, they cannot sit still or think the way others want them to. These things for the ADD and ADHD kids are impossible because of their inherited brain chemical differences unless they go on medication to alter those differences.

So that is a classic case of false guilt. The kids are made to feel guilty for something that cannot be easily controlled and is certainly not their fault.

False guilt is the trip we either lay upon ourselves or other people try to lay upon us that has no basis in truth. We are not really guilty of what we think we are. Everyone gets slammed with false guilt once in awhile, especially because some people are very, very good at laying it on others. It is a prime source of depression; you feel so very rotten for doing whatever it is you were led to think you did.

Teens get saddled with a lot of false guilt and shame by others, because teens do not think and act like older people, and older people are convinced that only their own ways are "right." That's the way older folks are. That's the way you're going to be when you get older.

But teens also build up a lot of false guilt all by themselves. Everyone does, in fact, but teens are especially good at it.

Let's say your best friend (if you're a girl) or girlfriend (if you're a boy) becomes deeply depressed. She takes up alcohol in a big way, stealing liquor from her father's cabinet, getting

141

her cousin to buy wine and beer for her. You know she's going over the top. She insists, though, that if you tell a single soul, she'll kill herself. And you get the strong indication that she means it.

She has just dumped ten tons of guilt on you. You know you're not helping her if you keep your mouth shut. In fact, you're contributing to her downslide. You feel extremely guilty for keeping her dirty secret. But what can you do? You know she's taking the wrong path. But you can't turn her aside from that path by yourself; she won't listen to you; and you don't dare tell anyone else so that they can try to redirect her. Again, you feel so guilty for not doing something. She needs you and you're letting her down. Now let's say that you can't stand it. You know she's going to get caught, and her situation is deteriorating worse and worse. So you confide in the school counselor. The next day your friend actually does commit suicide. Now you're carrying impossible guilt! The depression your guilt inflicts ruins your whole life.

Which statement is true? More than one may be.

1. I could have stopped this somehow if I were a better friend.
2. I let her down terribly by telling. I broke her trust.
3. If I had told right away, maybe this wouldn't have happened.
4. My friends blame me and they're right.
5. I just caused my best friend's death.
6. Not a shred of this is my fault. None of it.

You know what? Item six is the only valid choice. Every ounce of your guilt is false. Here's why.

True guilt does not come from the actions of people other than yourself. In the case above, your friend imposed a feeling of guilt on you not because of your actions but because of hers.

That's a powerful, powerful difference. Do you see it? It wasn't something you did or were doing. It came from something *she* was doing. You were not forcing her into her situation; in fact, you counseled against her course of action and she ignored you.

Our modern culture doesn't help a bit. In today's society, we've made an art out of blaming someone else. For instance, I have an acquaintance whose husband works in a major national park. One Sunday afternoon during a winter storm, a carload of teens drove around a road barrier up into a blocked-off parking lot. They wanted to play in the fresh snow. One of them slipped and broke an ankle. A week later, the guy's dad called the park and asked, "Where do I send the doctor bill?" Even though his kid and others illegally ignored a barrier; even though they went where they weren't supposed to be; even though they knew winter weather causes slippery conditions, but they took their chances anyway; he assumed the park should have to pay.

That's the attitude that prevails these days. Whatever happens to me, it's not my responsibility, so it must be someone else's. We have lost what is an important truth:

If I do something wrong or stupid, the consequences are my own responsibility, not others'. The exception to this, of course, is little kids who don't have a clear grasp of what is right or wrong and haven't had enough experience yet to know what's stupid. Running out into the street after a loose ball is stupid to a twelve year old but not to a five year old. You, though, are getting old enough to have a pretty good idea about what constitutes stupid actions, and I hope by now you have a good sense of right and wrong.

There's another reason teens are so vulnerable to false guilt. A very small child is totally self-centered, and that's quite normal. The child's needs are the most important needs. When anything happens, the child assumes that it's somehow because of him or her. That's why when their parents divorce, little kids are absolutely certain the divorce occurred because of them. In a different, very sad case, a little pre-school boy was abducted, horribly mutilated, and turned loose out in the country. When rescuers found him, his first words were, "I was a bad boy."

As the child gets older, this self-centeredness dwindles. Basically, we call it maturity. The child begins to think of others' needs as well as his or her own. The child sees that people do things over which the child has no control. By adulthood, Lord willing, that person has a good sense of personal responsibility and also realizes that the actions of others—that is, most of life—are beyond changing.

Teens hang betwixt and between on the maturity scale from total self-centeredness to total maturity (is there such a thing?). And that's good in some ways! That's why teens are still ready to change the world. They think they can do it, and if it weren't for us older folks getting in the way, they probably could. Teens are still ready to pick up burdens of responsibility—and guilt—that are not theirs to bear, just as do youngsters. Deep inside, the attitude of that poor, disfigured little boy still operates; "No matter how rotten or uncontrollable the actions of others, somehow, it's my fault." When other persons lay a guilt trip on the teen, that just reinforces the little child down inside. "See? It *is* my fault!"

True guilt can come from either doing wrong or failing to do right. Some people call them sins of commission (actively doing, or committing, wrong) and sins of omission (omitting an act, or failing to do the right thing when called upon). *However:* True guilt never comes from doing your best, whether your best is effective, or good enough, or not.

I saw a headline in a paper a while ago that illustrates this perfectly. By chance, a young man was first on the scene of a major car wreck. One vehicle with three teens in it caught fire. He managed to drag one girl out, but the other two burned to death—if they weren't dead already. The headline: "Man who saved teen haunted by other deaths." He was kicking himself because he had neglected to bring his cellular phone with him that day and thus lost precious time calling the accident in. And he couldn't save the others.

Here is a true hero who did the best he could, and he still isn't satisfied. It's human nature. We all get those feelings. But we all must recognize the feelings for what they are. False guilt.

While you are doing your best, you might leave out things you should have done as well. After doing your best, you might discover later that you did the wrong thing altogether. Good news! God doesn't expect you to be perfect. He does indeed appreciate when you offer Him your best efforts. But you aren't omniscient. You aren't all-powerful. And He of all Persons knows that.

Therefore, any guilt arising from doing the wrong thing in good faith, or failing to do something even though you were doing the best you could, is false guilt. In the situation I described about the best friend's suicide, you did the best you could think of to do. In a phrase, you "acted in good faith." God honors good faith. Whether it was right or wrong, you did what you thought best at the time. Don't let others lay a false guilt trip on you.

True guilt almost invariably comes from a lack of self-control. Let's call a spade a spade here. The kind of self-control I'm talking about is the kind that resists temptation and sticks to what's right despite pressure to do what's wrong. Plain and simple, yielding to temptation and doing wrong is sin.

This isn't someone else's self-control, either. We're talking about your own.

Probably the two most common sources of sin are sex and greed—not the only ones, but the biggest ones. When you fall to temptation in either area, your conscience jumps right on you. Then you do one of two things: Either you acknowledge that bump by your conscience or you blot it out with a big fat glob of denial.

"It's wrong for most other people, but it's all right for me in this situation." That's denial. It muffles conscience, but it doesn't change the fact of sin. Your conscience continues to grind along, covered up but still alive. The result: depression.

The classic example is King David.[1] Without air conditioning in Jerusalem three thousand years ago, people spent a lot of time up on the flat roofs of their houses, especially in the evening. David was strolling along his, looking out over the city, when he saw on another rooftop below a beautiful woman taking a bath. What an awesome lady!

So he sent a servant to find out who she was. Her name was Bathsheba and she was the wife of Uriah, a soldier who was away at war. David invited her into the palace and, smitten with lust, slept with her. Not long after, she sent him word that she was pregnant. Obviously, tongues would wag, since her husband hadn't been home for months. David's denial mode kicked in and he started calculating how to cover the scandal up.

He had Uriah sent home on leave, but the loyal soldier refused to sleep with his wife since all his buddies couldn't have the same privilege. Finally, David got his commanding officer (it was, you see, David's war being fought) to put Uriah in the front ranks of a suicide charge. That worked, and Uriah was killed, along with other innocents. David took the freshly widowed, pregnant Bathsheba into the palace, out of the public eye. Their nasty little secret was secure, and David's denial kept a lid on the whole thing.

Soon thereafter, David's trusted advisor Nathan told him a story. "A rich, greedy man with lots of sheep stole the only sheep, a treasured little ewe, of a poor fellow." He really tugged at the old heartstrings.

David roared, "That man ought to die! And pay through the nose!" Even then, David's denial was up to full strength.

And then Nathan said, "You are the man," and prophesied misery for David from that day forth.

Finally, the wall of denial broke and the enormity of his actions hit him. David wailed, "I have sinned against the Lord!"

Lack of self-control in one situation brought grief to thousands in Israel for years thereafter. And yet, although her child died soon after birth, Bathsheba ended up being the mother of Solomon. That brings up the one great thing about true guilt, which David's was.

True guilt can be cleansed by forgiveness. I see it happen over and over in my practice. A person comes in to be treated for depression. The usual causes don't seem to be *the* cause. Then as we talk, a major source of sin or shame emerges. We identify it and discuss it. The patient asks God's forgiveness. The patient asks forgiveness of the persons injured by the sin. The sin situation is ended one way or another so that the patient is not continuing the practice of sin. The depression disappears.

The conscience was there all along, nudging, but it was stifled by denial or stubbornness.

Shame

Incidentally, I mentioned "shame" in the chapter title because shame so often goes hand in hand with guilt. Addictions are nearly all shame driven.

Addictions aren't always what you think, either. You think of drugs, cigarettes, and alcohol. Addictions can also include "good" activities. Workaholism, for instance. The person neglects other aspects of life—family, friends, recreation, rest—in order to spend more time and energy at work. Churchaholics have to be at church whenever the doors open. They go to church so many times a week that even God gets a little put out with them. They sit on half a dozen committees, always make their feelings known at meetings, make certain they are recognized as super-duper-dandy Christians.

People can be addicted to an inability to say no to others. Girls might let boys take advantage of them sexually; that's an addiction also, called "codependency." Boys think they just gotta sleep with girls. Sexual addiction goes both ways.

How does shame drive these actions? In two ways.

One we call the addiction cycle. It was first described in reference to alcoholism, so we might as well stick with that as an example. The alcoholic drinks. Gets drunk. Is shamed by others and feels ashamed himself or herself for losing control. That person gets drunk again to ease the pain of feeling ashamed. The person feels even more shame for this lack of self-control. He or she drinks more to blot out the pain. And so the cycle goes on, spiraling downward. It works for any addiction that our society does not approve of.

The other is shame about that old bugaboo, feeling like a nobody. I long ago learned that the more dysfunctional (that is, riddled by alcoholism, extremism, denial, or legalism) the family of origin, the more shame and feelings of nobody-ness that child-victim will experience as a teenager. In order to prove he or she is an okay person, the addict may go overboard with alcohol etc. or perhaps in a socially acceptable way (church and work, for example), then feels ashamed about the lack of balance. The poor shame-driven victim just can't seem to win.

What "cures" shame? A decent sense of self, which can come with therapy. To an extent, arguing with yourself works. When your heart cries, "Shame!" you say "Oh, no you don't. I know better than that!" Much shame is based upon false guilt, too. Now that you know a little more about false guilt, you can, we hope, avoid that aspect of shame altogether. Remember that Satan is called the accuser of the brethren.[2] He loves to create false guilt.

In our example above where the friend committed suicide, what would have been the course for you to take?

1. **Recognize the false guilt. This person was imposing responsibility for her actions upon you. That's not possible, because she will do what she wants regardless of**

what you do. To confirm if this is false guilt, reverse the situation. If you made demands of someone else, and that person followed them, would you be obligated to act in a particular way? Not really. If you want to do something, you're going to do it. Or not.

2. Take a stand immediately. "You are the only one who can make yourself do something or keep from doing something. I cannot. I care about you! I hope you don't choose to kill yourself. But if you think you want to kill yourself, nothing I do or don't do will make you change your mind. I will not go along with this." It's a tough, tough thing to do, to stand up to someone you truly care about. In this case, it's your best bet.

3. Tell your friend how you feel, what you think, and what her dangers are. Then give her the chance to find help herself. But set a cut-off time. If she isn't finding help by such-and-so time, you'll tell someone. Put the responsibility for her actions squarely in her court.

There is one other item that afflicts teens heavily. Pregnancy. It hits guys indirectly, but it hits girls forever. Let's talk about that.

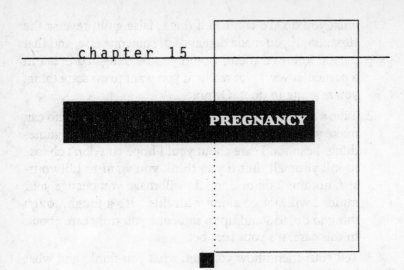

chapter 15

PREGNANCY

As part of my psychiatric training, an instructor showed us a
videotape about three minutes long. A sort of hidden-camera
thing, it depicted an actual family coming in for a session with
a psychotherapist. By analyzing those first few minutes, which
included the family entering the room and sitting down, we
were then supposed to tell the instructor what the problem in
that family was.

Oh, one other thing: There was no audio. We could see but
not hear. We would have to observe body language and facial
expressions—visual clues only.

It's an interesting exercise. How good would you be at
guessing the situation? Here's what you would see:

On one side of the room up against the wall stands the therapist's desk. Its naugahyde chair is swung around to face into
the room. A sofa sits against the wall to the chair's left. In front
of it is a large, stylish coffee table. To the therapist's right, three
wingback chairs are arranged along the other wall, facing the
sofa. They are served by small end tables. A thick, shaggy carpet, a potted palm, and large, beautiful paintings complete the
scene.

The therapist comes in and sits down. The family troops in right behind her. As they enter the room, the extremely overweight mother directs everyone, telling them all where to sit.

On the sofa, she places their teen daughter closest to the therapist and the father right beside her. The daughter is a frail kid with rather stringy hair and a woebegone droop to her face. She'd be pretty if it weren't for the sad look. The mother settles the two younger children into wingback chairs and she herself takes the wingback farthest from the therapist. She and the smaller children, a boy about eight and a girl ten or so, face the sofa.

The mother's mouth never quits moving for long. When the therapist says something to anyone in the room, the mother responds.

The dad looks uncomfortable and pretty much resigned to doing something he obviously doesn't want to be doing. He displays nervousness, fiddling with the pencils in his shirt breast pocket, adjusting his tie. He doesn't appear to say anything.

The little boy fidgets constantly and the little girl looks like she is whining, twisting her head and squirming as whiny kids do.

It's the teenaged girl who grabs your attention. She seems so uncomfortable sitting beside her dad, and yet she doesn't try to move away or put any distance between them. She looks like a kid torn by impossible circumstances, as though she were tossed into a shark tank. Should she float virtually motionless so as to attract no attention, or swim like mad for the shore? And which way is the nearest shore, and should she swim for it? She sits rigid on the sofa, her arms crossed tightly.

The tape ends.

"Okay," says the instructor. "What's the problem here and what are the interpersonal family dynamics that precipitated it?"

Here was my guess, and that's what it was, was a pure guess.

The mother's bossiness says "control freak." She was directing every detail of her family's behavior. Control freaks often suffer through out-of-control childhoods to get the way they are. Too, she was extremely obese. She could be using that fat pad to keep people at a safe distance, and to prevent herself from being attractive in the surface sense. I guessed that she was probably sexually abused as a child—a horrific experience over which the child has absolutely no control (but is always led by the abuser to believe she or he is the guilty person who caused it).

I further guessed that the mother had a poor sexual relationship with her husband, since she sat on the opposite side of the room from him. She also directed him around as if she were his mother rather than his wife. All that suggested to me that the mother may have been unconsciously pairing off daughter and father in a sense, fostering a relationship of emotional incest.

Now emotional incest is not the incest you automatically think of when you hear the word. It is usually not sexual in nature. In sexual incest, the daughter becomes a surrogate wife image to the father. In emotional incest, the daughter becomes the nurturer and friend of the father, a role the mother/wife ought to be playing and is not (or the son becomes confidant and nurturer to the mother; works the same with boys). You see, in a normal family, the parents do the nurturing and the children receive that nurturing and grow thereby. In the family governed by emotional incest, the relationship is twisted inside out. The children cannot grow normally, for they are sapping their own strength nurturing rather than being nurtured. Our book *Love Is a Choice*[1] explains all this in greater detail. I strongly recommend it—and not just because I had a part in writing it.

So here, I guessed, was a woman afraid of close relationships and especially of close sexual relationships, unconsciously encouraging her daughter to become the primary female friend of her husband. I also guessed that because she was displacing her normal wife-husband relationship with something more distant, they probably slept in separate bedrooms.

The girl's body language—the tightly crossed arms, the discomfort—suggested to me that she probably sensed that this family relationship was unnatural, even though there is no way she would see what was actually going on, and even though she seemed to love her father in a daughterly way.

So then I took a really wild guess, adding up these further observations also: The girl was placed closest to the therapist and the mother sat farthest away. The dad seemed to be rolling along for the ride without any active input. The little kids, the boy especially, were acting out great stress in the family.

"The girl's pregnant," I said to the instructor. "Below conscious level, she feels ashamed of her closeness to her father, yet craves the male attention she got used to. So she acted out her confusion on an unconscious level by getting herself pregnant. Maybe it's even her ticket out of the family and into a premature marriage. And now the family doesn't know how to handle this pregnancy crisis."

Turns out I guessed right, straight across the board.

• **PREVENTING MISERY** ■

If that sad, confused teen girl had read this book a year earlier, I hope she might have figured out her family's interpersonal dynamics and taken conscious control of her own life. You see, that's exactly why I'm writing this book for you. You are now old enough and strong enough and wise enough to take an active role in shaping yourself the way you want to be. But you have to know about your baggage. Even if you have a healthy, wonderful family, none of us is perfect. We all carry some of this "codependency baggage," at least to a limited degree.

Your Deepest Influences

"Baggage" is what people call all the emotional kinks and other shaping forces that exist in every person below conscious

153

level. Some folks have more than others do. And those shaping forces color every single decision you make. Every one.

You see, we've learned that 80 percent of the so-called "rational" decisions a person makes—that is head decisions which they think through—are actually made by the heart, below conscious level. "By the heart" is another way of saying "by those deep-down, undetected shaping forces." They are not subject to reason. They do not care about what is best for you. Dark and secret, they do whatever they want, regardless of your well-being. As a result, they can help you or they can drastically harm you.

This baggage controls every aspect of your life if you let it. Why do you choose the clothes you wear? Why do some people end up with certain tattoos? Why do you like one kind of car and not another? All the fruits of baggage. Spend a little time reflecting on your preferences and why it might be that you have them.

I often do Bible studies for the Texas Rangers baseball team and the Dallas Cowboys football team, and I like to ask the players the same question I'd like to ask *you*. "Why do you play the position you play in sports?" "Well," you say, "I just seem to fit there." So now you ask yourself why you fit. What does the position require and why do you fill the requirements? Do you have the personality of a defensive end whose goal in life is to knock down opposing quarterbacks? Literally. Or do you have the personality of a wide receiver who just loves to make spectacular diving catches and get creamed by defensive backs the size of a Chevy Blazer? Are you the quarterback, ready to make fateful, instantaneous decisions in the heat of battle, and then listen to other people pick your choices apart after they've had two days to think about them?

See? Now you've learned a little about your baggage.

Thwarting Baggage

Here's why that's important. You still have that other 20 percent to work with, the part of you that actually makes reasoned decisions—truly based on reason instead of on baggage and emotion. If you can get that 20 percent to kick in when you need it, you can save yourself an awful lot of misery. Much of what we psychiatrists and other therapists do is help people discover what their baggage is and learn how to get past it.

But that 20 percent, what we'd call head knowledge, has to have facts and conclusions to use when making decisions. And so, for one thing, you must teach your head facts to work with. You find them in books like this, in reliable magazines and newspapers (by reliable, I mean journalistically responsible and not sensationalistic; sensational magazines and papers feature headlines such as, "Elvis was secretly married to aliens for two years." That kind of nonsense)—everywhere.

Of course, the best book of all to help you understand your unconscious is the one God wrote, the Bible. Back when Saint Paul was writing his epistles, they didn't use words like *unconscious* and *emotional baggage*. But God, who knows us completely, referred to it in words they could understand. He tells us, in essence, that His Word is sharp and powerful, able to reveal our own unconscious motives.[2]

You also have to learn what your personal baggage is so as to work past it. For example, I have seen this situation many times: A girl who is the daughter of an unwed teen mother, a girl who never even saw the birth mother who gave her up, gets herself pregnant at the same age her mom was. She has no conscious knowledge of when her birth mother conceived her, and yet she reenacts what her genetic mother did. Then, still below conscious level, she "proves" that she's better than her birth mother by keeping her baby. That's how powerful this baggage is.

The best way to begin this process of learning is simply to watch and think about what you see, and also to search your memories. Your family is your primary shaping influence. I analyzed the family above by observing closely who seemed stressed (everybody did!), facial expressions, body language,

155

who ran the show, and who ended up next to whom. What do those kinds of observations look like in your home?

Who really runs the home (this may not be the same person who thinks he or she does!)? Who decides what videos come into the home, what movies you go out to, which restaurants you go to, if any? Think. Analyze. Teens are extremely good at seeing beneath the surface like this.

Go through the family photo album, looking at the casual snapshots. Who is always on the outside edge of the picture? That person is probably often on the outside edge of the family also. Who looks aloof? Whose arms are crossed (a great subconscious don't-get-near-me defense mechanism)? I remember looking at a friend's snapshots of an infant dedication. There were the happy godparents beaming at the squalling month-old guest of honor, and in the background cringed the saddest-looking little three-year-old, watching. It was the older sister, totally left out and feeling it. That snapshot spoke volumes about the occasion.

Check out your relationships with friends as well. What kind of people do you like to associate with? Who likes to associate with you? You realize, we tend to choose boyfriends and girlfriends that are like our parents (not in a physical sense necessarily; I'm talking about deep traits and values). Who runs the show, who makes the choices, who hangs back, who's the goofball?

Through all of this, remember the power of projection. You're doing it now, you've always been doing it, and the rest of your friends and family do it. Be aware of it as you think this stuff through.

The luckless girl in that instructor's video could have avoided the unwanted pregnancy if she had understood her family's interpersonal dynamics and how she fit in. She would then have a clearer idea of her own motivations. "My family's situation is messing me up. But I'm not going to mess myself up even more just so I can get back at them or even get away from them. Now that I see what's happening, I'll either figure out how to live with it or how to get around it. And, with God's help, I'll plan my own future for when I'm on my own."

If she read the books and watched her own behavior, or the behavior of an older sibling, she might also have figured out that she probably only had crushes on passive boys like her daddy. So she might realize she stood a good chance of becoming much like her domineering mother, who needed a docile man to boss around . . .

Taking Control

Do you really want to become like your parents? It might be a great idea, if they're good parents. It might be a terrible idea if they're messed up the way that girl's were. You have to pick and choose the traits you see in them that you want for yourself. You must identify the traits you want to avoid, too. That's that 20 percent of your thought processes at work, to your benefit.

Some particularly thoughtful people even make a list.

"The traits I admire in my parents."

"The traits in my parents that I want to avoid, or perhaps improve upon."

"Things my friends do that are harmful or wrong."

"Things my friends do that are good. I should too."

Even more, you have to keep an eye out for projection. But then you already know about that.

Most of all, you have to watch out for antennae.

Avoiding Antennae

I was in a professional seminar one time when a fellow therapist raised her hand and told this story on herself. "I was at some social function—a lawn party of some sort—and I saw this guy across the yard. Perfect stranger. I'd never seen him before. Didn't know who he was. He looked at me and I looked at him, and bingo! I knew I was in love. Later he said he got exactly that same feeling.

"We were going steady the instant we met, weird as it sounds. A month later, we got married. On the honeymoon we found out we had both been deserted by our fathers when we were six."

Love at first sight always, always comes from baggage. The trick is finding the baggage.

That's right. Love at first sight is not really true love. It can develop into a true love, but it starts out as a psychological phenomenon.

The woman whose story I just told had a terrible time attaching. She deeply feared that her man would leave the way her father did. Her husband felt the same, and for the same reasons. And you know? The truth is, chances are excellent one would have left the other. The lessons of early childhood persist all life long. People so often play out all over again the dramas of their own childhoods. Moses knew that when he wrote God's warning that sins of the parents would be visited upon the generations to follow.[3]

Fortunately, this woman and her husband knew about baggage and got their fears out into the open where they could deal with them. Then they vowed to stick with each other for the long run (this was a conscious promise in addition to the wedding vow) in spite of the baggage and they kept that vow. They're still happily wed today.

If baggage played a determining role—that is, if you were condemned to do what it directed—no one could stay married for long. Those antennas would help you pick out a baggage-laden mate, and then the deep forces would mess you up. The psychological "romantic crush" that our world foolishly calls "love" seldom lasts more than eighteen months or so.

But you are *not* condemned! Any couple can make marriage work if, like the woman here, they are willing to look at the truth, ferret out the baggage, and understand what that baggage can do if it's left to go its own way. True love based on an intimate friendship and firm commitment can grow deeper and deeper over many years—over a lifetime.

Stockpile Facts

And since our society is moving so rapidly, you'll want to keep up on facts as they change. Some statistics that were true ten years ago, or five, are way out of date today.

Some facts to ponder:[4]

- We have always had unwed teen mothers. But this year in America, 10 percent of all teenage girls will get pregnant and one million of them will become mothers; more than two out of three of these mothers will be unmarried. They face raising the child by themselves. Twenty years ago, the percentage was less than half that. Eighty percent of unwed mothers end up on welfare rolls within five years. In the United States in the early 1990s, more than a third of those were still on welfare.
- Young bodies (early to mid-teens) are far more susceptible to sexually transmitted diseases, such as pelvic inflammatory disease (a very painful internal infection that can render women barren), than are older (twenties) ones. A twenty-four year old can often escape a disease that will infect a fifteen year old at the same level of exposure.

Some of the diseases teens are at risk of contracting:

Chlamydia. This one-celled organism is a major cause of the pelvic inflammatory disease just mentioned. Condoms do not prevent the inflammation. Out of every ten sexually active teens, two to four carry the organism.

Human papillomavirus. It causes warts in the region of the genitalia. It also causes almost all precancerous Pap smears (the Pap smear is a test for the presence of cervical cancer) and a variety of cancers, including that of the penis. It crops up in nearly half of sexually active college women and about two-thirds of them will develop abnormal Pap smears. Condoms provide virtually no protection whatever against this virus.

Herpes. This disease hits one in every three unmarried sexually active people. If a mother passes it to her baby at delivery, the baby will probably either die or suffer severe brain damage.

AIDS. AIDS kills. Period. Once you're infected, you have maybe five or ten years left of your life and the last few years of that life will be an absolute hell. Trust me on that; I've seen the disease's ravages. One fourth of newly diagnosed HIV infections will be found in people younger than twenty-two. This year, seven thousand babies will be born to HIV positive mothers. More than one thousand of those babies will die of the disease. Every single one of them will end up motherless, perhaps even before they start school.

Condoms have a 30 percent failure rate in the prevention of HIV transmission, for the viruses are many times smaller than sperm. Condoms fail 15 percent of the time in preventing pregnancy in girls who are sexually active and in the fertile phase of their monthly cycle.

More than twenty other diseases are spread primarily through sex. I won't bother to list them. By now you have the idea. Two things make infection much more likely: sexual activity, which starts early—around age fifteen—and multiple partners. The person who experiences intercourse only once is still vulnerable to any and all of the infections discussed above; don't get me wrong. But the odds zoom upward as sexual activity expands. Also, statistics show that people who get started with sex early have more partners than do people who wait. When you add in the point already made that young kids become infected more easily, you can begin to see the size of the problem sex causes unmarried teens.

Remember also that because transmission of diseases happens so often, if you have sex with only one person, then—medically speaking—it's like having sex with everyone that person ever had sex with, and all the people they had sex with, etc.

Know What You Must *Not* Believe

Beware these myths! All are false!

- A guy has to have sex periodically or he'll get [sterile], [bald], [pick an adjective; I've heard some lulus]. The truth: Celibacy, which is abstaining from sex, does no damage whatever.
- A condom (a rubber sleeve for the male genital) prevents pregnancy. The truth is, it sometimes prevents pregnancy. But condoms fail, or they're not put on right because everyone's in a hurry, or they break, or something else goes wrong. The truth: there is no such thing as "safe sex."
- You can't get diseases if you use a condom. You now know that's false.
- A girl can't get pregnant until her breasts get big.
- A girl can't get pregnant until she has periods. This one is normally true, but there are exceptions. You can't count on it.
- A girl can't get pregnant if she's drunk.
- Older guys know best. Let's say you're a fourteen-year-old girl and a college-age guy comes on to you. He might have half a dozen different pitches: that he loves you, that it's safe because he knows what he's doing, that you need an experienced partner at first . . . There is only one thing you can be sure of about anything he says: *It's a lie!* Over a third of unwed teens' babies are fathered by men over twenty-one! Bet he doesn't tell you that.

Please, don't ever let an older man take advantage of you! The minute he suggests sex or starts to lead toward it is the minute when you can be absolutely positive the guy's a creep!

Love? Hah. He doesn't love you, and he's proving it as he speaks. He wants to use you and have some mastery over you so that he feels like a somebody, because deep down he feels like a nobody. If he actually loved you, truly, he'd be thinking about what is best for you, because that is real love. And what is best for you, because of both pregnancy and health considerations, is always to confine sex to marriage. Always.

The same is true, of course, for guys enticed by older women. Sure, they're not going to get pregnant, but they can pick up some wicked diseases instantly, or cause a pregnancy. With its pithy discussion of getting enticed by a woman, Proverbs chapter five is gorgeously eloquent. The part about springs and wells toward the end, verses fifteen on, is talking about the dangers of sex outside marriage. Drinking water from your own cistern says symbolically and poetically to remain faithful to your spouse. It even mentions the ravages of venereal (that's sexually transmitted) disease.

Expand this list. What myths have you heard around school? I'll bet you've come across some beauts from time to time.

All right. I admit that all the facts in the world won't prevent *every* pregnancy. But I hope you can see why so many adults say "abstaining altogether is the only safe policy." Sure, morality is involved here. But far, far more, health and happiness are at stake too.

Our daughter Elizabeth said it well. Simply, "Whatever you do, don't get pregnant. I've seen girls trying to raise kids. You can't imagine how badly it drains you and robs your happiness."

So let's say a friend who didn't listen to Elizabeth or me confides to you that she's pregnant? What do you tell her?

· IF IT HAPPENS
■

In today's newspaper headlines, abortion is a hot political issue. The pro-choicers and the pro-lifers get arguing and roaring. They cite legal cases and fume about morals and right and wrong. They try like mad to influence legislation. In the process, they sometimes forget all about the actual girls getting pregnant.

Okay, right now I'm ignoring all the political stuff. In fact, I'm not even going to talk about right and wrong. Instead, let's talk about the women (any girl capable of motherhood is a woman, as far as I'm concerned). Forget the thunder and lightning, the idealism and pragmatism. What is best for a teen (presumably unwed) mother or mother-to-be? By "best," I mean "how can that woman choose the wisest route toward good health and the best shot at happiness?"

Deliver the Baby

I see it over and over. Abortion causes women more stress and pain in the long run than delivery does. The major fallout will come five to ten years in the future, with an extraordinarily high incidence of depression. We have a name for it: Postabortion syndrome.

We treat adults all the time who were teens when they underwent abortions. Some didn't get depressed at the time. Some did. Although they can never forget that lost baby, some put it behind them successfully. But then some incident much later reminds them of the child whose life was snuffed out, and a deep, clinical depression slams them. I even see psychotic depressions.

There is also the health problem. Getting an abortion makes it more likely that you'll have a variety of physical difficulties later, often including the inability to get pregnant again.

And then there's guilt. Always. So many times, a woman will tell me, "I never realized I'd have to live with such heavy guilt." And this is true guilt, not false. Fortunately, true guilt is what Jesus died to forgive. But some psychological scars always remain, and often physical scars as well.

Decide Whether to Adopt or Keep

That's a question with no right or wrong answer, but some answers will be better than others. At those times when our counsel is asked, we say it has to be an individual decision. What's right for one person may be wrong for another. When the mother is very young and unwed, it is often more kind to mother and baby both to give up the child. Each individual must pray that God will assist in the decision.

Adoption these days is more enlightened in many states. Sometimes the mother even gets to choose the parents she wants for her baby. That makes it easier to settle on a wise decision. For various reasons I personally recommend that you stick to committed Christian adoption agencies.

.... HOW PREGNANCY HAPPENS

This is not a sex ed. book. But I find it appalling how little a lot of teens know about their own bodies. Here is information you should have so that you know what's going on. A lot of people get in trouble by believing some of the weird, false information about sex that circulates in high schools.

Male genitalia are the penis, the scrotum containing paired testicles right behind it, and some glands and tubes up inside the pelvis. This system produces the male cells, sperm, which fertilize female cells, the eggs. The sperm is carried in fluid called semen. Whenever semen comes in contact with an egg, a baby is likely. No ifs, ands, or buts.

Female genitalia are shaped this way: The chamber which opens in front of the anus is connected at its back by a narrow neck, the cervix, to another chamber up inside, the uterus. From the uterus, a pair of narrow Fallopian tubes lead deeper into the pelvic area and flare out into wide funnel shapes. Nestled against these funnels are paired knobs, the ovaries. The breasts are called secondary sex characters because they are governed by sex hormones but don't take part in the fertilization—the actual making of the baby.

About once a month, one of the two ovaries will produce a tiny egg (very occasionally both ovaries do, and if the two eggs are fertilized, fraternal twins result). The egg enters the nearest tube via the funnel-shaped opening and travels down into the uterus. This takes several days. All month, the uterus has been building a blood-rich, spongy bed in which the egg will plant itself after it's fertilized. A fertile egg attaches into the uterine bed and grows into a baby.

If the egg is not fertilized—i.e., has no contact with semen—it shrivels and dies. The spongy uterine bed then sloughs off and is expelled through the vagina—what the girl calls her monthly period. Right away, the uterus begins preparing a new bed for the next month's egg. The complete cycle, from the release of one egg to the release of the next one, usually takes from twenty-eight to thirty-five days, more or less.

A woman can become pregnant anytime she has a live egg anywhere in the system. That can be four or five days at a time out of every month.

This whole process sounds terribly complex and iffy. Complex it is; iffy it's not. Pregnancy for most women occurs fairly easily whenever semen reaches an egg. In the act which should occur only in marriage, the male's genitalia make contact with the female's. That's the normal way semen is introduced into the female's system. But spilled semen anywhere near the vagina opening can do the job. More than one girl, still technically a virgin, has found herself pregnant just from messing around (she is a virgin so long as male genitalia have never entered hers. A male is a virgin until he engages in genital intercourse).

Caution: If there is any chance at all that you might be pregnant, and you suffer discomfort and pain in your abdomen that won't go away, get medical attention *immediately!* I mean *this instant!* Very rarely, a fertilized egg fails to reach the uterus, where it belongs. It becomes lodged up in the Fallopian tube somewhere and begins to develop into an embryo. As the embryo gets bigger, the tube stretches and eventually bursts. We call it "ectopic pregnancy" and it's fatal!

Enough about dismal stuff. Let's get down to the real nuts-and-bolts of choosing happiness. There are seven guidelines, and I know for a fact that they work.

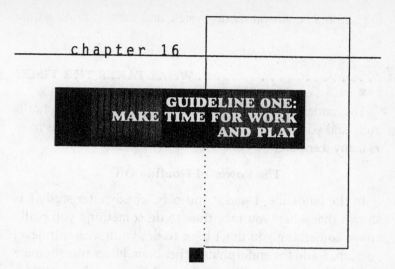

chapter 16

**GUIDELINE ONE:
MAKE TIME FOR WORK
AND PLAY**

A one-panel cartoon depicts a beehive office, with all those little cubicles set apart by low dividers, men in white shirts and ties, women in business attire. Busy, busy, busy. And in the middle, a guy in shorts and a loud Hawaiian shirt sprawls in his chair with his sandaled feet up on his desk, sipping a tall drink.

The boss is glaring down at him. "Smith, we'd all appreciate it if you'd take your vacation somewhere else."

Believe it or not, goofing off is part of one of the seven guidelines I offer to help you choose happiness. These guidelines have no particular order of importance. They all contribute. This first is no less intrinsically important than is the seventh. None of them is burdensome.

This first guideline might be phrased:

Establish for yourself a daily program, or routine, of work and play that will provide you with satisfaction.

Easy to say; almost impossible to do, as busy as your life is. So let's approach this in two ways: 1) figuring out what ought to go into a health-promoting week, and then 2) finding time to do it.

■
.... WHAT TAKES THE TIME?

The hardest activity to find time for we can call "doing nothing." And you may not be engaged in it at all, if you're as busy as many teens are.

The Power of Goofing Off

In the guideline, I said, "And play." Study after study has shown that when you take time to do something you really enjoy, something you don't have to do, your serotonin level goes up. So do the endorphins, other brain juices that promote good feeling. Play—call it goofing off if you wish—provides still other benefits. People who know how to relax and use measured recreation have fewer illnesses than do the busy folk—their immune systems work better. Too, play reduces stress. And you already know what stress does for depression.

I can't think of many lifestyles more stressful than a teenager's, except maybe the presidency of the United States (and even the president goes out jogging). Teens today have it much tougher than when I was growing up. Your life drags you to the thin edge far more than mine ever did. I don't have to get into all the reasons why. You already know them. The bottom line is, you have to be smarter than we were about combating stress, and at a much earlier age.

Taking time out for recreation *that is pleasant for you* is an integral part of fighting stress. It's not an option. You must do it for health. So let's figure out how.

Now I know that large numbers of teens don't have time for goof-off projects and therefore have never developed a hobby or interest along those lines. You may not know where to start. If you already have a hobby or interest, great! That's a good place to start. If you don't, I suggest you use the list below to get you thinking about something that you would want to try, something pleasant that might relax you.

Notice I'm not saying "Something someone else thinks you ought to be doing." Many times, I see parents push their kids into sports or other activities the parents think they ought to be involved in and the kids hate them. Try to avoid that trap.

Also, make sure some of the things you decide on provide physical activity. Exercise. Within certain bounds, the more your body exercises, the higher the brain juice.

These are some activities (and non-activity) that I, my family, and friends enjoy.

TV, sports. Watching sports on TV and sometimes attending games. My kids and I have shared some wonderful times going to games and watching our favorite teams lose (they don't always lose; it just seems that way sometimes). You yell and hoot and let yourself go. That's great for the old brain juices! Of course, you can yell and hoot at home in front of the TV set, too.

Every now and then, various groups complain that TV should be instructional. Viewers, especially children (of all ages; that includes you and me), should come away having learned something of substance, they say. In a way, they're right. But they're discounting TV's value as pure recreation. Vegging out in front of the tube is a legitimate form of relaxation, so long as it's not carried to excess. Don't be embarrassed if the educational channel is not the only channel you watch. Do be careful, of course, about what *morals* and *values* you are blotting up. Garbage in is always garbage in.

Taking part in organized sports is a great pastime too, providing you're playing for *fun.*

Consider also sports that aren't organized or even official. For example, I have otherwise normal friends who love birding. They tote huge binoculars out into parks, woods, and fields to look at wild birds who frequently don't want to be seen. Some birders build life lists of the different kinds of birds they see. Hiking, camping, jogging, horseback riding, and skating—all sorts of activities get you out and moving. Any of them is well worth the time spent on it.

Talk to your librarian about orienteering clubs in the area. Orienteering is taking a map and compass and getting from here to there—cross country—without street signs, or streets, or other handy indicators of where you are.

Making things. The creative process—making something from scratch or picking out and completing a kit—can be immensely satisfying. God creates. We are made in His image. We are born to create, to make.

There is a woodcarving club in your town with men and women eager to show you how to whittle and carve. They'll welcome you, and you'd be amazed at how many ways you can make wood look like something else. In fact, there are all kinds of such groups around—gem and mineral societies who cut and polish rock, and others who dig fossils. You'll find poetry groups, writing groups, quilting clubs, needlework and ceramic-painting groups. All of them enjoy creating.

You don't need a club in order to express yourself whittling, quilting, needlepointing, knitting, crocheting—pursuing any of the creative arts. You can learn on your own and follow your own interest in your own time frame.

How about building model planes, cars, boats, railroads? The elaborate models and kits are not for kids. In fact, dollhouses aren't for kids either. I've seen some dazzling dollhouses, all made by and for adults. One kid about your age built a model of a World War II bomber. But instead of the usual perfect airplane, he mounted it on a base to look as if it had just crash landed—scorched metal, parts lying around, the landing gear crumpled. And standing here and there were little human figures depicting engineers with clipboards!

How about cooking?

"Naa. I'm a guy. That's for girls."

"Oh, yeah? Tell that to the world's greatest chefs—98 percent are men." Guys can be excellent cooks and take great pleasure in it. A gentleman who cooks as a hobby recently won the Pillsbury Bake-off. And girls, it's still true; the quickest way to a male's heart is through his stomach.

Ever make a video? I mean the kind that tells a story—not just a two-minute "Funniest Video" sequence of the baby getting bowled over by an overly friendly Labrador retriever. If Stephen Spielberg can make a great movie, so can you.

Specialized activities and interests. They tell me ham radio operators have a wonderful time listening in on things like ship-to-shore communications and Coast Guard rescues. They love talking to each other and find radio pals in exotic places. Computer buffs will tell you that you don't need the latest hardware to get on line (but it helps). Sophisticated games are available either on computer or game-playing hardware. But you know more about that stuff than I do.

There are MG car clubs, Corvette clubs, vintage Ford clubs, and (ready for this?) John Deere tractor clubs. You name it.

A lot of teens, even those who never belong to FFA (Future Farmers of America), take pleasure raising fish, birds, or other animals. And it's not just cats and dogs. You can breed and raise anything from guppies through hedgehogs to ostriches. Check local zoning ordinances before you get too deeply into it.

Science fiction enthusiasts conduct some really weird conventions and collect all manner of fascinating memorabilia and artifacts.

Got the idea?

All this sounds frivolous. It sounds like retired geezers with time on their hands, people who don't have family plus sports plus school plus maybe a part-time job to juggle in a twenty-four-hour day. And if you're involved in church activities, there's a ministry that's more important than playing, right?

Not really. In our clinic, we've served hundreds, and I mean hundreds, of full-time Christian workers. Pastors. Teachers. Youth leaders. A lot of them are young. They come in burned out, depressed, angry, frustrated, sick. "What's wrong with me?" they wail. "I want to serve the Lord and He's turned a cold shoulder on me. I feel terrible, and guilty for not doing as much as I should for Him, and . . ."

And the first thing we counsel, even before we get into deeper issues, is, "Quit doing so much." These people neglect themselves, falsely thinking they are serving God. When you hobble and weaken God's servant—yourself—is that serving Him? If we can get them to balance their lifestyles with relaxing activities, the joy comes back and they return to service refreshed. More important, by balancing their lives, they maintain their strength over the long haul. You can too.

Important as recreation is, there must, of course, be more to your daily routine than that. Work is a biggie also.

The Power of Work

"Oh, yeah. Sure. Power of work in a pig's eye," people grumble. To most, including high school students (maybe especially high school students!), work is drudgery. And that's so sad. Work can be almost as good for you as play, if you do it right. Work teaches responsibility, humility, leadership, healthy interdependence, and teamwork with your coworkers. Work also gives us a sense of worth and accomplishment. Work develops our physical, mental, and relational skills. And eventually, work enables us to earn enough money to support ourselves and our dependents.

Pause and make a list, either in your head or on paper, of the work you do. Make the list pretty detailed. I assume school tops the list. You bet that's work, and it counts as work. For most people it's a duty thrust upon them by others. In addition to the courses themselves, there are special projects. Research papers, book reports, outside writing assignments. Extra-curricular activities such as concerts, plays, debates, and tournaments.

Homework.

Do you hold down a part-time job? Don't just put "job" on

your list. Spell out what you do. Let's pretend you work evenings at a nearby franchise fast-food store, the Guppy-Burger. You take orders, make change, wipe tables, empty the Thank You trash bins, bag fries, draw Guppy-colas, assemble Double Cheese Guppy-Burgers . . . It's go, go, go all night. And you might as well add "smile" to the list, because by the end of a shift, smiling at the customers is work.

What do you do around the house? That's work, whether you get paid or not. If you live in a condo, there's not too much. If your parents own a dairy farm, you're out in the barn at 5:00 A.M. Cleaning your room counts. So does taking care of younger sibs. Now think about all of the different types of work you do and think about ways you can do your work better and more efficiently. Think about how to balance your work with your play. Think about all the ways your work is helping you grow. Learn to *enjoy* your work and your play.

Some people call all that work "earning your daily bread." But, to quote Scripture, "Man does not live by bread alone." There is also the word from the mouth of God.

The Power of God

And now we're talking *power*.

We're also talking lots of time and effort, if you are heavily involved in the social and spiritual life of your church.

What do you do at church? Worship isn't supposed to be work, but perhaps you help clean up after Sunday school or watch kids in the nursery during worship services. You might as well make a third list to include all that.

You might wish to make a fourth and final list, "Miscellaneous." These are the time-eaters that don't fit into any other list. How much time do you spend riding on school buses each week? Going to and from church and work? Talking on the phone? Reading the paper? Worthy or necessary as these items might be, they carve chunks out of your day, so list them.

Pretty impressive lists you have there!

Now let's arrange time to do all that and more.

· · · · · · · · · · · · · · · · · **HOW TO MAKE THE TIME?**
■

Sorting through this pile of time-eaters and building a health-supporting weekly routine takes wisdom. Sticking to that routine in the face of what some people call "the tyranny of the urgent" takes powerful discipline.

And here I must make a confession on behalf of my generation. Somehow we never got around to teaching your generation that the fear of God is the beginning of wisdom. If you must find and develop your own godly wisdom it is because we've failed you. I'm sorry.

What I do know, and wish we all had taught you all, is that God is perfect wisdom and perfect love matched perfectly with perfect discipline. By discipline, I don't mean punishment. I mean self-control and self-guidance. On a performance appraisal, the person with discipline is called a good self-starter.

You are not perfect. I certainly am not. But we need to come as close to perfection as we can get, exercising love, wisdom, and discipline—all three, if we're going to make and keep promises to ourselves.

I suggest the first step now to building a really good weekly routine is to establish priorities. These are not first-second-third priorities. They're unranked: first-first-and-first. For myself, I decided to make spiritual health, physical and mental health, and work/service my three priorities. I combine work and service because they're not easy to separate. Service includes nurturing my family, something you probably don't have yet. With my work I serve others.

So do you, especially if you have a part-time job. You serve your boss, you serve customers either directly or indirectly, and you serve yourself by making money. Your school work serves yourself primarily; you're learning stuff that will help the world make more sense to you and help you go out into the world more productively. It's preparing you for the future, which makes it very important work.

So let's say for illustration that those are your three priorities also—spiritual health, physical health, and work/service. (Remember, I'm not asking you to adopt anyone else's, including mine; I'm saying tailor your priorities to your own needs and wants.) Although you'll make time for all three, you don't have to give them each equal time. Work, for instance, will consume much more time proportionately than will recreation.

For spiritual health, I build intimacy with God. Specifically, every day I read a passage of Scripture, then spend five minutes or more just sitting there thinking about what I read. What did it say as told in my own words? How does it apply to me? (When you hear from others that you should meditate on the word, this is pretty much what they're talking about.) Then I finish my devotions by praying. Other options might be to use a book or pamphlet of daily devotions, or to study a prepared lesson. The weekly routine for me includes Sunday worship and adult Sunday school (if your church doesn't have a study class for your age group, go in with the grown-ups).

To serve the overall priority of physical and mental health, I make three sub-priorities: Sleep, food, and recreation. I have to be up and out of bed by seven in the morning and I need about eight hours of sleep to function at my best. That means going to bed around eleven. You as a teen probably need nine hours of rest. So count back nine hours from when you have to get up and try to make that your bedtime.

Okay, okay. I know. You have tests to study for, term papers to finish, baby-sitting until midnight sometimes. You can't allow eight or nine full hours for rest. But you know what? If you do, if you force yourself with that self-discipline we were talking about, you'll absorb more in study and do work faster because your body isn't dragged down by lack of sleep. Trust me on that. I earned good grades in medical school and seminary, and getting enough rest was a key. Sleep builds up your serotonin, which in turn helps your memory, concentration, energy level, and motivation—all the things you need to do well in school and sports.

Certainly, there will be times when it just doesn't work. Try to limit those times, those nights without enough rest, to once or twice a week at most. Then try to sleep in a day or two later, if you can.

You'll be amazed at how much good nutrition sharpens you up. "Good nutrition" doesn't mean "stuff you hate." One of my kids is, by choice, a strict vegetarian. She has to be careful to get enough protein and certain vitamins, A especially. So, on her own, she's become quite sophisticated at choosing a diet she enjoys that gives her all the nutrients she needs. You can do that too.

"Good nutrition," on the other hand, doesn't mean "stuff you love indiscriminately," either. Sugar delights the taste buds, so have some. Fats provide the flavor in meat; enjoy your meat. But put a lid on the less nutritious stuff and get enough vegetables and bread. In other words, be sensible. The eating patterns you set up now will be hard to change later, so they should be good ones.

While you're looking at your nutrition, remember that a building block for serotonin is tryptophan. You have to obtain it from your diet; your body cannot manufacture it. Meats, dairy products, and bananas contain tryptophan.

And then there's recreation, the third leg of the good health footstool. It doesn't have to be pursued every day, though that would be nice. It doesn't have to take a lot of time. But it should be there, every week. Review your week when the week is over. Did you make time to kick back and relax a little? Good. But if you didn't, alter your next week's routine to provide that necessary break. I personally try to find at least a little time every day when I can sit back and say to myself, "I have everything on my short list done [that's the critical stuff] and nothing else I absolutely have to do right now."

. . . . THE HARDEST PART
■

Establishing a routine, a weekly schedule, will mean saying "no" sometimes. That is the hardest thing in the world to do.

It requires a great deal of maturity. I have heard good friends say, "I was forty years old before I learned how to say 'no.'" Some people never learn. And yet there are always many more demands upon your time than you have time for. You have to draw a line somewhere.

There are many reasons why "no," which springs so quickly and easily to the lips when you're two years old, is so hard to say when you're a teenager. For one, we are usually eager for people to like us. And when you say "No, I can't do that" to someone, that someone may well become angry or disappointed with you.

Is there a defense against that person's anger or disappointment, so you don't cave in and say, "Oh, all right. I will"? You bet. Let the 20 percent of your decision-making that comes from the head remind you, "This person is using dirty tactics on me. He/she is threatening me with disapproval if I don't do what he/she wants. And I don't like being coerced in an underhanded way."

Another reason "no" comes hard is that we don't want to let others down. We really do want to help, to serve, to do whatever is asked. On those occasions, your 20 percent headwork must step in and remind you, "You have twenty-four hours today. You'll get another twenty-four tomorrow, Lord willing. They're already full. You can't take on this new request unless you dump something else. And your priorities include some rec time, and time for rest. It's a worthy job they're asking you to do, but you just can't handle any more."

It's quite possible that at that time, your heart will step in and dictate that indeed you do dump something else in favor of this new request.

Fine. Always keep in mind that your routine, once established, is always open to adjustment and change.

In short, your routine should not be a rigid timetable. It's a framework in which you keep your priorities straight. The elements within it should be shifted to suit your needs.

Working example: at five feet three inches, you may not

quite be basketball player material, but you do love the game. So you're the varsity team's manager. You spend a lot of time making arrangements. You go on the road to all the away games and of course, you attend every game. It takes up a lot of your time (including sleep time; some of those away games are pretty distant), but you really enjoy it, and you're doing the school a fine service.

Now along comes the president of the debate team. She says, "You are a world-class organizer! You keep the basketball team humming. We really, really need you to organize our upcoming debate tournament. It'll be a piece of cake for you, and it will be over in a month." As the conversation unfolds, she may even hint darkly that if you say no, you can expect to be left off the top debate team. You enjoy debating. She's an influential person in your class and getting on the wrong side of her is not wise. And she's right; you could handle the job well.

Your heart says, "Take it. It's only for a month," and throws its weight—80 percent—behind the decision. Your head says, "Wait a minute."

May I suggest that in this case, you would step back and look at your routine as it exists now. You would look at:

1. **What's coming up in the next month that you have to do? Term papers? Special assignments? Big tests? Basketball playoffs? Driver training? These things may demand additional time and energy.**

2. **What might slack off in the next month? If your team is not likely to be in the playoffs, your managerial duties will be less demanding. Are your book reports done for the year? In short, can you make some time for the debating tournament?**

3. **What can you dump? You also run a paper route, but you can bribe your little sister to handle it for a month. It will be good for her to take responsibility on a limited basis**

(she's not old enough to handle it full time), and it will free you up for that month.

Something, naturally, will come along to mess up your best-laid plans. Things never come out the way we plan for them to. But no plan at all will mess you up. Keep in mind that your routine, your weekly schedule, is a guideline for choosing happiness. It is not a simple convenience.

As you work these things out with your priorities in mind, your head is working independently of your heart, because your heart has its own priorities and they aren't always best for you. Fearing being disliked, for instance, is not always in your best interests. You need your head to make your routine the priority. But it will pay off handsomely in two ways.

For one, the guideline works in promoting happiness. My own experience and the experience of the thousands of people who use these guidelines attest to that.

For another, as you become adept at holding fast to your routine, and saying "no" at times (it takes practice!), your self-confidence soars. You *can* control your own life, at least as much as it's controllable. It won't go perfectly, of course; no one's life ever does; but you can do things you wouldn't have guessed a year ago that you could.

Let me use myself as an example. As co-founder of the Minirth Meier New Life Clinics, the largest chain of such psychiatric clinics in the world, I have hundreds of demands on my time daily. Administrative needs and decisions are only part of it. We also do a daily national radio talk show. Because it's broadcast live so that we can take calls from some of our million-or-two listeners each day, we have to be in the studio every day; no recording five-at-a-time to be played through the week. I get thousands of phone calls and letters. If I were an obsessive-compulsive, I'd go nuts.

What saves me? Jesus said, "My yoke is easy and My burden is light."[1] When He says something, I take it literally, so I delegate as well as I can. By cutting out a lot of stuff that does not absolutely have to be done by me personally, I can live a balanced, productive life.

I love teenagers, so writing this book for you this very moment is pure joy for me. Jan and the kids can say the same. My life is fun and exciting because I'm doing what I think God wants me to do with my work, my sleep, my family, my fun, and my friends.

Some people get mad at me almost every day for not doing what *they* want me to do. You can bet that will happen to you as well. But I keep going with what I believe God wants and let the chips fall wherever they may as regards to everything else.

Let's go on to the next guideline. And I repeat what I mentioned earlier: I am not listing these in any particular order of importance.

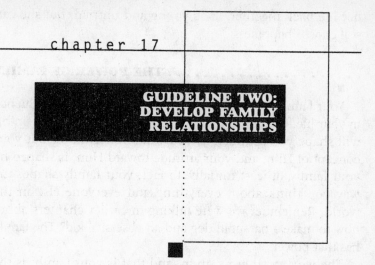

chapter 17

GUIDELINE TWO: DEVELOP FAMILY RELATIONSHIPS

"My family exploded," a teenage girl confided to me. "Ka Pow! It's gone." Her name is not Karen, but let's pretend it is.

Karen was not in counseling. She was not expecting my counsel, free or otherwise. She was just telling me what was going on in her life.

She is the daughter of an acquaintance in our church, so I knew a little something about what she was talking about. Explode was right. Her mom and dad were divorcing. It was a messy, acrimonious split, with bitter accusations flying all over. Her two brothers sided strongly with Dad and her sister with Mom. So the brothers and sister, all in late teens, weren't speaking to each other. If Karen stayed with her mother, her brothers and father were angry, and if she went with them, the mom was furious. When she tried to forge peace, they all turned against her.

She's the youngest in her family, so she's pretty much powerless. You know that nobody listens to the youngest, even if he or she is wisest. Was Karen depressed? She sure was, and I don't blame her for a moment. Her family had practically destroyed her life. And yet, she has it within her power to put her life back together. She's young and untried, but she can still choose happiness.

.... **THE POWER OF FAMILY**
■

Your family is the single most important shaping influence in your life, from birth to death. God, through His Holy Spirit, will shape you as much as you will allow Him to. But your concept of Him, and your attitude toward Him, is shaped by your family, at least initially. In fact, your family shapes the way you think about everything and everyone else in the world. Remember we were talking in earlier chapters about how to make a paranoid dog and an obsessive kid? The family has that power.

The world you grow up in, and that is your family, is the "normal" world. I put *normal* in quotes because no one can call his or her family truly normal. We're all oddballs, every one. Your family, though, humdrum or quirky as it may be, is the basis against which you will compare everything you come across in the world. Your life growing up is the yardstick with which you measure all other lifestyles, either to like them better than yours or to reject them.

Certainly, your friends influence you. But you weigh and measure them against what your family "taught" you at the deepest level.

Family attitudes also establish your own attitudes in thousands of ways you never think about. Example. An hour before you have to get up in the morning, your cat hops up on your bed and deposits a chewed-up dead mouse on your pillow. Love gift. You a) scream and yell for someone to come get this thing; b) grab a rolled-up magazine and bat both the mouse and the cat off your bed; c) mumble "thank you" grumpily and roll over (*away* from the mouse) to catch another hour of sleep.

None of those responses is right or wrong. Whichever you choose, though, will be largely influenced by your parents' and siblings' attitudes toward cats, rodents, little mangled bodies, sleep, being awakened themselves, and many other aspects of the situation.

"I can relate to that," says a girl we'll call Mary. "My mom is an emergency room nurse and my dad's a medical examiner. My brother and I grew up in a family where discussing really gross stuff, like dissections and murders, was normal, even at the dinner table. So picture me at a boyfriend's house, invited to dinner. Potential boyfriend; we'd only gone out once, but we liked each other. I started describing an emergency hernia-plasty and the whole room stopped dead. Freeze frame. They're all staring at me. No, make that 'glaring.'" Then she adds, "And hey! A herniaplasty is really mild, compared to some of the stuff I could describe."

I have no idea how the potential romance went from there. Quite probably, in college she'll date biology majors, who can wolf down fast-food burgers while they describe the intricacies of cat anatomy or something. In subtle little ways, you see, your family influences even your choice of romantic interests.

Your family is going to exercise power in the future nearly as strongly as it has in the past. Through the years, for instance, your relationship with your parents will change in ways you can't imagine now. Statistically, which is to say probably, there will be a day when they will become the child in a sense, and you will be their parent. That happens so much in our world today. Talk to some middle-aged adults with aging parents. You'll see what I'm saying.

Their situation is not unique. Parents, grandparents, brothers, and sisters may one day have to depend upon you. The opposite pertains as well; you may have to depend on them.

Until that time, they'll all have plenty of advice about how you should run your life. And they'll all be certain that you'd better follow their advice if you know what's good for you. And of course, you can expect all sorts of choruses of "I told you so!" when you deviate from their advice.

················ THE IMPORTANCE OF FAMILY
■

"I can do without the advice," most teens say. After all, you're not a kid anymore. And advice from siblings is especially annoying. Good news: that will change.

Your family is not your only shaping factor, of course. Your genes influence your personality and attitudes as well. So do your siblings'. That's mostly why, although you are growing up in the same family, you all have different natures. Birth order makes you different too.

That's good. You see, someday, you and your brothers and sisters, your mom and dad, maybe cousins and aunts and uncles, may have to put your heads together to work out serious family problems affecting everyone.

Let's make an example. Let's say Grandpa John has Alzheimer's, and it's getting worse. Grandma Lil, semi-invalid herself, can't handle him anymore. No one can take him in, for one reason or another, and no one can afford to place him in a satisfactory care facility; you're talking about $3,000 a month, minimum! He's likely going to outlive his insurance by many years, and will not be eligible for other insurance beyond a certain cut-off point. What is the family going to do? And what about Lil?

If the family pulls together, they can find a solution. Probably, by the time Grandpa John deteriorated to this point, you all have grown up. You pursue different careers, have had different experiences, and lived in different areas. That's a lot of knowledge about a lot of things. Pool that knowledge and you can rule the world! At least, you can help Grandpa John.

Your brother's a lawyer, so he works on the insurance aspect and other possible financial resources, finding out what options there are. Your sister lived in New Mexico and Arizona, and she knows some excellent nursing facilities for people like Grandpa John. At the very least, she knows how to evaluate them. Your mom wants to take Grandma Lil, her mother, in once Uncle John is situated. By putting heads together, you all discover that if each person will chip in a little bit to pay for his long-term care, he's covered.

Slowly, through give and take, welcome answers emerge.

But the family has to be pulling together. It has to be a unit.

The time to develop and strengthen family relationships is right now. When you're young. While the family structure is shifting and changing. And you, a "mere" teen, can contribute to that development.

This strengthening of family ties has practical value, as I just discussed, but it has far greater value for you as a teen. Family is where we draw our strength. Too, any rift in the family hurts us terribly, more than the deepest rifts elsewhere would.

You cannot imagine how many people walk through our doors either to find some way to mend family rifts or to undo the damage caused by them. Even people who say, "I gave up on my family years ago. We're not close. That can't be what's bothering me" are being bothered. You bet.

And when you do hit a rocky spot in life, nothing else helps you get over it like strong back-up from your family.

"That's easy for you to say," a teen might grumble. "But I go to Al-Anon twice a week because of my alcoholic parents. Don't talk about back-up to me. They didn't even show up for my graduation."

Abusive or neglectful family members are a whole other thing. That includes abusive siblings. At your stage of life, when you're still pretty much dependent upon your family legally, financially, and nearly every other way, your options are limited. But that doesn't mean you don't have any. Probably your best one is to avoid as much as possible the abusive person and circumstances that can lead to abuse (being in the same room with a person drinking heavily, for example).

In a case like that, by all means get help, as did the teen above who attends Al-Anon. There are strategies and resources available to you. Ask a counselor, a trusted teacher, a trusted church leader. Find those resources!

Books are a resource. May I recommend my book *Don't Let*

Jerks Get the Best of You.[1] The coping strategies it offers, including things like dealing with your anger, work on family just as much as on anyone else. In fact, there's a lot in it about families.

· **BUILDING FAMILY**
■

Even if your family are all total, complete jerks; even if you derive no benefit whatever from your family during your lifetime forever and ever; it is still worth building. Because of their pervasive influence, family members are usually worth helping. It will be immensely, *immensely* satisfying to you in years to come to be able to say honestly, "They're still a fractured gang of jerks, but I did my best." That's the worst-case scenario. Best case is, you can make a powerful, positive difference in their lives.

You see, the family you influence is not just you and your siblings and parents and maybe aunts and uncles. "Family" is them *plus* untold generations that aren't even born yet. I don't have to go any further than my own family for an illustration.

A hundred and fifty years ago, my distant ancestors, Germans living in Russia beside the Volga River, were unbelievers. Two missionaries came through their village in the 1860s. The missionaries traveled door to door repairing shoes and making shoes for people who wanted them. As they plied their cobbler's trade, they also shared with the people about God and His Word, and about how He can mend our human souls. These cobblers saved souls while mending soles.

A revival flamed up in that village, and about a third of its people became believers. Their new faith dramatically changed their lifestyles. My Meier ancestors were among those who converted. They taught godly beliefs and practices to their children, who passed them along to *their* children. Eventually, most of my immediate ancestors emigrated to escape the 1917 Bolshevik revolution. They traveled first to Germany; then most of them finally came to America.

I really loved traveling around the country on family vacations when I was a teenager, meeting far-flung members of the Meier clan all over America. And I do mean "far-flung"; they are scattered *all* over! What amazes me, and I think it's so really, really neat, is that almost a hundred and forty years after those two cobbler missionaries entered the lives of my ancestors on the other side of the world, almost every Meier I know around this country who is related to me is a committed believer in Jesus. We are still following the healthy and happy lifestyle that my great-great-grandfather chose on that distant yesterday so far away.

You may be the one who changes not only your own life but the lives of hundreds of your family's descendants. That's scary. The choices you make not only affect you but, given enough time, may affect thousands, even millions of people. Not only that, look at the phenomenal work two simple cobblers achieved in a quiet town on the Volga.

God knows how powerful the pressures of family are. Moses said that the sins of the parents would be visited on three or four generations.[2] That's not to say that God is a mean dude who looks at you today and says, "Your great-great-grandpa stole money at the store, so today you're going to pay for his stealing." What God is saying is that if Great-Great-Grandpa had the kind of moral structure that led him to his sin, those behavior patterns have a good chance of getting passed on for several generations.

Understand, it's not necessarily a sure thing from generation to generation. Often, godly parents will have children who go astray despite being brought up well. Kids rebel; you know that. But they rebel in both directions! Those rebellious, ungodly kids grow up and have kids of their own. That next generation may realize something is missing in that lifestyle; they regret not having loving and godly parents, so they go back the other way by turning to God. The cycle can go back and forth, generation to generation.

If you look at the history of the kings of Israel and Judah,[3] you see that this was actually the common pattern. Good kings were all too often followed by evil sons, followed then by a good son who rebelled against the father's ways. But in these general patterns, the godliness survives and eventually flourishes.

That's the kind of legacy David left behind, strange as his own family was, thanks to his powerful faith. It's the legacy you too can provide the generations to come.

Now you already see that it's plain stupid to be bad just because your parents were good or good just because your parents were bad. The smart thing is to take control of your life and send it the way you want it to go. Then help your family and extended family make a straight path for future generations. The fringe benefit, of course, is a better life in this generation for everyone.

Let me suggest some specific steps you can take to fulfill this guideline of improving family relations.

First: Take Inventory

What is your family like? To decide that, you have to get past wishing. "I wish my family were less stressful." "I wish our family were more like Marcie's." "I wish . . ." Forget that. We have to work with the way things are.

- Which members, if any, have emotional problems?
- Which if any have substance abuse problems (tobacco, drugs, alcohol, etc.)?
- Which if any are abusive toward you or another member? This includes verbal, physical, emotional, and other abuses as well as neglect. If you aren't sure what's abuse and what is not, talk to a trusted counselor or church leader. Much as you like your friends, trusting them with family secrets may be something you could regret later. The counselor or church leader is usually a safer choice.
- Which if any are near perfect? Nobody's perfect. I mean, which ones do you *not* want to change? Be honest.

- Where are points of friction in your family?
- Who communicates best with other members? Worst?

In prior chapters, you analyzed how you fit into various pictures. Review what you thought about and add to your observations if you can. How do you relate to other family members? How do they try to relate to you?

Second: Find the Hot Spots

Family feuds are terrible, terrible things. The roots of the Israeli-Arab conflict go back to the half-brothers Ishmael and Isaac, over four thousand years ago. On the frivolous side, think how many TV soap operas use as their theme the infighting within families. Soap operas almost always use stories that everyone can relate to, even if the stories are grossly exaggerated, with more furs and pearls, more money, more deceit, more glamour, more villainy than most families see. On the other hand, I have treated some families that have such hideous rifts, if you put their story into a soap opera, no one would believe it.

In your family, you want to understand the fights and the power politics for two reasons. One, it would be nice to help bring peace in rifts, and two, if you would mend anything, you must be tactful, and that means avoiding making a bad situation worse.

Karen, whose plight I described at the beginning of this chapter, could see her family's rift plainly. Many families, though, harbor secret rifts. The members tolerate each other but don't like each other. A key to these rifts is to watch how the member(s) of one "side" act when you do nice things for the other "side." Maybe Mom says she doesn't want you hanging around with Uncle Frank. Maybe Uncle Frank is a person to be avoided. Possibly, though, there is a rift there, and Mom's edict comes from jealousy and anger, not concern.

Use the inventory you worked out above to reach out to

members. That inventory can be a basis of understanding as you get creative about mending hot spots.

Let's look at some ways you can fulfill this guideline and thereby improve your own happiness. Then we can examine Karen's plight in particular.

·················· IMPROVING RELATIONSHIPS ▪

There are several important ways in which you as a teen can strengthen your family.

Spend Time with Them

Hard to do. Some years back, advisors were saying, "It's not the quantity of time you spend with your kids, but the quality." From that came the catch phrase *quality time*. The idea was, fifteen minutes reading a book to your child was better than two hours of just hanging out together watching TV or something. That "quality time" concept gave parents an out when they felt guilty about working long hours and spending so little time with their kids. It's hogwash. Quantity counts too. It counted when you were little and it still does.

When I recommend spending time, I mean two things. Do things together as a family. Also, do things with individuals that they (and, I hope, you) enjoy doing, one on one. Let's say you're a fourteen-year-old girl. Take your ten-year-old sister to lunch at the fast-food place—even better, at a "real" lunch counter or cafe. Go to the mall with your mom. Hang around Dad and talk to him while he's changing the oil in the car. Ask your brother to teach you how to do wheelies on a skateboard. Or teach him.

Make Peace When You Can

No one listens to you, just as they ignored Karen's pleas and needs. It's really difficult for teens to make a difference, but it can be done. Karen was on the right track. One way to ease conflict is to refuse to take sides. But she could go one step further. In private conversation with her mom, and at some other time privately with her dad, she can explain that she won't take sides, and why. They both belong to her and she loves them both.

Too, never take vengeance. Getting back at family members, no matter how justifiable it seems, never does anyone good, you most of all. It's tempting. A family member slights you or does you wrong, and you see a chance to pay back in kind. Don't.

Lastly, don't wait for erring family members to realize they did you wrong, repent, and apologize. It will pay dividends for you to take the first step in resolving conflicts. I've a true tale to tell about a woman we'll call Lynn. She was the oldest of nine kids in her family. Virtually her whole childhood was spent helping her mother. Basically, her childhood was taken away before she could enjoy it. She told once how bitterly she resented it every time Momma came home with yet another baby. It wasn't just sibling rivalry. She knew even at a very tender age that a new child meant even less time with Momma and still more time being a substitute mother herself. She grew up practically a stranger to her mom.

Lynn was grown and had kids of her own when one day she received a letter from her mother. "Dear Lynn, I'm so sorry I robbed you of your childhood. I didn't realize it at the time. You weren't sickly and you didn't have problems, so I didn't pay any attention to you. Please, please forgive me. And if it's any consolation to you, know that I could never have made it without you. I love you."

Lynn bundled her children in the car and drove right to her mom's house, two hundred miles away, to hug her. From that day on, they've enjoyed a beautiful and growing relationship. Tears still come to Lynn's eyes when she talks about it. And she deeply regrets not approaching her mother years before. Had she mended the rift earlier they would have had years more of happiness.

Peace and intimacy with your family, whether they are at

peace with each other or not, will work immense benefits for your happiness.

Practically speaking, there is probably no hope that Karen could orchestrate peace in her family. Through counsel, she should learn—should be absolutely convinced—that she did not cause the fracturing; teens often feel responsible for events that are none of their responsibility. As best she can, she should continue to keep peace with both sides. Grieving her loss is appropriate. And despite the fact that her world is temporarily shattered, she should forgive. Forgiveness will heal her own wounds better than will any other course of action, and it will heal others'.

Those steps will work for you too.

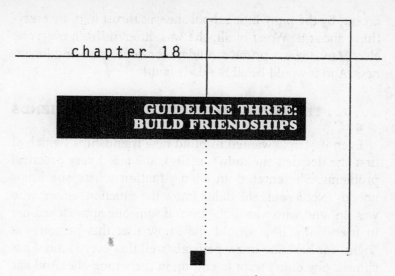

chapter 18

**GUIDELINE THREE:
BUILD FRIENDSHIPS**

Marcia Galen's parents did the next-to-the-worst thing in the world to her. The very worst thing would have been divorce, but this was almost as bad: They moved to Muskogee. The wilds of Oklahoma. This was only her jaundiced view, of course; people who live there love it.

Marcia, you see, had spent the first fourteen years of her life quite happily in Downer's Grove, a suburb just west of Chicago. Her school, with seven hundred students in every class, played big games against the despised rivals of Clarendon Hills and Hinsdale. Malls abounded. Her friends all spoke with the crisp midwest accent of people in a hurry. She loved Downer's Grove, where nobody would be caught dead in a Stetson.

"Muskogee! That's not nowhere. It's less than nowhere! Nowhere is somewhere compared to Muskogee!" Her wailing made no difference, of course. Her electrical engineer father moved his family to his new job location and that was that. They didn't even live in town; they lived outside town near a hydroelectric facility.

Marcia was appalled by the isolation, by everyone's Okie

accent, by the puny little school she was thrust into. By everything about it. Worst of all, she was different from everyone else. Marcia was a prime candidate for depression and loneliness. And it would be all her dad's fault!

...... THE PROBLEM OF FINDING GOOD FRIENDS

Even if Marcia wanted to build new friendships (which at first she decided she didn't, really), she faced very practical problems. She entered an alien situation where she knew nobody. Not a soul. She didn't know the situation, either; who was "in" and who was "out." Even if someone approached her in friendship, how would she know that this person was "right" for her? She knew perfectly well that every school has cliques. She didn't want to end up in the wrong one. And she also knew that strangers from outside are not warmly embraced. She herself had snubbed strangers in Downer's Grove. Now she was on the receiving end.

Her situation looked utterly bleak. She sat on her bed staring at the stack of cartons in the middle of the floor and cried.

.... THE NITTY-GRITTY OF MAKING FRIENDS

How can we help Marcia out of her dilemma? How can we help you? You may have faced exactly what Marcia faced. Perhaps you've always lived in one place and have never had her problems. That doesn't really matter. What matters is that people need friends in order to function well and be happy. We're programmed that way by God. For the sake of our own happiness, we need to find and nurture good friends.

Sociologists and others claim that the ideal human group consists of about fifty people, those fifty representing all ages and comprising both friends and family. Curiously, that's about our capacity for knowing people well. And that works greatly to Marcia's advantage and yours. Here's how.

You need not please everyone. Face it. Because of projection and other personality irritants, some people turn us off. Others seem very desirable. That means that you yourself are going to irritate some people and be attractive to others. You can't please everyone. That's a hard fact to accept.

Everyone fears rejection, but teens tend to take it far harder than do more mature adults. With time, you learn that rejection is inevitable, and you learn to dismiss it. As a teenager, you haven't had enough time and experience yet to learn that valuable lesson.

A few weeks of observation showed Marcia which kids she wanted to be with, who the groups were into which she would fit best. Getting them to accept her would be the tough part. She faced rejection not from people she didn't care about but from the people she wanted to care about.

It's okay to pick and choose. Most people have a very, very wide circle of people they recognize and that's about it; a wide circle of casual acquaintances, the people they smile at and speak to but don't know deeply or intimately; a circle of close acquaintances, usually people they work with and for, go to school with, see on a regular basis; and then there are friends. Friends know us intimately and we know them. Friends stick close despite circumstances. Friends are the people we turn to first when we want to share good news, and the people we turn to first when we need solace.

Surprisingly, a person does not need many friends of the sort we're talking about here. The lucky person has two or three. Usually but not always, those two or three pretty much share our views about life, though they may differ strongly on various points. The differences are freely accepted on both sides. Those two or three usually share common interests.

You can therefore pick and choose in the sense that you don't have to convince the whole world that you're lovable. At first it seemed to Marcia that she had to befriend the whole school. That's natural. Once she realized she didn't have to, life brightened a little.

Then she made a wise, wise move. She decided that rather than zeroing in on cliques, she would focus on people with common interests. She found them in her denominational church and youth group, by attending club meetings that interested her, and also by simply keeping her ears open. When she learned that Andrea was the class's reigning shopper, she approached Andrea with a sincere, "I love shopping and I don't have a clue what's here. Can you show me the stores to go to?"

Marcia loved malls. Andrea loved malls. Andrea also loved showing off her deep knowledge of where the snazziest clothes and best prices could be found. The two girls soon became fast friends through their common interest.

Marcia's school in Oklahoma was much smaller than the one she came from, so she had a smaller pool of strangers from which to find a few friends. But there are some out there. There always are.

The responsibility for building circles of friends and acquaintances, incidentally, rested squarely on Marcia. Certainly people are supposed to extend the hand of welcome to strangers, people in the church especially. But you can't count on it. Marcia could not sit and wait for a circle of wonderful new friends to spontaneously gather around her. She had to step out. So do you.

Making friends is part of the guideline but it doesn't stop there. Being friends is what intimacy is all about. Being a friend is a key to happiness.

•••••••••••••••••••••••••••• BEING FRIENDS
■

No one was more surprised than Marcia when she discovered that less than four months after she moved to Muskogee, she had built an interesting circle of acquaintances and one good friend.

Quite by chance, she was in a stall of the girls' west end bathroom when she overheard two of those acquaintances talking about her!

One said, "That new girl sure talks uppity. But I guess she can't help it, being raised up there in Chicago and all."

Said the other, "She doesn't act uppity, though. And you can trust her." Then they left.

Be the kind of friend you want to have. *You can trust her.* What a wonderful thing to say about anyone! Marcia didn't spread gossip and was careful not to believe rumors. She didn't tell secrets. When a close acquaintance named Cassie accidentally wet her pants, Marcia quickly stashed her in a rest room stall and brought her a clean pair of walking shorts from her own locker. She never told a soul. In short, Marcia was herself the kind of person she would want as a friend. Do people notice? They sure do!

Judge wisely. Solomon, king of Israel and Judah, had plenty to say about making friends. Most of the wise comments in the book of Proverbs are his; perhaps all of them are. Proverbs is a good guide to judging the people with whom you would develop intimate friendships.

Solomon claimed that the person who associates with wise people will be wise, but if you hang around with fools, you'll suffer harm[1] (my paraphrase). That means that if you are a Christian, you should be associating primarily with Christians. I've found this to be true just as Solomon did: You will become increasingly like the friends you associate with, whether you want to or not. For your own sake, then, you must exercise good judgment in choosing friends and close acquaintances.

Non-Christian friends will dampen your faith a lot quicker than you will improve theirs. Trust me on this.

Solomon also says that good friends keep each other sharp,[2] and that happy hearts are like medicine.[3] Basically, you want to develop friendships that let you stretch and grow, friendships with people who are upbeat and positive.

Marcia got to know a couple girls who were negative, constantly complaining, and depressed. Certainly, they could use a friend. But Marcia was vulnerable at the time, subject to depression herself because of the drastic life changes forced upon her. Her best bet was to stay with positive, bright people and let them buoy her up. She needed strength before she could impart strength.

And so she had to exercise good judgment when choosing associates. On the other hand:

Withhold unwise judgment. Marcia found herself discounting people's abilities on the basis of their Okie accent, just as some kids in her school wrote her off because of her clipped Chicago speech. If the person spoke with that drawl, she sort of instantly dismissed that person as having a room temperature IQ. Nothing could be farther from true. It was foolish of her, and she didn't even realize she was doing it.

She learned the truth when one of their classmates was injured in a major car wreck and she and Andrea were riding in the car right behind his. She watched super-competent medical people pull his crumpled car apart to get him out quickly and whisk him off to intensive care. She later learned heroic efforts in the emergency room saved his life. When she and Andrea visited him at the hospital a week later, she no longer noticed that the highly competent and caring doctors and nurses talked in that funny way. She had learned to judge the tree by its real fruit.

She was certainly not alone. After the Oklahoma City bombing, a noted news journalist got into trouble by assuming that the city's public safety personnel (that's fire department, police, and medical services) were less than competent simply because of that accent. The journalist was politely removed from at least one interview site because of that judgmental attitude.

Persons who did not judge on externals found an extraordinary welcome among the hurting Oklahomans.

It is so easy to judge by externals, such as manner of speech, that mean nothing. You don't want to be judged in that way yourself. Can you think of ways you might be doing that?

You can't be phony. When we say that everyone needs a few close, intimate, true friends, it goes without saying that you're not going to build rapport by being false in any way.

You can't buy friendship. The prodigal son had plenty of friends until he ran out of money. They all disappeared when hard times came and he needed them.[4] Throwing parties and spending freely will get lots of people to tag along with you. But you don't need that. You need real friends.

And so, out of fifty or so people with whom Marcia developed some sort of acquaintance, two relationships—Andrea's and Cassie's—blossomed into close, intimate friendships. It doesn't happen overnight. And Solomon mentioned that too. "A man of many companions may come to ruin."[5] You only need a couple.

To fulfill this guideline, superficiality—that is, surface—simply won't cut it. A real friendship must be genuine.

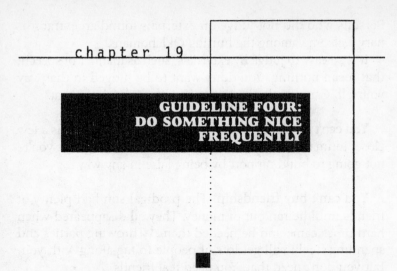

chapter 19

**GUIDELINE FOUR:
DO SOMETHING NICE
FREQUENTLY**

What's the nicest thing anyone's ever done for you?

Were you ever able to return the favor?

If you did, you were lucky. Most of us can't. It's interesting the way nice deeds (recently some have come to call them "random acts of kindness") circulate. That is, they don't bounce back and forth between two people so much as they bounce from person to person all over the place, often to total strangers. And they happen much more frequently than most people realize.

If you read the newspaper regularly, you come to believe that everyone is eventually going to be arrested for murder or mayhem, burglary at the very least. All you see is crime and disaster. Crime and disaster are news. Kindness is not. It's a sad commentary on human nature, but that's the way it is.

People who are victims of crime and disaster often need psychological help coming to terms with their emotional trauma. People who are victims of random acts of kindness don't. So if you want to put us psychiatrists and psychologists out of business . . .

I'm being silly. But you see the point. Good results come

from good deeds. However, the results are not just the receiver's. They are even more so the giver's.

············ THE GOOD FRUIT OF GOOD WORKS

Let me tell you about Jason (that's not his real name). He was a brand-new Christian and typical of a lot of new converts. Jason was as eager as a person can get about telling everyone else about his new faith. Do you know that almost all new converts to the faith hear the gospel from other new converts? Apparently after being in the faith two years or so, most Christians quit actively telling others the good news they themselves have found.

The exception to that generality is new believers who feel called into full-time Christian work. Jason was certain God called him and insisted that everyone else who knew Christ as Savior ought to be in full-time Christian work as well. His was a common attitude among new believers. But he couldn't afford seminary, and everyone else seemed reluctant to bankroll him. He felt betrayed.

Also in our church was an amazing woman, Anna. Anna was Russian by birth and older than dirt. Had to be in her nineties, but she was still spry and living independently. She called herself "Double-old Grandma," an honorific she once heard applied to Corrie ten Boom, because in most parts of the world, age is greatly honored. Her Christian family couldn't live with Communism, so they fled Russia in the thirties. They crossed the frozen Amur River in a sleigh in the dead of winter and took refuge in Hardin, a frontier Chinese city. They eventually arrived in America. If ever our church had a *yenta*, an old lady matchmaker and busybody, it was Anna. Nothing escaped her notice.

So one day this Anna took Jason out for coffee after church, sat him down with a sweet roll, and said, "I hear you take Mrs. Perkins out to the grocery store every week."

"Yeah. She can't drive." Jason shrugged. "Everybody's gotta

buy groceries. She helps me pick out the best fruit. She's good at it."

"Ya, she is that. Her husband was a greengrocer once, you know. She says you drive all right, for a teenager."

"I'll be happy to take you too, if you need it."

"Why thank you. And I hear you helped Charlie finally prune that terrible hedge of his. It looks much better now."

"He couldn't reach the top without help; it was too overgrown."

"After so many years, of course it was. Charlie. That man. He puts off too much." She wagged her head. "And I heard lots of other things you do. So you want to enter full-time Christian work. Preacher, eh? Youth leader?"

"Yes, but every door into seminary that I try seems to slam in my face. And I wanted to work at the church camp, but they had to cut back this year and all their slots are filled. I don't understand why God called me to His work and then doesn't let me do it."

"What is this you're saying?! You are doing it. Why do you complain?"

"Doing what?"

"His work. Some He calls to preach, ya. Pastors and missionaries He raises up. But all of us He calls to be a full-time Christian. You do that now. Three thousand new believers at Pentecost,[1] eh? How many of them were preachers? Only Peter we know about, and eleven others. The rest, they get assignments to wait tables.[2] They are full-time Christians, all the same as preachers. Already you are a lovely full-time Christian, Jason, doing God's work. And so young. The whole church is proud of you. We want you to know that. I am proud of you."

I am proud of you. One thing you knew of Anna; she never ever said a word that wasn't true. Jason saw the light.

He is still doing full-time Christian work. His career is not preacher but skilled auto mechanic. He's trustworthy and good, and he makes a fine living at it. He also makes house calls for old people in our church who depend upon him to keep their vehicles running. Those on social security get billed only for parts and oil.

Do you realize how valuable and needed a skilled mechanic is?

Being in full-time Christian work as a pastor, etc., makes you neither more nor less spiritual than the equally committed Christian who does piece work in a lawn mower factory. Service to others is the key. God loves to serve, to give. And since we are made in the image of God,[3] whether we are Christians or not, service fulfills us.

When you do nice things for others, then, you reap an emotional benefit. Emotional ups encourage brain juice production just as emotional downs discourage it. See the connection to happiness?

Let's assume you give yourself this guideline as an assignment. Find a few things to do for other people. As you start looking for favors to do for others, you turn your focus away from yourself and outward toward the rest of the world. One of the big problems of a depressive is that the whole focus is turned inward, into the self. A little introspection is good, more is kind of good, but total inward-looking gets pathological. Focusing on others breaks that extreme introspection.

But how do you go about it?

· · · · · · · · · · · · · · · · · **GIFTS FROM THE HEART**
■

Let's use Jason as the example. He performed several kinds of kindness, both random and non-random—that is, scheduled and unscheduled, you might say. Both kinds present excellent opportunities.

Random Acts of Kindness

When Jason drove by Charlie's house, he saw the old man struggling with the pruning shears, the rickety ladder bobbling. So he stopped. Charlie held the ladder, and Jason, whose arms were longer by six inches (Jason is a really lanky kid), lopped branches as Charlie directed. Ten minutes later, Jason continued on his way and Charlie handled the rest of the pruning job, the branches he could reach from the ground.

Ten minutes out of Jason's day made Charlie's job possible and prettied up the whole neighborhood. That hedge was really an eyesore. Even more important, had the ladder tipped as it kept threatening to, the old man could have been seriously hurt in a fall.

Jason stumbled upon that good deed. It was a one-time thing that just sort of happened. That's what I mean by random.

A friend of mine picks up litter when she goes walking. She scoops up gum wrappers, scraps of paper, plastic bags—whatever she happens upon. Surprisingly often, she says, stuff is tossed on the ground within ten feet of a litter receptacle. Is hers a Christian service? She insists it is. It counters an illegal and immoral activity, littering, and it improves the neighborhood. Although it's her constant habit, it is also random.

What about you? Can you think of some situation you passed in the last couple days where you could have offered an act of kindness?

A kid in the hall, struggling with an armload of books, drops a pencil.

A teacher is trying to get a box of papers out of the back seat of her car, close the car door, and lock up.

The woman behind you in the check-out line only has a quart of milk and you have a grocery-cart-full.

At a busy fast-food counter, a woman with three small children is trying to handle her order—not one but two of those flimsy, bendable paper trays full—plus get straws and napkins.

And then there are the non-random acts of kindness. When Jason took Mrs. Perkins to the grocery store, and also Anna, as it turned out, he was acting on a regular basis. He dropped by their places every week. That's non-random, or scheduled.

Non-Random Acts of Kindness

There are even greater varieties of opportunity for this kind of service.

Like Jason you might end up helping someone on a fairly regular basis. Can you think of opportunities in your neighborhood for that kind of thing?

Don't neglect your family. And they don't have to be big, spectacular things, either. The smallest kindness can mean an awful lot. I'm thinking of a high school sophomore, Carrie, who spends two or three minutes each morning threading needles. Her great-aunt lives with the family, and Auntie Bess quilts. Most of the day, she hand-sews gorgeous quilts. But she can no longer thread those little needles. So Carrie threads thirty or forty needles for her and sticks them in a couple corks. It keeps Bess in handwork until Carrie's mom comes home in the evening to thread more.

Carrie laughs, "Me? I can't sew a stitch. But man, can I thread a needle!"

Many young people who think they might be interested in medical work when they graduate volunteer in hospitals. Some hospitals have formal programs, and the people who volunteer are called candy stripers. Others are less structured, but they need the help, all the same.

And that brings up another point. When you do acts of kindness, you get all the benefits I mentioned above—better focus, a sense of accomplishment and good feeling, an emotional upper. But if you obtain other benefits, that's fine too. You may want to volunteer in a law office if you're thinking of a career in that field. Sheriff's departments often have patrols made up of high school students. The volunteers are official, and they are used for non-hazardous (i.e., no use of firearms) law enforcement such as crowd control at official functions. It's a great way to serve the community and also get a true, inside look at law enforcement (and no, you do *not* get that from television!).

Jason found out that it's very easy, once you get into the

habit of doing things for others, to overdo it. As you become attuned to others, looking outward rather than inward, you'll see more and more opportunity. Jason booked into too much for a while, and found it extremely difficult to back off.

After all, there is so much to be done.

But you can't do it all.

I suggest zeroing in on one special thing to do for someone else each week. It may be a service. It could be simply buying a helpful book for a person who needs the information. You might join someone for devotions together.

Giving is godly. And that brings us to the next guideline.

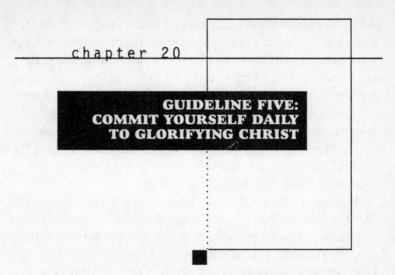

chapter 20

**GUIDELINE FIVE:
COMMIT YOURSELF DAILY
TO GLORIFYING CHRIST**

"No thank you."

You'd be surprised how many teens say "thanks but no thanks" when I suggest this guideline. From a worldly point of view, they actually have some good reasons for saying no.

········· **WHY NOT TO FOLLOW THIS GUIDELINE**

Committing yourself to Christ on a daily basis can make you look pretty much like a dweeb. Laughed at. Ridiculed. Snubbed. Sometimes even sabotaged by so-called "friends." Saying the word *Jesus* out loud can make you an outcast, unless you use it as a blasphemy, of course.

That's not at all your fault in any way. The media and too many other Christians in this country make the faith look spineless. Nerdy. Dweebish. Anyone who doesn't keep his faith hidden is considered a fanatic (although shaven-headed militia people who wear camouflage fatigues and tote guns are not fanatics but just regular joes with a mission). Real faith is not the least bit like it is pictured.

Unlike Anna's committed Christian family, these glib

detractors never faced hardship and death for their faith. Had Anna's sleigh been intercepted before it got across the river (and that was a very likely prospect), her family would have been imprisoned, probably tortured, possibly killed. Certainly separated, the children made wards of a godless state. Russia felt that all good citizens should be good Communists, and good citizens don't flee the country. Packing everyone you love and everything you own into a sleigh and then driving the horses out across a frozen river into a foreign country is a supremely gutsy, frightening thing to do.

A woman named Brenda Lange runs an orphanage in Mozambique. Fellow Christians and the orphanage's dogs keep thieves, rapists, and plunderers at bay. The crops that are their food are constantly threatened by wild hogs and baboons. She faces continual harassment and physical danger from local men of other faiths. Hardly Nerdy.

Christians in the former USSR, in China, in Africa, in Southeast Asia can tell you whether committing yourself to Christ is spineless. People in many countries consider Christians an enemy or a dire threat; they think the faith foolish or horrible; but they don't belittle and mock it. Only in our "Christian" nation does that happen.

So when you commit yourself to Christ, yes. You're going to hear about it and get laughed at. Especially in school.

What if you decide to lead a righteous, upstanding life without actually openly declaring a commitment to Jesus Christ? No booze or drugs, no cheating on tests, no slipping around with the opposite sex. You're going to get laughed at anyway. "Sister Christian." "Miss Goody Two-Shoes." "Mr. Perfect." And they say it with a sneer. It looks like you can't win.

. . WHAT HAPPENS IF YOU ADOPT THIS GUIDELINE ■

Look again.

"Blessed are those who are persecuted for righteousness' sake, for theirs is the kingdom of heaven."[1] You're laughed at in school, but you're only going to be in school a couple more years. You're going to be in heaven for eternity. Which is more important?

Do you know what Jesus said? "Blessed are you when they revile and persecute you, and say all kinds of evil against you falsely for My sake. Rejoice and be exceedingly glad, for great is your reward in heaven, for so they persecuted the prophets that were before you."[2]

Of course you knew what Jesus said! You memorized the beatitudes years ago, in Sunday school. Well, this, as they say, is where the rubber meets the road. This is exactly what He was talking about. Notice that word "exceedingly." He means it, too!

The only immediate advantage you have for committing daily to Jesus Christ is never easy to hang onto when you're being laughed at. The advantage is, you know you're doing the right thing, the courageous thing. It takes real guts, not phony courage, to make a stand for Jesus and stay there. You know, though, that Jesus asked you to. You know that His followers' trials, as described in Acts, were a thousand times worse than heckling by silly, shallow, blind classmates.

But you know what? Sometimes it's easier to stand firm in the face of death or beating than to stand firm in the face of a thousand sly little digs and giggles. The church has always done best under persecution. When the opposition is great and glaring, your response is pretty obvious. But when it's a constant trickle, shadowed, and vague, it wears you down.

So even with the best of intentions, there will be times when you just plain blow it. Don't worry about it. Jesus isn't asking for perfection. He's asking for you.

It makes things a little easier if you can remember that you're not alone in this. You have an international family of believers just like you, people living all over the world. Two of the Meier teens went to a public high school of three thousand students; three hundred of those people attended a weekly Young Life Bible study. It was a great place to not only stand for God, but to also meet similar friends of both sexes and have lots of fun.

How do you go about completing this guideline?

● ● ● ● ● ● ● ● ● ● ● ● ● ● ● **MAKING A DAILY COMMITMENT**
■

Here's how I and my fellow Christian workers at the clinics go about it. Use our method or adapt it to your own needs.

First, when we wake up, we speak to God first thing:

1. **Thank You, God, for another day. Help me to become more like You today.**
2. **I commit this day to You. I want it to bring You glory and honor.**
3. **I'm going to need Your strength to supplement my own self-control, so that I don't yield to temptation. Thank You for it in advance (that's one you know He will deliver).**
4. **Please forgive me when I make a mistake, particularly if that mistake does not glorify You, or if it fails to benefit the people You bring into contact with me.**

Then we get on with our day. Whenever possible—that is, whenever I think of it—I remind myself, "Does this bring glory to God?" Or, "No one knows I'm doing this except God and myself. But if this deed were described over the public address system, would it advance God's glory?"

If the answer is "No," the second question is, "Is what I am doing neutral with regard to glorifying my Lord?"

If that answer is no, there's only one choice left; it would bring dishonor to God were it known. It takes strength and guts to change your activity right then and there. Can you do it?

For Him?

The sixth guideline makes this one much easier.

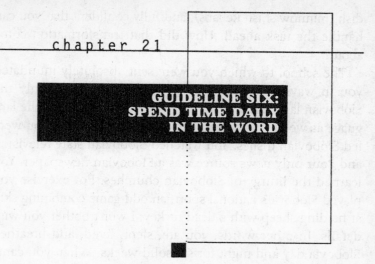

chapter 21

GUIDELINE SIX: SPEND TIME DAILY IN THE WORD

Let's say you are a college professor quietly minding your business in some university when the president of the United States calls up. His ambassador to Slobovia died and he wants you to take over the position. You'll be perfect for the job, and he needs you! Oh, well, uh . . . what can you say?

For one thing, you've never heard of Slobovia. You'd have to look it up on a map. You have no idea what the customs are like or what the state religion is, and you've certainly never seen their language, Slobovian, in print, let alone heard it spoken.

But the president understands that. He's sending you to a language school.

"I've never been very good with languages," you protest weakly. "I never had to be. I'm a botany professor."

No matter. "Pack your bags," says the president. "You leave for Slobovia in eight weeks."

"*Eight weeks?*" you shriek, but he already hung up.

Eight weeks later, you step off the plane at Slobovia's only airport, fluent in the language, understanding the gestures and customs the people around you use, ready to eat the national dish (minnow shish kebabs), and fully confident that you can handle the task ahead. How did that transformation come about?

The school to which you were sent absolutely inundated you in ways Slobovian. All day long, you heard only the Slobovian language and nothing else but. You studied the language as well as Slobovian customs and traditions. You were fed Slobovian dishes. You watched Slobovian state television and your only news source was a Slobovian newspaper. You learned the liturgy of Slobovian churches. For exercise you played Slobovia's national sport, an odd game combining skill at herding sheep with a dead turkey; I won't bother you with details. In other words, you ate, slept, lived, and breathed Slobovia day and night for six solid weeks. When you came out of that crash course, you knew a thing or two about handling yourself well in Slobovia. And you had two weeks to spare, to speak English and read American papers.

But by now you were so comfortable in Slobovian, you didn't need two weeks of normalcy. Slobovia was normal. You were ready to go.

There is no Slobovia, as I'm sure you know. But there is in fact a school like that. Government legates, corporate bigwigs who will be working abroad, some missionaries, and others who must know all about a country in a hurry attend the school. In six to eight weeks, they learn what regular college courses would take years to teach.

This magic happens because the student is totally buried in the thing to be learned. If the student is not going to the country immediately, the learning will wear off unless he or she keeps up intense contact with the language and culture. By intense, I mean hours daily, every single day.

The school succeeds so well because it takes advantage of two basic human traits:

One, people are influenced the most profoundly by the things they come in contact with most frequently.

And two, today's influence, whatever it is, tends to push out yes-terday's.

· · · · · · · · · · **PROBLEMS FROM THOSE TWO TRAITS**
■

These traits of human nature can cause us severe problems when they are used wrongly. You're too young to remember first hand, but some years ago a misguided religious leader named Jim Jones built himself a "church" empire in California. He demanded twenty-four hours a day of his followers' time and 100 percent of their energies. They gave it. Paranoid of authority, he moved most of his group down to South America and established a camp in the jungle. His paranoia grew worse and he ended up slaughtering many hundreds of his own fol-lowers, nearly the whole group, with poisoned Kool-Aid.

In a book titled *Deceived,* long out of print now, Mel White interviewed some of the people who got out of the cult before it left the country. He asked one young woman who had been raised in an extremely religious home how long it took her to shed her old religion and adopt Jones's "new" one. "About two months," she replied.

Two months is all it took to unseat a lifetime of teaching, because Jones immersed his followers, day and night, in his own programs and preaching. That is how powerfully those two human traits can work against us. Fortunately, they can work for us just as powerfully. Perhaps even more so.

· · · · · · · · · · · · · · · · **KEEPING CONTACT WITH GOD**
■

You can use those two traits to your eternal advantage. Think about it. You're going to be in the company of God forever. He purchased you with His only Son's blood. Wouldn't it be great, since He already took care of you so beautifully, if you could take care of His concerns while you're down here on Earth?

To do that, you have to keep His concerns at the front of your mind, so to speak. That's terribly hard! The pressure of daily living, of going to school, rushing around, studying, watching TV, whatever it is you do, can easily crowd out thinking about Him. That's why it will help you in very practical ways to spend time with Him every day.

Just as evil people use those two human traits for their own purposes, and that intense-education language school uses them to impart enormous amounts of information quickly, you can use them to keep contact with God.

In Chapter 16, wherein we discussed using a weekly routine in order to keep important priorities straight, I explained how I build intimacy with God. Briefly, there are four elements to the daily devotions I described:

1. Every day I read a passage of Scripture.
2. I spend five minutes or more (sometimes hours) thinking about what I read. (In fancy Christian-ese, I meditate on the Word.)
3. I try to work out how the passage applies to me personally. That's actually part of the meditation.
4. I pray. In fact, I carry on an ongoing, silent conversation with God off and on *all* day, *every* day, and even at night while lying in my bed.

Some of those books and pamphlets of daily devotions are excellent; a few are lousy. Whether you use prepared material or not, try also to read daily in the Word itself. There is no substitute for God's unfiltered voice.

I and several others at the clinic like 3″ x 5″ cards. We write very special passages of Scripture on them. Then we carry them with us to review when we get breaks in the day. I memorize many of them.

· · · · · · · · · · THE NECESSITY OF KEEPING CONTACT

See how important that is?

The very human trait of letting today's thoughts and influences push out yesterday's makes it imperative that you keep regular contact with things that are important to you.

Let's say you fall in love. This is your One True Love! But then your One True Love moves to another town. Do you want letters from him/her at Christmas and Easter? Sure. But you want a letter every day in between, too! If your One True Love writes to you twice a year, you two won't stay close for very long. Another person, another love whom you see daily or nearly so will inevitably push out your One True Love. Deep inside, everyone knows that. That's why people in love write and call so often.

And that trait of being influenced most by the things you are in contact with the most applies to God as well.

Pause a moment. Let's count all the things that you are influenced by and surrounded by most during the day—family, TV, classes, the kids you hang around with at lunch and so on. Use the fingers of one hand to count those that are likely to bring you closer to God, and on the other hand count those that are either neutral in spiritual value or tend to separate you from God (for example, most prime time TV would count on that hand).

Do you see the problems that the everyday world brings? Some ugly influences there! They must be countered—pushed back—by putting other things in our lives that do bring us closer to God, and Bible reading is the best and quickest way to do that.

But there is an even more important reason to spend time every day in the Word. Happiness requires that we reprogram our computers.

.... REPROGRAMMING THE OLD COMPUTER

People liken our brains to computers. The analogy isn't very good. Computers can calculate, and that's about it. Of course, they do it lightning fast, which our brains cannot. Check out a computer program that will do your taxes. You plug a number in on, say, line eighteen, and the machine instantly recalculates everything in order to come out with the correct answer—your tax. Change an entry, any entry, and *zip!* The correct new total appears virtually instantly. Amazing.

However.

We may have to divide using a pencil and long division, but our brains are masters of what computer folk call "fuzzy thinking." If two plus two equals four isn't good enough, our brains allow a little fudging, a little adjustment. Computers can't do that. Their calculation is rigid, black and white. More important, they can't think creatively. That's not adding two and two; that's pulling a little memory from here, a bit of data from there, a few totally unrelated facts, and coming up with an entirely new idea *that works*. Computers can't come close to doing that. The human mind can create a computer; the computer will never create a human mind.

Example: Ice cream became all the rage around the turn of the century. In 1904, a clever entrepreneur envisioned an ice cream container you could stroll along with. Then you wouldn't have to sit down in one place with a dish and spoon. Do the boardwalk at Atlantic City, and eat ice cream as you go. Tour the St. Louis exposition with ice cream in hand. Afterwards, you could simply eat the container also. He invented the ice cream cone.

A computer could never have seen the need for a portable ice cream holder, or picture someone eating it as well as the ice cream, or . . . That's creative fuzzy thinking. We call it "brainstorming" or "ingenuity" or "stroke of genius," and it is the gift that made civilization.

Fortunately, we all have the gift. Unfortunately, like every other gift it can also work against us. Fortunately, we can counter the bad aspects because we also have something else a computer does not—a will. Not the testament that's read to your survivors after you die, disappointing all of them. I mean the desire to do a particular thing. I *will* change my way of thinking to line it up better with God's desires for me. I *will* choose happiness.

Here's how it works. A neurosurgeon named Penfield became famous for a series of experiments.[1] He would stimulate various areas of a person's brain with electrodes and the person would tell him what came to mind as a result. Just by touching a tiny point of the brain he could make that person fully recall a past event. Sometimes the subject only remembered the feelings of an event without the memory of the event itself. Sometimes it was merely an aroma, or a glimpse of something. But one thing became clear. Everything in that person's life was stored away in the brain. Everything!

Now along comes our brain in everyday situations as well as special occasions. Operating almost exclusively below conscious level, it takes bits and pieces of all that information and uses the data to make sense out of what is happening and plan what to do next. The problem is, a lot of that info is damaging. When people yell at you, put you down, belittle you, and curse you, it all goes into the computer memory bank. Then the brain uses that false information to decide, "You're a worthless blob of sea foam," and you act according to the brain's erroneous conclusion.

Think of all the garbage you dump in from TV, videos, and the like. It may be entertaining, but it probably does not emphasize good values. The brain doesn't care. It uses that data too whenever it thinks.

Even worse, your brain gathers info in that way to support greed, jealousy, worry, lust. . . . Is everyone like that? God says so. "The heart is deceitful above all things, and desperately wicked."[2] In other words, the desire to sin is pretty much programmed right in. It's human.

Reprogramming draws us away from these human brain-failings, if we would call it that, and closer to God's healthy brain functions. Failure and sin bring on depression and self-disgust. Godly behavior spikes the old brain juices and allows happiness and feelings of self-worth.

You reprogram by shoving God's Word in on top of the human nature, pushing it back. You use the principles that school uses in order to give the brain new, wholesome information that displaces the bad programming that accumulated through time. It counters the odd info and bad info our current culture dumps on us constantly. Too, it reinforces the good programming of the past.

But you have to keep at it, every day. Sure, read helpful books like this one, but don't forget to have daily input from the pure Word. Nothing else can help as well.

There is one last guideline. It's also first—remember, there's no rank to these. All are important. It's the shortest, and it's the hardest.

chapter 22

**GUIDELINE SEVEN:
GET RID OF GRUDGES
DAILY**

The Canadian cartoon strip *For Better or For Worse*, by Lynn Johnston, does the greatest job of depicting its characters' emotions (so did *Calvin and Hobbes*, R.I.P.). Elation is palpable, with the characters' faces open and joyous. Anger visibly smolders, their eyebrows a low, flat line. The mother in particular, El, gets shot down so often.

In one story line, she wanted to try a vegetarian lifestyle, so of course the whole family had to eat veggie. She fixed beautiful dishes that happened to be just about all beans. When her husband cheated on the veggie diet with fast-food fried chicken, she erupted like St. Helens. In the final panel, he's staring off, bewildered, while she rages. And he's thinking, "Remind me never to have an affair."

That comic strip, as well as some others, teaches some pretty deep things about anger and grudges. In fact, you might find it interesting to actively take note how various media deal with the subject of anger. TV, films, the funny papers, comic books, novels, and short stories will give you a varied slant on what makes people angry and how they deal with it.

· · · · · · · · · · · · · · · · · · · UNDERSTANDING ANGER
■

It's important to understand how anger operates and how to manage it. In Chapter 3 you saw the importance of getting rid of grudges. Grudges cause so many, many cases of depression. Nine out of ten. But we never did talk much about how exactly to do it. That's what I want to talk about here, and understanding anger is the first step. Incidentally, understanding how anger operates will take you a long way in dealing with jerks, also.

That cartoon episode I described above illustrates several truths about anger.

Like beauty, anger is in the eye of the beholder. Something makes you angry only if you personally care about it.

El was furious because this vegetarian experiment was dear to her. It loomed large in her life *at that moment.* She was mad at her man because he broke a rule even though it was only a temporary, artificial rule most of the world doesn't even know about. Six months before her experiment, or six months afterward, she would never even have noticed the chicken on her husband's breath.

A man who takes great pride in his lawn and spends lots of time on it may well be furious if you walk on his grass. The guy next door whose lawn looks like he raises dandelions for a living probably doesn't give a rip, unless kids in general annoy him. An older woman who lives alone and feels vulnerable may go ballistic if you startle her. Startle the girl sitting beside you in class and she'll jab you, maybe, but she probably won't feel threatened.

Little things can provoke a big reaction. A person's anger response will not usually be governed by the size of the reason for it.

You might think that a severe offense, such as breaking one of the Ten Commandments, would trigger wild fury, while a minor offense, such as getting dirt on the kitchen floor, would cause a small, temporary outburst. You know and I know it doesn't work that way, especially if your mom just washed the floor. When anger boils up, the size of the infraction that caused it often means nothing.

Which is more serious, committing adultery or eating a drumstick? El exploded in fury even though her husband's slip transgressed no biblical or moral law. The artist made a nice gag line out of a serious truth about anger.

That then is the nature of anger. Basically, anger is sometimes irrational, not behaving according to reason. There is also much to learn about the causes that generate anger.

A lot of anger results from selfishness. And it isn't pretty.

A kid breaks into your garage at 1:00 A.M. to steal your mountain bike. However, you were up getting a drink of water, saw him jimmying the door, and called 911. The cops nail him cold with bike in hand. Is he mad at himself for breaking God's law? Not at all. Is he mad at the cops? Always. Mostly he's mad at you! *You* messed up his selfish plans. *You*, in his faulty way of reasoning, are the reason he's in jail!

A youth leader who spends eighty hours a week at the job needs a van for still another retreat and can't obtain one. She needs more parent participation in her latest Kids' Night Out and they aren't cooperating. She needs money; the church isn't financing half of her ambitious plans and people aren't giving as much as they ought to at her fund-raisers. Does she take that as a signal that maybe she's planning too much for the size of the church? Naaa. She's mad at the parents, at the car dealership who won't loan her a van again, at the church elders, and at God. If you were to tell her that maybe she is going overboard in order to prove she's somebody instead of nobody, or that she is pretty selfish in her demands that everyone dance to her piper, she'll be mad at you, too.

Projection generates much anger. You know all about projection. That's assigning your own traits and feelings to someone else, whether that other person possesses them or not.

A sad case we often deal with is the person with paranoid personality traits—the person who thinks the whole world is against him or her. That person—let's call the person a "he," for convenience—is angry at life and probably at God. He projects his anger onto the people around him, which means he thinks they are angry with him. Then he "sees" them cutting him down, getting back at him, doing other things that anger can lead a person to do. They aren't, really. He's reading the signs wrong. But they don't take kindly to his constant accusations and slights, so pretty soon they really are angry, not at him so much as at his attitude.

Things and accidents generate anger. Get mad at a table? You just might, if you stub your toe against the table leg. You slop peanut butter on your sociology book and explode with a colorful word. A small child spills sticky grape juice in your lap, and you're wearing your good jeans.

Much of that kind of anger is frustration with pain, damage, or the mess. Still, it's anger and should be recognized as such. It's not appropriate. None of those events was intentionally planned to hurt you. But it's there.

Anger at genuine wrongdoing is appropriate. There are times when anger is fully justified.

You thought she was your best friend, but she steals from you the watch she's been coveting. When you confront her, she says you're being childish.

The guy next to you in English tells lies about you and trashes your reputation. He thinks it's funny.

Of course you're furious, and rightly so!

The bottom line is that there are, then, two different kinds of anger, appropriate and inappropriate. The last named example above, the one mentioning sin, is appropriate. *Others usually are not.* This understanding about the nature and causes of anger is about to come in very handy. Anger creates terrible problems in its own right, but it also creates grudges. And grudges, as we've seen, rob your happiness quicker than anything.

Now that you know a little something about appropriate and inappropriate anger, you can get an idea which kind of anger is gripping you by the throat at any particular moment. Is it appropriate? In other words, was true harm done because of some sinful act? Or does it follow the pattern of one of those inappropriate kinds? Learning to tell the difference is a great step forward for a couple reasons.

One reason is that inappropriate anger is usually the result of immaturity. The one thing you, a teen, have to be quickly in this day and age is mature. The faster you can develop maturity, therefore, the better off you are. The faster you can develop true Christian maturity, the better off you are for eternity!

The other reason is, gaining insight into your anger can help you stave off depression, and that is the name of our game.

So let's pretend you just blew your stack. I know, it's hard to imagine, but try. There you are, fairly unruffled, and this event we'll call X happens. Suddenly you're enraged! But instantly you stuff it, because you know it's stupid to be angry.

Step One: Admit You're Angry!

You'd be amazed how many people in our counsel come in claiming, "I'm not angry; I gave up on so-and-so long ago." Or, "I'm not angry; it's not Christian to be angry." We hear that so much!

You can't deal with anger until you recognize that it is there to be dealt with. Often this is no easy thing. Anger is a cheat and a robber and adept at hiding. These two facts may help you find it:

1. Everyone gets angry. Everyone. That includes you. It's an immediate, automatic response, like yanking your hand

away when you accidentally burn it. It's down there somewhere, rest assured, so you might as well dig it out.

2. Anger is not unchristian. God gets angry.[1] Jesus.[2] Moses.[3] David.[4] God programmed it into you, so there must be a reason for it. There might even be a good reason, so let's haul it out and look at it.

Step Two: You've Acknowledged Your Anger, Now Decide If It Is Inappropriate

Which of the items above describing anger does it fit into best? Is X, the thing you are angry about, generating appropriate anger? That is, have you been incensed by a moral violation? Jesus saw the moneychangers' greedy practices as being immoral, particularly inside the holy temple. Righteous indignation is appropriate. Everything else—that is, inappropriate anger—was either triggered by or intensified by strange things from the past going on below conscious level.

Let's make up a theoretical example. Here's Joe Blow, who was yelled at and belittled long ago when he was small. It seems his mom would make him help in the garden and then really rake him over the coals when he'd do something the least bit wrong. Now your dog takes off chasing a squirrel. The squirrel runs through a corner of Joe's corn patch and your dog runs after it. You'd think that the dog and squirrel had combined forces to rip the whole garden apart, the way Joe carries on. He chews you up one side and down the other. Actually, neither the dog nor the squirrel damaged anything at all. It was a minor non-event. What's Joe's big problem?

Well, you know because I told you. His present anger, all out of proportion to the infraction, is actually past anger erupting again. If you know the situation, you realize that Joe never dealt with his original anger and it keeps coming back to haunt him. Of course, you probably don't know about his childhood, so you have no idea why he's so touchy about his garden. But you can see, I trust, how a person's personality and past experiences can uncork in the present, given the right trigger.

Here's the key: Inappropriate anger may well stem from, or at least be greatly intensified by, the past. If you realize that, it will be much, much easier for you to overcome inappropriate anger. You know where it's coming from, and you know it's not legitimate.

That's a big step toward maturity, and a lot of adults haven't made it.

What is its cause? I don't mean the event we're calling X, but the real cause. The basic cause. Selfishness? Are you angry because you didn't get your own way? Is it projection (that takes some thinking-about!)? Are you mad at an accident, or an inanimate object, or an innocent person who simply made a mistake? It's a lot easier to put a lid on anger (*not* stuffing it, but rather acknowledging it and controlling it) when you realize that deep down, it's pretty stupid and petty.

But how about a major accident? Let's pretend your friend is out biking in the country and a deer leaps out across the road in front of her. She falls trying to avoid it and breaks her neck. She's paralyzed; no feeling or voluntary motion whatever from the top of her shoulders to her toes. That can hardly be called stupid or petty. Will you feel sad and angry that it happened, even though it's no one's fault?

Of course you will, because you care about your friend! It's part of the normal grief process. It is also a part of life. The "rain," figuratively speaking, falls on the just (innocent) and on the unjust (the jerks of this world).[5] Truly inappropriate anger stems from three things: 1) *selfishness* (no need to define that; we all know what it means); 2) *paranoia* (thinking everyone else is out to get you and projecting your fear and anger on others), or 3) *perfectionistic expectations* (that is, allowing no margin for error or variation).

How do you handle inappropriate anger? Once you figure out what it really is, that takes out some of the steam right there. If you ought to apologize to someone else, by all means do so. Clear the air.

Be sure to forgive yourself. You got angry when it was not

really appropriate; you let your past do your thinking for you. Those things happen. Now it's over. You deserve forgiveness, so make sure it happens.

The matter has been acknowledged and handled. Next time will be easier because this time has given you some practice dealing with inappropriate anger. Next time you'll be quicker to clue in to why anger is happening. With time and practice and insight, incidents of unbridled inappropriate anger will diminish.

But that's not the way you handle appropriate anger.

Step Three: Give Appropriate Anger
the Special Treatment It Requires

Since a moral problem is at issue, another person is necessarily involved here. You will want to handle your anger by taking two steps. One is to verbalize it. The other is to forgive the perpetrator promptly.

"Yes, but . . .!" you roar. Surely you can't just forgive like (snap of the fingers) that.

Here's how. And it is for your sake more so than the perpetrator's.

First, verbalize. That is, get the offense out in the open by describing it. You will eventually verbalize it in three directions, upward, outward, and inward. At first, you may not tell another soul other than yourself. That's inward. But tell it out loud. The truth emerges much more easily when we talk about the problem. That was the rehearsal. Now that you have the problem clear in your own mind, take it to the perpetrator and tell him or her about it. That's outward.

Please do it tactfully. Don't come on like gangbusters with, "You stupid zucchini, do you realize what you did to me!" You need not accuse. The Holy Spirit will accuse if accusation is appropriate. Your goal is to reconcile the situation, never to get back at the perpetrator. Tell the person why you are angry and keep the telling in your point of view. "I am feeling angry because . . ." "This happened, and I'm feeling angry toward you about it, but I would like us to talk it out."

Maybe the perpetrator realizes the transgression, maybe not. Maybe the perpetrator thinks your anger is appropriate and maybe not. You have aired your grievance to the appropriate person. That's what counts. You're doing what God wants you to do.[6] That counts even more!

There's another benefit most people never think of. It reduces your desire to gossip. When you are wronged, you feel the most powerful need to tell someone. Telling anyone other than the perpetrator is likely to generate gossip, because other people love to spill what they know, particularly when discord is involved. Is any resulting gossip going to go your way? Don't count on it. You know how distortions can twist the truth completely around. You avoid that whole can of worms by keeping the problem in house, so to speak.

Certainly there are times when you cannot verbalize your anger to the perpetrator. That person is your boss and you'll lose your job; the principal and you're in hot water up to your ears; the president of the United States and the FBI will cause you all sorts of grief.

In that case it may pay you to vent your anger and frustration in some way. I have a friend who throws stovewood. His household heats with wood and there's usually a cord or two behind the shed. He tosses it out into the yard stick by stick, and then he tosses it back. He sometimes yells while he's doing it (they live way out in the hills). You can't do that and probably don't want to. But you can go running, hit a tennis ball, pound on something, or perhaps watch football, rugby, or some other hard-contact sport. Do something to vent it.

Finally, verbalize it upward, to God. Pray also that He will reveal to you any anger and grudges you're penning up inside you that even you don't know about. He knows about them, of course. He knows everything that's going on within you. Tell Him about it anyway.

By now, you have a good enough grip that forgiving the perpetrator should be easier. It may not even have been possible before. If you cannot forgive the person in your own strength, it is perfectly acceptable to use Christ's strength as a supplement or even wholly.

"I forgive you for . . ."

"With the help of Jesus Christ, I forgive you for . . ."

"Through Jesus Christ, I forgive you for . . ."

Forgiving is not forgetting. Forgiving is *not* condoning what the perpetrator did. Forgiving is not instantly healing the emotional wounds involved. Forgiving does *not* mean that you subject yourself in the future to any more sinful acts by that perpetrator. Forgetting may never happen and healing takes time. Forgiving is a deliberate thing you do because you know you ought to. It is a step, not a cure-all. But it is a crucial step.

Exactly, it is a step in which you give up any right or desire to get personal vengeance on that perpetrator and instead leave all the decisions regarding vengeance to God. He has promised to take care of every act.

Once you have forgiven, you may or may not trust the person again. Trusting is not a part of forgiveness either. Let's say you forgive the girl who stole your watch and then called you childish. That doesn't mean you can trust her alone with your possessions, and if you are wise, you will not. She is projecting her own childishness on you and may well steal again.

Forgiveness means only that the past is dealt with. You have every right to be cautious about the future.

Remember, leave the vengeance to God.

I love the story of David and Nabal, which is pretty much all of chapter twenty-five in First Samuel. Nabal was a world class jerk with hardly any common sense or tact. What an ultra-jerk! He insulted David, who at that time was trying to elude King Saul. A rising warlord is not a person to insult, even if he is on the outs with the king at the moment. Particularly when that warlord, David, protected your shepherds and flocks for you out in the hills.

David mustered four hundred crack soldiers, experienced

guerrillas, and hit the trail, intent on wiping out Nabal and every single male on his estate. Nabal's wife Abigail, both beautiful and one smart cookie, intercepted David with a peace offering. When she addressed him, David perceived that he would have sinned terribly if he had taken vengeance on his own. He backed off and let God have the vengeance which was His in the first place. Less than two weeks later, not only did Nabal die, David married Nabal's smart and beautiful widow.

When Paul quotes Scripture, "Vengeance is mine, I will repay, says the Lord."[7] he adds, "Beloved [readers], do not avenge yourselves, but rather give place to wrath."

It's hard. Maybe God will forgive without taking vengeance. Maybe God will take so long about it that your perpetrator practically gets off scot free. Maybe God's vengeance isn't as severe as what you would have inflicted. And God's vengeance almost never brings satisfaction as immediately as you want it to. All sorts of doubts cloud your ability to turn everything over to God.

You've heard about faith your whole life. This is it, right here. Trusting Him to do the right thing. Letting Him handle the whole show. Resting in the confidence that He'll inflict appropriate vengeance and no more or no less. Your head knows you can trust Him. Now make your heart do it also.

This faith is extremely comforting if you work it backwards. Other people, justly or unjustly, have it in for you from time to time. They might be calling God's vengeance down upon you! You want it to be appropriate to your wrongdoing, if you did wrong in the first place. You don't want Him to be careless about handling your enemy's case. You can trust Him to be just as careful about handling yours.

• GOOD-BYE GRUDGES!

"It's about time you started talking about grudges," you chide me. "This whole chapter has been on nothing but anger and it's supposed to be the seventh guideline, getting rid of grudges every day."

And I reply, "Ah, how right you are!"

Now you know how to get rid of grudges before they can plunge you into depression. Identify anger, deal with it one way or another, and forgive, whether the perpetrator deserves your forgiveness or not, whether he or she admits anything or not. Forgive the person for God's sake and for the sake of your own serotonin level. Then turn the outcome—vengeance and all—over to God. The grudge never has a chance to take root and grow. It's gone before it starts. Forgiveness is the key.

There is one other kink in the plow line that can keep you from choosing happiness, and that is anxiety. I'd like to explain it and show you how to get past it.

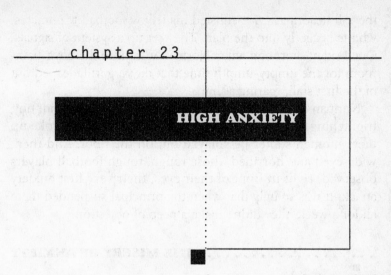

chapter 23

HIGH ANXIETY

When I was a kid in high school, we called his kind "Nervous Norvus." That guy was always acting like he was about to fall off a tightrope. His name was Norman (not really; I changed it for the book), which didn't help. "Nervous Norman" is just about as bad.

He couldn't relax. He talked all the time, as if he were afraid of what would happen if he stopped. He fidgeted. He crabbed at everyone. He went to the bathroom half a dozen times just during school hours. He was constantly on the alert, constantly looking around, constantly acting like someone might try to sneak up behind him. And then, someone did.

One of his classmates—I'll call him Harry—took it upon himself to either cure Norman of his constant irritability and wariness or drive him out of his tree. Norman really bothered Harry, who was a solid, stalwart, football player type. Harry was sure Norman was just acting nervous to get attention; nobody could really be that goofy down inside. Harry didn't like people who put on phony airs. He decided to teach Norman to straighten up and act right.

And so Harry rented a gorilla costume, but he only needed

the full head mask. He enlisted his fellow football teammates, who fell eagerly into the plan. They set up a system of signals. One Friday afternoon when Norman went into the boys' bathroom for the umpty-umpth time that day, a gorilla leaped out of the first stall, roaring at him.

Norman quit breathing. Then his breath came in rapid, tiny, frightening gasps. He wet his pants. He fainted. He woke up mere moments after he splayed out on the floor. And then, wide-eyed and horrified, those rough, tough football players observed, right in front of their eyes, their very first anxiety attack. It was so ugly that when the principal suspended them all for a week, they didn't make a peep of objection.

····················· THE MISERY OF ANXIETY
■

Harry and his cohorts did not understand beans about anxiety. Poor old Norman certainly wasn't faking it. In fact, he had additional signs and symptoms that didn't show up at school. Some of them are difficulty falling asleep, poor concentration and memory, headaches, tight muscles, and excessive perspiration (especially the hands), diarrhea as well as frequent urination, "heartburn," gut-ache, fluttery heartbeat and butterflies in the stomach. There will probably be excessive worrying and fretting about inconsequentials.

Sounds like what you feel like when you're terrified, right? Or watching a really good horror movie.

Well, that's it exactly. Anxiety is a kind of fear. To over-simplify the picture, when we say a person fears, that person knows what he or she is frightened of. You fear a vicious dog. You fear that you'll earn failing marks in a class. You fear for your mother's well-being when you learn they've found a lump in her breast.

Anxiety is fear that occurs when you *don't* know what you're afraid of.

No matter how bad a fear is, at least you know what's going on. Imagine being terrified all the time and not knowing why. Not only that, the anxious person is likely to feel anxious about being so unexplainably anxious, and the anxiety multiplies upon itself.

Because the fear has no conscious object that the mind can focus on, the anxiety often translates as worry. That worry almost always concerns itself with insignificant little things other people don't even think about. Often too it dwells upon things in the future that are probably never going to happen.

Harry, with his I'm-better-than-you-are insensitivity, made a bad thing horribly worse. Norman's anxiety attack was completely beyond his ability to control. We would say, "Wow! He's really losing it there!" He totally panicked. Freaked. And he couldn't help himself. That helplessness is in itself terrifying.

He was screaming and he couldn't quit. He was running in circles in the halls and he couldn't slow up. He was making a fool of himself while the whole school watched open-mouthed, and he couldn't stop. He felt like his pounding heart was going to give out and there wasn't a thing he could do save his own life.

· · · · · · · · · · · · · · · · · · **DEALING WITH ANXIETY**
■

Obviously, the person with an anxiety problem isn't going to be choosing happiness anytime soon. Too, anxiety very often keeps company with depression.

Unfortunately, anxiety is hard to deal with because it's so nebulous; you can't put your finger on anything specific the way you can with an actual fear. But we know some things about it that may be able to help you come to terms with it in yourself or in a friend.

So let's pretend you're Norman's buddy and . . . No. That won't work. Norman didn't have any close friends. He was too antsy, too cranky, too hard to be with. He seemed like a nut and people felt uneasy around him.

Let's pretend instead that you are Norman's classmate. You don't like him any better than Harry does, but at least you're not going to knock the poor guy clear off his rocker, the way

Harry did. You want to genuinely help him just so you don't have to put up with his squirreling around so much.

Causes of Anxiety

Since Norman has no conscious grasp of why he is so anxious, you guess that the roots are probably deep below conscious level. You guess right.

One root lies in childhood. Remember Penfield's experiment that I described in Chapter 21? People whose brains were stimulated by tiny electrodes might remember only the emotional response to an event rather than everything about it, and one of those responses is fear. We believe that sometimes, something happening at the present moment triggers a memory of a childhood fear. It happens below conscious level, but the body reacts all the same. Anxiety results because the person doesn't know what the object of the fear is. All kinds of childhood fears could be candidates.

Present anxiety and former anxieties might be buried below conscious level only to erupt as obsessive worry and phobias (intense, extreme fears).

Another root might be Norman's parents or other close family members. If they worry excessively and are anxious about the future or what might happen, Norman gets that same response to life programmed into him from birth. For Norman, being anxious and worried is the normal response to life because that's what he grew up with. Remember that whatever your family is as you're growing up, that's what "normalcy" is, whether it's anywhere close to average or not.

Still another root could be fear of facing the truth. If you want to look at this root from a spiritual level, picture this. Our messed-up minds are afraid to look at the truth that they're messed up. But the Holy Spirit presses the issue, trying to get us to face up to how our minds really are. Our minds below conscious level push it down where we need not deal with it; the Holy Spirit shoves it upward. This constant tension is a big source of anxiety. In fact, the vast majority of what we psychiatrists call *true anxiety* is a *fear of finding out the truth about our own thoughts, feelings, and motives.*

Countering Anxiety

But knowing causes isn't going to help you help Norman much. He may be able to gain some insight into his anxiety that way, but that's head knowledge. You'll get farther faster if you help him develop some new behaviors.

First, you ask Norman if he's a Christian. You can still help him if he's not, but if he is, it makes your job and his a whole lot easier.

Know what his answer is? "I try to be."

So what's your response? "No, Norman, you can't try to be a Christian. Either you are or you aren't. If you allow Christ's blood to pay for your sins, you are. It's God's work, not yours."

"Okay, then I guess I am. But—"

"You can't try to be a Christian, but if you are one, you're supposed to try to be a better one. In this case, a less anxious one. See the difference?"

Actually, trying to be a less anxious one was what Norman meant in the first place. He just didn't phrase it well. He needed reminding that the fruits of the Holy Spirit are love, joy, and peace—not bitterness, depression, and anxiety.

That out of the way, you can then offer him insights, one at a time, from God's Word. As he gets better and better at putting them into practice, his anxiety will ease. Again, it's largely a matter of reprogramming the computer-brain to process the same old material in new ways. Instead of reacting with anxiety, Norman has to learn to react differently. He can do it.

Here are some insights you can offer him. They also work well for non-Christians, of course, but the non-Christian is not likely to take God's Word as being authoritative. Most especially, the non-Christian will not be able to tap into the help of the Holy Spirit, the *real* Higher Power.

Follow the Philippian road. The fourth chapter of Philippians offers great counter-programming for anxiety. It's a neat way to get Norman moving in a different direction.

Verse 4:4. Rejoice in the Lord! What a bright way to start any day! Norman needs it, but then, so do you. So do I.

Verse 4:6. When God tells Norman not to be anxious here, Norman is getting marching orders. A smart Christian decides it's best to obey God. Good motivation.

Still in 4:6. Frame everything as prayer. Instead of worrying about the math test coming up, make an urgent appeal to God regarding the math test (and be sure you've studied thoroughly too, of course!). Send the concerns upward rather than inward. This refocuses Norman's worry beyond himself.

Verse 4:7 promises peace as a result, and of course that's exactly what Norman needs.

Verse 4:8 asks Norman to think positively and meditate on the best and brightest of human endeavor. This is no easy thing for an anxious person to do; in fact it's a reversal of Norman's usual doom-and-gloom thoughts. But you can see how it can refocus his attention from "The sky is falling!" to something praiseworthy. Chicken Little needed verse 4:8.

In verse 4:9, the Apostle Paul urges Norman to follow Paul's example of a godly life. It's an interesting line in that Paul was certainly nowhere near perfect in his own walk. His temper was too quick and he even held an occasional grudge.[1] But he was virtually fearless! He'd walk into any situation anytime, and more than once paid the price.[2] His was the opposite of the anxious heart. This is the kind of persistent, flawless courage Norman needs, and Paul is an excellent example to give Norman a model and encouragement.

That verse also suggests, though it doesn't actually say, that Norman become associated with mature Christians. That way he can hear and see Christ in Christlike people, thereby having a model and goal for becoming more Christlike himself. We all need that. When counseling anxious patients, we suggest they join small fellowship groups. Loving and being loved—human relationships—will go a long way to reduce Norman's fears.

Verse 4:10 extols helping others and thinking about others. That gets Norman's attention off himself. The anxious person really needs that, but it cannot be imposed from the outside. Others cannot make him quit focusing on himself. He has to reorient his own thinking.

What a great lesson in 4:11! Whatever condition you find yourself in, that's okay. No matter what economic class you end up in, it's okay. No matter what kind of classmates you have and what kind you are, it's okay. God sticks you in a particular place under particular circumstances, and it's all okay. This attitude is the exact opposite of the kind of fretting the anxious person indulges in constantly. Norman might work on making this his life verse—the verse he depends upon, the verse that would describe who and what he wants to be.

Philippians 4:12 is an expansion of verse 11.

Now you point out 4:13 to Norman. He probably can't pull off his anxiety-reduction program by himself, but he doesn't have to do it by himself. Jesus is right there to lend a hand, supplying the mental muscle Norman doesn't quite have yet.

So that's the Philippian road. Two other verses in that chapter can be of particular help to Norman. God in 4:19 promises to take care of Norman's needs. Not his wants, understand. His needs. And in the end, 4:23, see the beautiful blessing. "The grace of our Lord Jesus Christ be with you all." Not just Norman. You and me also.

Follow the lifestyle discussed in Chapter 16. Anxious people have a lot of trouble with priorities because everything takes on the same oversized, overblown, overly frightening urgency. Ask Norman to review 16 and strive especially to get enough rest, exercise, and recreation.

Be the opposite of a procrastinator. The longer Norman puts off doing a thing, the more he frets about it. Because of his anxiety problem, he must pay more attention to deadlines than do most people, and if possible, *turn in projects on time or even ahead of time.* There is no law against submitting a book report a week early. Then Norman must put the project behind him and think about the next one down the line. Otherwise, he's likely to worry, "Did I do a good job? Could I have done better? What if . . .?" You know how it goes.

Sometimes psychiatrists will ask perfectionistic worriers to try to do *average* work on their assignments. Their "average" work is usually way above average. If they try to do a perfect, 200 percent job, they often never finish it, because it is never prefect in their eyes.

Play mind games with himself. Other people try to mess with our minds all the time. Here's Norman's chance to mess with his own mind.

When he catches himself worrying about something, he catches himself in mid-worry, as it were. Then he imagines the worst-case scenario. What could go wrong-est? What's the worst that could happen? Now think why that worst outcome might not be so bad after all. Here's a rather silly example:

"I'm afraid Dad is going to lose his job. We won't have any money. Worst case: We'll get kicked out of our house, and we'll starve to death! Why it wouldn't be as bad as it looks: If we die, we'll go to heaven and see Jesus. And it will be He who sent us there, since God promises to take care of us."

That's a bit over the top, but you see the method.

Another mind game Norman might try involves cooking up solutions to something he finds himself worrying about. The wackier the solution, the better he will feel as he diverts himself from worry to fun. He ought also, of course, to think of possible practical solutions as well. Example:

"I'm afraid Dad is going to lose his job. We won't have any money. Mom can take in wash and I can string the clothesline between the coat hook in my closet and the maple tree outside my window. That way we'll have line to dry laundry on, rain or shine. I can clip poodles at my cousin's veterinary office. My sister can get a paper route. Dad could sell apples on the corner. They did that in the thirties; I saw an illustration in my history book. We could eat the cat. I don't understand what my sister sees in that stupid beast." And on and on it goes.

Another fruitful mind game is to use anxiety not as a trigger for more anxiety but as a signal to relax. When Norman feels himself getting especially uptight, that is his cue to himself: "I'm supposed to relax now." No matter how much a hurry he's in, he stops and takes slow deep breaths. If he's going somewhere, he walks. If he's sitting there, he puts his hands in his lap and perhaps closes his eyes to block out all the frantic stimuli around him—kids moving, papers rattling, and so on. If the teacher is lecturing, he concentrates only on that voice. If he really wants to play mind games, he might imagine a trickling stream gurgling past his desk. Water is extremely relaxing.

Practice living one day at a time. Norman knows he should prepare for tomorrow. But he doesn't have to worry about it. Most of the time, the stuff we fret about never happens tomorrow anyway. This is a mind-set that has to be cultivated. It doesn't come naturally, especially not to a person like Norman.

Talk to someone about frustrations—a close friend, a counselor, a sympathetic teacher—at least once every week. This airing of fears and frustrations brings them out in the open so they can't eat at Norman. He'll likely get some pretty good advice, if he listens.

Deliberately limit the time spent worrying. Crazy as it sounds, this actually works. Norman finds himself worrying about his math test tomorrow. He can't put it out of his mind completely. So he decides he'll put off worrying about it until it's time to study math at 7:00 P.M. Then he can worry for two hours on purpose while he studies math for his test.

Another method, and Norman can train himself to use it, is

to set aside a particular time period each day that will be used primarily for worry. Norman might start out designating an hour in the evening and, as he gets better at it, pare it down to fifteen minutes or so. Then when a concern or worry pops up during the day, he writes it down on a 3" x 5" card and postpones thinking about it.

He might tell himself, "I can't worry about this item right now. But tonight, from 9:00 to 9:15 P.M., I sure will. You, item, will have to wait until then."

Yes, it works. Telling an anxious person not to worry is like telling a baby not to burp. The person simply cannot do that. But often that person can very successfully postpone fretting, just as you postpone eating until a particular TV show is over, or postpone going to bed in order to study for a test.

It's incredible how much mental energy is wasted in worry. It saps strength. It destroys concentration. Whatever time Norman can delay worrying, that is energy and time he can use on other things—positive things.

If you and Norman could handle anger and anxiety well a hundred percent of the time, and turn everything over to God completely, you'd almost never need help with depression. But real life doesn't work that way. You can handle some of your responses some of the time, but it's very possible that now and then, depression sneaks up on you and grabs you.

Let's say that right now you are languishing deep in depression, a darkness so thick that you don't want to take the effort (nor do you have the energy) to dig out. How can we help you recover enough to be able to choose happiness?

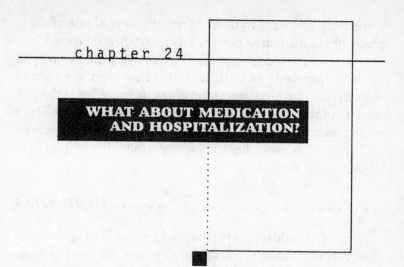

chapter 24

WHAT ABOUT MEDICATION AND HOSPITALIZATION?

"New Miracle Drug Cures Everything from Colds to Flat Feet!" cries one headline.

Right beside it another headline rages, "America Is Turning Her Children into Drug-zonked Zombies!"

What a battle! Those who see drugs as the first line of cure for emotional problems butt heads with those who claim that drug psychotherapy is wrong, wrong, wrong.

When I see these essays and opinion pieces, the first thing I think is, "So what ax is this guy grinding?" In other words, what are the writers' hidden agendas, their purposes that they don't want you to know about? The purpose that is always hung out front is concern for others' welfare. Sometimes, that's genuine. Usually, though, the real heart of the matter is an ego trip or power issue, with the writer trying to sway people to his or her way of thinking. Sometimes there's actually a financial consideration you never hear about.

Also, almost never do I see both sides adequately defended on an issue. So often, the author conveniently leaves out little facts that would change the whole argument, were they known. You're almost never getting the whole picture. It's

241

something you want to think of when you read one of these pieces about the curing power of drugs or their dangers.

Whatever the hidden agenda, these essayists get so wrapped up in tooting their particular horn that they often lose sight of the real goal of any consideration about drugs: What is the best interest of the person who might need a drug regimen? That's what I want to talk about in this chapter. What is best for *you*?

The truth, as usual, lies somewhere around the middle. Let's discuss drugs first.

· **MEDICATION**

When I'm evaluating a patient, and the use of drugs is a possible part of treatment, I have three options. One is: No drugs are needed at this time. The patient will do just fine without, though counsel will be appropriate. Two is: Drugs are necessary, and then I have to have a good reason why that's so. Three is: The drugs will be used in combination with other therapies to bring about the best results for this individual.

Let's expand on those three options.

When Medication Is Essential

A girl in her late teens whom we'll call Anne slipped into such a powerful depression, her mom couldn't make her get out of bed in the morning. She was so deep in the pits she wasn't considering suicide because it would take too much effort.

Her parents tried a psychotherapist. No success. They tried another therapist who recommended medication and had her put on Prozac. Anne perked up a little, but her limited improvement was sure nothing to write songs about. When her Prozac regimen ended, she fell right back into the pit. They brought her in to see me.

Psychotherapists, including those holding a Ph.D., can recommend the use of drugs, but they usually cannot prescribe them (except in certain states under specific conditions). Psychiatrists, being licensed medical doctors, can. We can also more thoroughly explore the possibility of physiological causes of emotional problems. Anne wasn't responding well to other therapies, so we did a complete medical workup. We found a problem with Anne's thyroid.

The thyroid is a gland which wraps around your windpipe in your throat. It produces a cleverly named hormone, thyroxin. Thyroxin, released into your blood, travels all over your body and chemically controls growth and metabolism. Too little thyroxin leads to lack of growth and sluggish metabolism. No energy. Too much makes you nervous and jumpy and damages metabolism. The ultimate "bosses" are the pituitary gland and the hypothalamus, which release hormones telling the thyroid what to do.

Anne's thyroid was producing not quite enough thyroxin. The thyroxin level in her blood tested near normal, but there is another test for thyroid activity and we did that one also. She had an abnormally high level of the hormone with which the pituitary gland directs the thyroid, thyrotropin. It indicated what we call subclinical hypothyroidism—a shortage of thyroxin too slight for clinical tests to pick up but great enough to cause depression.

Anne went on thyroid medication to adjust her thyroxin levels, and within a week, her depression dissolved away.[1]

Anne is typical of those patients who suffer depression caused by physiological problems. She may spend most or all of her life on medication to correct the thyroid problem, but she does not need medication for the depression as such. In fact, low thyroxin levels reduce the effectiveness of antidepressant medications. That's why they didn't work well in her case.

Investigators are busily at work trying to find connections between depression and levels of other hormones as well.[2] We do know this: A tiny alteration in any of a number of the body's natural chemicals can cause profound effects, and one of those effects can be depression. Correct the hormonal defect and you correct the depression. And of course you also correct the other problems that imbalance was causing.

It's so tragic. Teenagers have killed themselves because a hormone imbalance that could have been corrected was making life unbearable for them. Not just teenagers, either. You've heard about Dr. Jack Kevorkian, who assists suicides. Patients requesting assisted suicide should be treated for depression, which is curable, even if they have an incurable disease. Suicide is wrong for any reason.

Medicines given to help other emotional or psychiatric problems may also ease depression as a side effect, so to speak. When bipolar patients or those experiencing psychosis are put on Depakote, lithium, Risperdal, or an equivalent, many will remain on the chosen medication thereafter, if they have a life-long, genetic imbalance of one or more chemicals. The medicine is used to counter a range of problems and not just depression specifically, but it does that job as well.

It works in the other direction also, so to speak. We might put a teen diagnosed with Attention Deficit Disorder on an antidepressant. "But I'm not depressed!" the kid insists, and it's true. However, the antidepressant helps the Attention Deficit problem. And although the patient is never given the medicine in order to prevent depression, it sometimes does that.

I probably don't have to mention this but I will anyway. Doses are always carefully adjusted and monitored, tailored to fit the patient well. We are especially careful with teens' dosages, because their physiology is shifting so rapidly from child to adult. What was right yesterday may not be right tomorrow. The trick is to find the perfect level, not too much, not too little to do the job right.

Sometimes medication is useful as a temporary tool for making other therapies quicker and more effective.

When Medication Is Useful

Let's say a fourteen-year-old boy we'll call Michael displays a lot of the serotonin-depletion symptoms discussed earlier—lethargy, irritability, and all that. His dad divorced and moved out. His mom, who's not a real strong woman anyway, can't handle him. At school he's a pill, constantly testing the limits, breaking the rules, and bugging people.

He's old enough to respond to psychotherapy. And he's been through a lot that can cause depression in a kid—the divorce especially. We may recommend that Michael take an antidepressant medication for a limited time, usually six to twelve months. But antidepressants don't cure. They will restore a normal serotonin level, but the root problem will still be there, lurking below conscious level. They should be used to get people started on recovery, combining them with other therapy, most particularly counseling. Therefore, we *never* recommend antidepressant medications unless counseling is part of the cure. By "we" I mean most psychiatrists[3] and certainly the Minirth Meier New Life psychiatrists.

There is an exception to that. When genetic differences cause lifelong depression the patient will probably benefit from a lifelong regimen of medication but certainly not lifelong counseling. People with significant ADD also need lifelong medication to live a normal, maximally productive life.

Without counseling, Michael or any other patient is rarely aware of the grudges, repressed anger of some sort, or whatever else the cause may be. Within about ten days to two weeks, the patient feels better on the meds, which is fine. But then, whenever he or she comes off the antidepressant, the serotonin will just deplete again because the root problem has not been eased.

Antidepressant medications like Prozac, Paxil, Effexor, Serzone, Imipramine, etc., are *not* addicting and can build the serotonin up much quicker than can counseling alone. Persons who are depressed cannot, to use the hackneyed expression, see the light at the end of the tunnel. They can't concentrate well. They can't care about themselves enough to do the necessary work. Progress is slow when depression is putting on the brakes so heavily. Antidepressants restore the teen's natural zest, ability to concentrate, and hope for the future. Also, the medication makes good sense. Why spend a year or more in counseling, when with the temporary help of antidepressants, the same effects can usually be achieved in a few months?

Very occasionally, we prescribe medications for the long term, even for life. Some people, for instance, have naturally low serotonin levels, as governed by genetics. It runs in the family. If it presents a serious problem, the persons thus afflicted may need maintenance dosage of an antidepressant and/or lithium or Depakote for life. It sounds daunting, but usually it's not the big deal it seems like. True, it's somewhat of a hassle and somewhat expensive, but maintenance medication is well worth it if it restores the teen to a normal life.

When Medication Is Not Needed

That does not mean that every time we see a case of depression we pop some antidepressants into the patient in order to make therapy go faster. Not at all.

Generally, if a teenager in the early stages of depression is still doing well in school, sleeping normally, and enjoying a reasonable energy level, then counseling alone is fine with no meds. In fact, the vast majority of the thousands of teens who come to our clinics each week don't receive *any* medication— just good Christian counseling.

Also, if the patient has misgivings about taking medicines, we honor that reluctance and work around it. We don't force the issue. There is an exception to that: If the patient is suicidal or seems to pose a threat of some sort to others, then we can get pretty adamant about using drugs to get past the danger point. Human life is nothing to take chances with. Suicidal ideation and other threats to life also indicate hospitalization.

. . . . **HOSPITALIZATION**
■

When a girl we'll call Megan left a suicide note and took a dozen aspirin tablets, her classmates snickered at her behind her back. "Babe, if you're going to check out, do it right! A dozen aspirin won't off you."

Her classmates had all heard that feeble attempts at suicide are actually cries for help, so they dismissed it as that. Megan had been crabby and moody for months, lashing out viciously at friends, alternately withdrawing and sticking herself in everybody's face. Maybe some shrink would fix her up so she'd be easier to live with.

Megan is one of those people we hospitalize immediately, whether her attempt was sincere or not. What if she tried it again, this "cry for help," and by miscalculation actually died? Or what if she decided to "do it right" the next time? It happens often. In fact, 10 percent of teens who make a suicide "gesture" end up dying of suicide later in life.

Another situation in which we hospitalize immediately is psychosis. The person who breaks with reality in any way is a danger to both self and others. But there are other reasons for hospitalization in addition to safety concerns.

The Benefits of Hospitalization

The patient and others are protected. No more suicide attempts, successful or otherwise. The staff in a medical or psychiatric facility have seen it all. They know the precautions that are necessary to prevent suicide attempts or attempts on others, as in a psychotic who's out to get someone. Everyone is safe.

Psychotherapy is intensive. In a hospital setting, not only are various therapists on staff and available, but psychotherapy is intense. You get help for hours every day, drawing on the skills of several different people, instead of going in for an hour a week. If you need help or have a question, you're not on your own until your next counseling session; you can get the help or answer immediately.

The patient is monitored closely and well. Knowledgeable nurses keep an eye on the patient's behavior all the time. They can report helpful observations that most folks don't notice.

Medication is monitored also. If you need an adjustment, it happens immediately. Close monitoring, incidentally, is the best way to put patients on the road to long-term drug therapy, such as the use of Depakote for bipolar disorder. We can fine-tune the dosage very precisely if the patient is right there to watch and talk to.

The patient is in a less stressful environment. Whether or not the teen's home environment (or the street, if that's where he or she was lately) is making the problem worse, the hospital environment is structured, safe, and predictable. Too, the staff is friendly, helpful, and supportive. They understand, which the outside world often does not.

Where it's insured, hospitalization is usually less costly. Treatment proceeds rapidly, rather than being drawn out over months or years. For a kid who has to keep up in school, for a person who has to support himself or herself, the speed usually makes up for the high initial cost.

The Problems with Hospitalization

Of course there are problems. And one of the biggest is:

The cost. You're looking at over $1,000 a day. Insurance companies often apply caps, limits above which they will not pay and you are on your own.

The stigma. You go into a regular medical hospital for an appendectomy or broken leg, and nobody blinks an eye. They send flowers and sign your cast. Go into a psychiatric facility to shake a persistent clinical depression, and the whispers start. Don't count on receiving as many get-well cards. The hospital stay may damage your social standing and some misguided people may avoid you. In reality, though, most of our teen patients are pleasantly surprised by the genuine love and support of their friends, especially if they attend a healthy church.

The tension. Picture yourself being discharged from a facility, say, three to six weeks after admission. You go back to school feeling good, over your depression, ready to really live life! Your friends don't know what to say. Some will be afraid to mention your hospital stay, so they pretend it never happened. Some will ask terrible, horrible questions. Some will make abysmally ignorant comments. It's best to just be honest about going through some depression and getting intensive counseling for it. Most of your friends will probably be very supportive. Those are the friends you want to keep for life anyway. My high school friends are still my friends thirty-five years later.

Day Hospitals

I mentioned day hospitals back in Chapter 7. You enter the hospital for the day and go home at night. In the day hospital, your medications are monitored, you stay caught up on your schoolwork, and you get intensive therapy. As long as you're not in any significant danger to yourself or others, it's an excellent arrangement and much less expensive than a twenty-four-hour-a-day psychiatric facility. Day hospitals are not taken as seriously by the outside world, either. That is, there is much less stigma attached. I suppose, the outside world figures that if they let you out at night, you can't be off your crock too badly.

It's really strange, how the outside world thinks sometimes.

· **AND IN CONCLUSION**
■

Congratulations. You now know more about how the heart and mind work than do most adults. Obviously, you don't know it all. There is much, much more to the subject than we've touched upon here. But you now have the keys with which you can make happiness a choice.

Let us close with some suggestions that will put the principles in this book together in a general way.

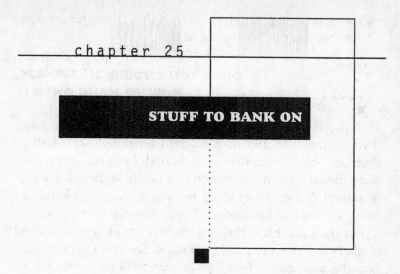

chapter 25

STUFF TO BANK ON

Life for you, today's teen generation, is infinitely harder than it was for my generation when we were your age. The way the world, and that includes my generation, treats you, I'm surprised any of you can make it into adulthood without losing your happiness and maybe your health as well. You get lousy advice from adults. The culture surrounding you gives you lousy advice and then tears you apart with impossible demands. Other teens give you lousy advice because they don't know enough about the world yet to understand it.

You are provided with excellent, terrible, bad, wrong, and right entertainment and messages. Inundated with them. And then you're expected to be able to discern which is good for you and which can damage you. You're expected to act like an instant grown-up without being allowed any of the adult privileges and responsibilities. Be a kid, but whatever you do, don't be a kid.

If there's any consolation, you have one crew of sympathizers who understand a little of what you're going through—the Meier clan. In these next two chapters, we can offer you some parting thoughts that are based on our accumulated experience with teens and with life. We trust these thoughts are wise, advice that you can take to the bank.

ONCE YOU CHOOSE HAPPINESS,
. . . . **HOW TO HANG ONTO IT**
■

Kathy is the girl I mentioned in Chapter 2. Her mom divorced her dad and then married a prime loser—Kathy's opinion. She and the new man, Rob, did not get along a bit. She suffered a severe depression that nearly set her back a year in school. When Rob kicked her out of her own home for being spoiled and insolent—his opinion—she hit bottom.

But she came back, through the support of her friends and teachers and also, eventually, her mom. She spent her sixteenth birthday in a shelter, homeless because of "that potato brain." She spent her seventeenth in Yosemite National Park, having a ball. And believe me, Kathy was smart enough to know that her reversal of fortune was a gift of love—God's love, her friends' love, and her teachers' faith in her.

People who are depressed have a high chance of becoming depressed again. How can Kathy keep herself from slipping back into a depression the next time life smacks her one upside the head? For that matter, how can you? Let us suggest some things that will help you maintain a happy life.

Don't chew yourself out. Kathy gets out of her car, hitting the lock button as she stands up. As the door slams, she remembers that her keys are in the ignition. And the radio is on. And the motor's running. Mercy me, what vile expletives she rains upon herself, starting with, "How could you, you dumb enchilada! What a stupid kazoo, you—" etc.!

The rest of the world is quick to find fault with you, often when the fault is not yours at all. And you can bet your brain records your own bad thoughts toward yourself, just as if it were someone else yelling at you. You therefore must be the first person to excuse and forgive yourself when you make honest or careless mistakes. Everyone makes them. If Kathy were your best friend when she accidentally locked her keys in the car, would you chew on her as viciously as she ranked on herself? Or would you sympathize, knowing that next time it might be your own keys behind that locked door, and set about helping her?

The person at risk for depression must always be his or her own best friend. That means *no* harsh criticism of the self. This is one of those things the 20 percent of your brain is going to have to remember to do, because the automatic response to any error is to be harder on yourself than you would be with anyone else. Certainly, you admit and confess true guilt. But do treat yourself as you would treat your very best friend (because that's exactly what you are!)—with respect, affection, and reasonable expectations.

Influence your feelings with your behavior. Within certain bounds, if you do cheerful stuff, you'll feel more cheerful than if you did not. If you do downer sorts of things, you'll feel down.

It doesn't work that way always. I read of a police officer who acted heroically after the Oklahoma City bombing. The pressure of being singled out for attention, plus intense personal problems, led him to commit suicide about a year later. "He always kept you laughing," a co-worker recalled. "That's why you didn't know he was hurting."[1] Cheerful outside, tortured inside. A lot of people do that.

But if, like Kathy, you are no longer depressed inside, keeping the outside happy will greatly help the inside remain happy. And we repeat once more, if you are hurting inside, get it out! Write it in a journal. Tell someone about it. Get help!

To put this whole point another way, neither Kathy nor you dare let feelings rule your life. You can't control your feelings directly. Neither can I. I can't say to myself, "So, Paul, you're feeling sad, huh? Well quit." And bingo! I quit feeling sad. We both know that won't work. *But!* We have near total control over what we do. And by *doing,* we control our feelings indirectly.

You remember about Cain (the italics will be my own, for emphasis):

. . . Cain was very angry, and his countenance fell [in other words, he sulked].

So the LORD said to Cain, "Why are you angry? And why has your countenance fallen? If you *do well*, will you not be accepted? And if you *do not do well*, sin lies at the door. And its desire is for you, but you should *rule over it*."[2]

There it is. God gave Cain the key to getting past his anger and sulkiness, which is depression. Do well. Well, Cain didn't do, because a verse later, he killed his brother.

You've heard, "Don't just talk the talk. Walk the walk." Cain and Abel talked; the Bible says so.[3] As helpful as talking it out may be, it's the doing that gets you out of hot water or into it.

Make a definite plan for staying healthy. Let's use Kathy as a theoretical example. As part of her initial recovery, she developed a weekly schedule that afforded her time for sleep, work, and recreation. Right! That's our first guideline, back in Chapter 16. Her schedule works well for a little while, and works sort-of for another while, and then quietly disintegrates as the end of the school term comes near and she has to study for final tests. She stays up too late, then sleeps longer, getting up too late to eat breakfast. Ramming off to school with a Pop-Tart and a can of soda is not nutrition. And it's not going to get her to 10:00 A.M., let alone lunch. Just about the time she thinks she can get her schedule up and running again, she takes a summer job that wrecks it altogether.

I'm sure your plans never go astray like that, but Kathy's do. Now she feels depressed because she can't stick to a schedule, and she's not getting enough rest, and she hasn't had any time to herself for five weeks, and she's depressed about getting depressed again, and . . . You get the picture.

It seems to people in her situation that they have no options. Discouragement blurs their thinking. But she does indeed have some choices here. We suggest in counsel that the discouraged person sit down and work out some possible options. Write them down. Then choose one of them and try it for a couple weeks. If it doesn't work, you dump it and try another. And another. And another, until your life is in order again.

The trick, you see, is to get off dead center. Get moving on something, and give God something to guide, then ask Him to guide it.

In Kathy's case, as the school year's end approaches, and she finds herself getting off schedule, skipping breakfast, and otherwise wearing herself down, she might set up one of several plans:

■ Since she gets sick if she tries to read on the bus, and therefore can't study on the half hour ride to school, the first time through her textbook material, she reads it aloud into a tape recorder. Then she listens to it on the bus. Receiving the info by both eye and ear, she retains more. It cuts study time two ways—the bus time is redeemed, and she doesn't have to work at the material as long.

■ The prime pest in her life is her little brother. So she gives him leave to bug her when her alarm goes off. She hates it! He loves it. She regrets having said that the first morning he shows up to jump on her bed. But it works. She starts eating a good breakfast again.

■ What is a suggestion you might make for her?

Try something new. Although getting into a rut doesn't usually depress you by itself, it can make life pretty humdrum and encourage depression. Not only that, exploring new areas of interest keeps you sharp. It stimulates you.

Kathy expanded her horizons literally and figuratively by, with a friend's help, going on line. Over Rob's objections ("The kid is still a pill; she doesn't deserve special favors until she shapes up better," he said.), Kathy's mom financed her basic monthly cost. Once Kathy started drawing a paycheck, she could buy her own time. She learned how to research a paper and how to E-mail an application to a prospective employer or send a letter to the editor.

She learned from a friend about job opportunities in national parks, working for the restaurants, hotels, and gift shops serving park visitors. In December, she applied to a concession company serving Yellowstone National Park. Imagine! Yellowstone! They turned her down. And there's another lesson. Keep trying. Four applications later she landed a job in the Yosemite Valley. She spent her summer working with the distant roar of waterfalls as background music and playing in ways you can't imagine—floating down the Merced in an inner tube, hiking, learning wildflowers, taking art lessons, and seeing bears.

You might not consider on-line access of interest at all. Or seeing bears, for that matter. What else might you like to dabble in and never have? Pigeon raising? Quilting? The works of Edgar Allen Poe? Photography? Try your hand!

Surprisingly often, these oddball interests pay off; you've learned something that you find useful some time in the future. A friend of mine who writes romance novels tells about putting together an elaborate model kit of the clipper ship *Cutty Sark*. Apparently she had to use up some merchants' trading stamps, and this kit was on sail, so to speak. Until that moment, she'd never given sailing ships a thought. A year later, she found herself using the information she gained from the model when she wrote a period story that took place on an old-time sailing ship.

You never know.

Tap into God. Prayer and Bible reading—you can't beat 'em for good anti-depression support.

Prayer is nothing less than calling up the power of God. Who but He can provide the perfect strength and help because

He knows every aspect of your situation? The people who are most consistently effective are the ones who make prayer a priority.

The Word of God is just as great a source of power. We discussed earlier the importance of staying close to the Word as an antidote to depression. Staying close to the Word is just as crucial for continuing in good health and happiness.

Staying close entails more than just reading. Since the beginning, the Bible has been meant to be used. As you read, ask yourself, "What's God saying? How can I do what he says today? Right now? How can I use this information?"

Grow a friend. Friends don't just happen. Friendships aren't arranged in advance, for convenience. Making a good friend means being a good friend. But the rewards are enormous.

Back in the second World War, as with all other wars, when one side caught a soldier from the other side, they wanted to extract as much information about their enemy's movements as possible. They wanted that prisoner to dump everything he knew. Often, they also wanted to punish. And of course the soldiers, both sides, were trained to resist interrogation. You provide your name, rank, and serial number. Period. They found by trial and error that the best way to crack a man was to slap him into solitary confinement. No sight of another human being, no sound. Food was delivered by faceless, voiceless, unseen entities through a slot in the door. It didn't take long for the prisoner to turn to mental mush.

We people need people. We absolutely must interact with others. And the more intimate the level of interaction, the more rewarding. One of the best ways to guard against further depression is simply to build a solid friendship.

Stay away from wrongdoing. Now that, you insist, is a stupid thing to say. And I agree. Everyone knows you're supposed to avoid sin. Why state the obvious? Here's why.

Sin can be extremely enticing. "Just this once" or "I can always forgive myself later" is just as appealing. But doing wrong, whether you provide yourself with excuses for doing it or not, is a major source of depression—or repeat depression, since that's what we're fending off now.

In addition, many people sin again and again in order to blunt or counteract the emotional pain caused by the first misstep. It's like hitting your thumb with a hammer, so you figure you can make it stop hurting by hitting it again.

Keep observing the seven guidelines. They worked then. They'll work now.

Laugh. "You're kidding," Kathy would say. "That's crazy." Again, it won't cure depression. Some of the world's most depressed people are stand-up comedians. But it can keep your spirits buoyed once they're up.

Laugh at yourself. Laugh at funny videos. Laugh at horrible puns. Laugh at this ludicrous world. Laugh at a six year old's pitiful attempts at humor, not because they're funny but because it's a nice favor to do for the kid. Please, please, never laugh *at* other people, but by all means laugh *with* them.

Avoiding depression requires maintenance, just as avoiding a ruined car engine requires keeping the oil level up.

I opened this chapter by mentioning the rough time teens have in this day and age. You face terribly difficult circumstances and you face them virtually alone. Your parents have no idea what your life is like because they didn't grow up in the kind of world you live in. You can navigate it! But you're just going to have to make some pretty tough choices. I'd like to close with that in the next and last chapter, not to end the book on a downer, but to help you through the minefield of today's world and cheer you on to happiness.

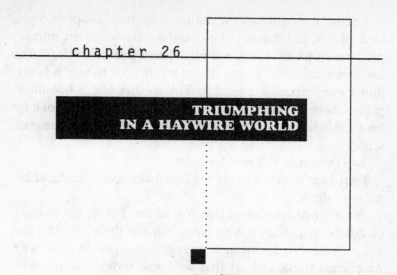

chapter 26

TRIUMPHING IN A HAYWIRE WORLD

Rural Kentucky, eight miles out of town: In the chill of predawn, Lottie and her brother Ben walk down to the barn. They turn on the radio while they work. As rock stars they've never heard howl out songs about sex and loose girls, Lottie feeds and milks their cows. Ben slops the hogs, tosses hay to the horses, and lets down silage for the feeder steers. He starts to replace a flat tire on the tractor but runs out of time and leaves it for after school.

Pa has gone to work by the time they get back to the house. Ma is putting a load of laundry out on the line before she goes to work also. They eat a breakfast of cereal and walk half a mile out their lane to the road where the school bus will pick them up.

Meanwhile, in a suburb of a major city in Kentucky: Chessie and her brother Jason argue over which one gets the shower first. Their mom and dad leave for work. The kids turn on MTV while they're eating breakfast and getting ready for school. Performers howl out songs about sex and loose girls, as around them gyrate young women with more skin than costume.

259

Chessie goes through the outline sections of chapters fourteen, fifteen, and sixteen of her social studies book, last-minute preparation for a test this morning. Jason channel-surfs (sixty-five channels) to the sports station where a sports star is being interviewed about his sex life. The mother of a schoolmate picks Chessie up at the door. Jason rides his bike a block to his friend's house and the friend's older brother drives them to school.

Two extremely different lifestyles.

Four kids who are being walloped alongside the head by today's culture.

You are being walloped also. We all are. But it's not as hard on adults, usually, as it is on teens. For one thing, we who are older have lived through enough changes in the way Americans think and act that we know today's culture will change as well. Because we've had more experience dealing with a variety of other people, as well as with our own selves, we've learned to read people and yes, to manipulate them. Experience has given us a clearer view of what is permanent and what won't last long, of what is valuable and what is not. Our views will differ from each other's, but we are solid in them. We have confidence in ourselves and in what we believe. Also, our various hormone levels have pretty much steadied.

Rarely is any of that true for teens. A generation ago, you would have been worried primarily about whether you were going to get caught chewing gum in class, or maybe whom you'd be seen with at the sock hop. Today, by the age of twelve you will be making major decisions about booze, drugs, and sex that can change your whole life, or even cost you your life!

And you know and I know, many of the cultural messages in which you are drowning encourage the very lifestyle your parents are begging you to stay away from. Also, the culture that surrounds you affects you more than it would a few years ago because you are getting out into the world more now, and home has less influence. Sadly, in many ways it's a terrible culture to have to grow up in.

There is another factor that's giving you problems now, and it goes hand in hand with culture—the two yous.

····················· THE TWO FACES OF ME

Every person in the world is two people. You get split when you're very small because you have to be. There is the "nice" one and the one you really are. To illustrate:

You're three years old and here comes your two-year-old cousin. The cousin picks up your favorite truck. With a shriek you snatch it back. That's yours! Then your mom intervenes and insists that you share. When you slug the two year old, she insists that you apologize. You don't want to share. You don't want to apologize. That's your true self. But you do both because you really have no choice. The person who apologizes and shares is the false self, a person not acting in a way that reflects true feelings.

In grade school a kid splashes paint on your favorite shirt and it won't wash out. The kid apologizes and means it, and your false self says, "That's okay." Your true self knows it's not okay. But the kid didn't mean to, and you're not going to make him or her feel worse than he/she does already. Your false self is doing the right thing, the loving thing, even though it is functioning contrary to true feelings.

We call normal splitting of the two selves *socialization*, because it's necessary to some degree if we are all going to fit in socially with each other. We learn what to say and do, whether we always actually say and do the right things or not.

The false self is validated only from the outside. That's psychological talk meaning the false self exists only to please and impress other people. When they are actually pleased or impressed, it makes you feel good and justifies that false self.

True self, on the other hand, pleases from the inside. It's how you really feel, and when it is rewarded in some way (by others being pleased and impressed, or simply by you yourself being pleased), it *really* makes you feel good.

Brent Verkler, my nephew, put it this way. "I spent a couple years in California schools and a couple years in Texas schools. The social scene in my particular school in California was pretty casual. Accepting. You could be yourself and natural. I tried to fit in some, but I didn't try too hard. I was mostly myself.

"But the Texas school was different. I stopped just being me and started wearing what the others did and getting a haircut like everyone else. I didn't enjoy it. I liked myself a lot better when I wasn't trying to fit in. I just plain didn't like myself anymore."

His lesson: Who are you going to be living with your whole life, yourself or these other people? Brent, and you also, had to learn that pleasing and being your true self pays off.

The happiest people use the false self carefully, even sparingly, in order to help others (perhaps to make them feel better, or to excuse them, or let them know they are forgiven) and to smooth a rough social situation. But they also keep a good, close contact with the real self, the true feelings and desires. As much as possible, they serve the true self's likes and dislikes.

Obviously, you can go overboard with this splitting. Deny the false self and let only the true self show, and people call you rude, undisciplined, nasty, anti-social. Deservedly. What a jerk!

But more often, especially in counsel, we find the opposite. A person tries so hard to be accepted socially and to please others, the true self gets buried. Lost. The person no longer remembers what it is that makes him or her special, what he or she especially likes. That person's life hinges entirely on the approval of others, and happiness flees. The problem hits teenage girls the hardest by far, because the culture ridicules and denies girls' true selves.[1]

·········· WHAT OUR CULTURE IS TELLING YOU
■

Let's personify culture for a minute—that is, think of the country's current culture as an actual person. We'll name this unpleasant person Culture (how clever). This will be a young person, because youth prevails. It is a harsh, judgmental person, unforgiving of mistakes or individuality. This person will judge others on outside appearance only. Motives and emotions and caring count for nothing. This Culture is especially powerful in your school.

The judgment will depend greatly upon whether you're a girl or a guy. For instance, picture what this pseudo-person, Culture, would say in these situations involving kids in your school:

1. A guy belches aloud in a restaurant.
   A girl belches aloud in a restaurant.

2. A guy becomes sexually involved with several girls.
   A girl becomes sexually involved with several guys.

3. A guy makes A's in science and math.
   A girl makes A's in science and math.

4. A guy is a little overweight.
   A girl is a little overweight.

5. A guy wears $10 discount-house jeans.
   A girl wears inexpensive discount-store clothes.

6. A guy gets really angry and starts yelling furiously.
   A girl gets really angry and starts yelling furiously.

7. A guy says, "This is what I want, and we're not done here until I get it."
   A girl says, "This is what I want, and we're not done here until I get it."

8. You're the editor of a guys' magazine, buying articles. What subject matter do you publish?

   You're the editor of a girls' magazine, buying articles. What subject matter do you publish?

Do you see the differences? Girls' and women's magazines deal almost exclusively with looks (or cooking). Appearance is everything. This person Culture doesn't allow girls to be their natural weight unless that natural weight is unnaturally slim. A girl is expected to look perfect. If not, she's a dog. Although looks certainly help, boys don't have to be physically perfect to be attractive. They don't have to wear make-up to correct "flaws" or to improve upon perfection.

Culture demands that a girl completely bury the true self and be nice. Smile a lot. Girls who are naturally aggressive, even in extremely positive ways, are put down. Shall we say, the girls are called "female dogs," and nothing makes a girl cringe quicker and hurt more than to be called that. Boys can argue. They can develop a strong position and maintain it. What do you call a girl who does that? Yep. You guessed it.

The burden of making relationships happen falls upon the girl, a burden that extends all through life. Culture says that if the boy dumps the girl it's because she wasn't good enough. If the husband strays, it's somehow the wife's fault.

Girls lose popularity rapidly if their true selves like to make good grades and enjoy math and the sciences, and they don't hide it.

And the sexual criteria that Culture sets! Females are valued primarily for sexual purposes. Consider the MTV video which Chessie and Jason watched that morning. The sole purpose of the female presence in that video was to titillate. Window dressing of the lascivious kind. That, says the unspoken message, is what women are for. Chessie's history text that she's studying is a history almost exclusively of men. Save for a few female hereditary heads of state, women do not take part in shaping the world, according to her schoolbook.

Is Lottie going to be better valued in society because she gets up early to milk the cows? Not at her school she's not. Does anyone even notice the double workload her mom carries?

When you hear an opinion-maker say that much of modern American culture devalues women, this is what that person means. It's the whole pervasive attitude. And that's why

Culture is harder on girls. Their true selves are so much more than Culture wants them to be. Girls your age have already picked up on the message "You're not worth much, Girlie," whether they consciously realize it or not.

Not just girls suffer. Guys are expected to meet standards also, especially in high school. But Culture doesn't tell you what those standards are until you violate them. Then Culture comes down on you hard.

Guys have to show they're tough. Culture insists that it helps the tough image to smoke, drink, shoot up, and swear a lot. And guys who wait until they're eighteen to get a driver's license are considered real losers. Guys who maintain their virginity? You can say better than I can what Culture thinks of them.

Guys have to agree with the other guys. They have to wear exactly the right clothes. The right haircut helps. And guys are victims of cruelty as much as girls are. You're too young to remember back when, but our culture today seems more mean-spirited than it used to be. Teasing takes on an acid edge, a desire to hurt. So does sexual innuendo.

"Everyone teases," your folks say. "You just have to learn to live with it." But it's not like it used to be. Your parents will either not realize that or will keep forgetting it. Remind them.

I have a suggestion. This week as you're watching TV, pretend that our Culture person has to okay what goes on the tube (that's true, actually).

When you watch a series episode, ask yourself what it says on the surface about teens, about females, about substance abuse, about sex. Also ask yourself what the underlying message is. In other words, what does it say without actually saying it? You're looking for meaning beyond what's shown.

When you flip through a magazine, what do the ads think you need in order to be happy? What do they suggest you can't live without? What do the ads recommend you buy or do in order to be well liked by others? In order to impress others?

Persons of which gender peddle which products? Example: A chain saw ad shows a beautiful young woman in scanty attire, testing the sharpness of a chain tooth. What relationship, exactly, does that model have with chain sawing? Does she wear that costume in the woods chopping down trees?

Compare models in car ads with models in domestic appliance ads. Compare models in teen mags with models in eco-conscious mags such as *National Geographic* and with models in special interest mags (such as a knitting or quilting magazine, *Car and Driver*, *Cat Fancy*, *Sports Afield*).

When you listen to the radio, pay attention to the lyrics. What are these songs saying, really?

See what's working against you? Lottie and Ben out on the farm can't escape it. Neither can you. You, they, Chessie, and Jason—everyone must learn to cope. And when you do, the whole world opens up, for the things Culture tends to value least are the things that make you strong. Remember that Satan is the father of this world, so don't be stupid enough (like most people are) to believe him.

• • • • • • AVOIDING CULTURE'S DAMAGING EFFECTS ■

You can beat Culture. Though it isn't easy, and there are some rough bumps, you can chart yourself a course that will bring you to genuine happiness. Now is when you can take control of your life and your future.

Let's assume that you pretty much understand what we talked about so far—causes, effects, and prevention of depression. Now you know to some extent how your mind (and others'!) works. In fact, you already understand a lot more clearly what's going on within and between people than do most folks.

Now let's nail that final bugaboo, Culture, that builds such high walls against happiness and can hurt you so easily. First, get the big picture.

Keep the Rest of Your Life in Mind

Danielle, Brian's wife, said it well. "When I was in high school, I couldn't imagine any other world." Junior and senior high were her only "now." A false self took over completely. She developed a lifestyle and personality to fit in with people she wanted to fit with, and that person was not she at all.

Every teenager is certain that if teens are not popular right now, they never ever will be. If they are shamed or hurt today, they will be shamed and hurt throughout all their tomorrows. Too many teens, consumed by the present, find themselves going along with a lifestyle they don't like, doing things they don't enjoy, simply so they will not be cast out by the "popular people." If they are not a somebody now they will always be a nobody.

I am going to paraphrase a newspaper columnist's piece here because I cannot remember specifically who it was. He attended a high school reunion some years after graduation and fell to talking with a quiet man from his class. He recalled that this person had been quiet in high school too. Not all that popular, not a standout in any way. The columnist and the other popular kids pretty much ignored the fellow. That quiet man was now a highly successful pediatrician who was doing great good with children's diseases. "How," the columnist mused, in essence, "could we, the so-called popular crowd, so completely overlook such a splendid person?"

Very frequently, a person's popularity in high school has absolutely nothing to do with what that person is destined to become. The popularity and social acceptance teens seek so eagerly won't last. When you leave high school, you enter a larger world where, essentially, you start anew.

It is hard—some would say impossible, but I know that's not true—for a teen to see beyond high school, beyond today. But if you do, you will reap rich rewards.

If you do look past today to adulthood, all of a sudden, Culture in your school no longer has a grip on you. You can let your true self come through, thereby finding deep personal satisfaction, and put the false self aside. You no longer have to go along with the "popular" people unless you really feel like it.

For instance, you know drugs can mess you up, so you stay off them. The in people laugh at you, and really cut you off. So what? They're messing themselves up not just now but into the future. You have a bright future ahead. Who's going to end up laughing?

This saying has been around so long it's become a truism: "Living well is the best revenge." You'll be living well long after they're burned out.

You know what booze can do. I'll bet right now you can name off at least three people from your school who died in alcohol-related accidents before they were twenty. That's not just "had an accident." That's "died." No future whatever. Gone. You say, "Yeah, but that wouldn't happen to me. I'd be careful." They were careful too—thought they could beat the odds. You're no different. So you avoid alcohol, and suddenly you're not invited anywhere anymore. But that doesn't matter. You consider that high school and junior high make up less than 10 percent of your total life on earth and less than the blink of an eye in your eternal life; giving up booze parties in the company of stupid people doesn't seem so difficult anymore. I wrote two novels, *The Third Millennium* and *The Fourth Millennium*, to help teens and adults get their lives in eternal perspective. Read them some time.

Jaime Escalante, the math teacher who led hundreds of "unteachable" kids to math excellence, said of one of his female students, "She makes more than I do now." She made A's and took the risk of being unpopular. Those A's got her into a good school and gave her a jump-start on mastering the college material. She is enjoying a comfortable life with all the things those "popular" high school kids would be salivating over.

Sex? When I asked Brian (now in his twenties) what he would say to a teenager, based on his experience, he didn't hesitate. "Save sex until marriage. Experience proves over and over that's it's really worth waiting."

God made sexual guidelines because He loves you and knows what works best in human beings, not because He's trying to deprive you of having fun.

I and many other psychiatrists and psychologists have found this to be true: The kids we talk to who are most mature in their attitudes and thought processes almost all claim that they feel they are not ready for sex. Put another way, the kids who know themselves best are convinced that sex ought to wait— that they aren't ready to handle all the problems and the emotional rips and tears that early sex causes.

In essence, Culture is forcing you to grow up before your time and to make mature, adult decisions long before you are either adult or mature. In a paradoxical way, the most mature teens recognize the limits of their maturity level and work within those limits. They avoid decisions if they don't have enough information to make them wisely, and they proceed cautiously with any action that cannot be reversed.

You can exercise that kind of wisdom also. To achieve it, you must really use your brain.

Use Common Sense

Picture riding a horse. Whether you ride much or not, you understand how to control the animal. You use reins connected to the horse's mouth. But what about a farmer plowing with a horse-drawn hand plow—you know, the kind of plow you walk behind? He has to guide the plow with both hands and the reins are draped over his shoulders.

He uses voice commands, of course. "Gee" and "Haw" turn the horse to right or left, and "Whoa!" stops the animal. A well-trained plow horse not only obeys voice commands instantly, it follows the furrow straight and true and anticipates problems, such as big rocks ahead.

That's exactly how you want to train your mind. You don't have physical reins with which to control your thoughts, so you control them with mental voice commands. Problem ahead? The best protection in the world is a prompt, solid, "Whoa!"

"Stop and think!"

It takes practice. Good plow horses aren't made overnight either. The more you exercise control over your thoughts and decisions, the easier it will become. Let's make up some for-instances:

Four people are going out for pizza Friday night and invite you along. The only one old enough to drive clowns around a lot and has already been arrested once for reckless driving. You really like these people, and eagerly look forward to . . .

Whoa!

There's a potential problem here and you've already spotted it. You are already stopping to think. Good for you! Now, do you turn in a different direction or go straight ahead?

1. **You can refuse to go because of the potential for being involved in an accident. You know the fine and reprimand didn't change the driver's careless hot-dogging a bit.**

2. **You can go and hope you all get home tonight in one piece, car included (earnest prayer is no doubt involved here).**

3. **You can tell the driver you'd love to go, but his driving habits make you nervous. You're going to sit beside the passenger door. He must promise that if you tell him to pull over and stop, he will let you out instantly.**

Which is the correct answer? Any of them, depending on the driver's personality, which you know better than I do. Number two is a fairly iffy choice. If three serves to wake the guy up to the danger he's putting people in, it might be best.

He'll listen to you quicker than he'll listen to the judge. Maybe you have to go with one. The important thing is that you've stopped to consider options. Here's another.

Your state conducts scholarship tests each May in which the best students of each school, three per team, can compete for scholastic honors. All through April, most of the teachers drill their candidates after school and during study halls, preparing them for the rigorous exam. Your English teacher targets you as one of her top students, destined for greatness in the state test. You're flattered. All you have to do is . . .

Whoa!
Huh? Why Whoa?
There is certainly no problem here, but that does *not* mean you don't stop and think. Any big decision, and this is one, merits some serious thought. Deep down inside, you've always dreamed of being a paleontologist. You're good in math and science. In fact, you're taking a college-level honors course in geology this year. Do you turn aside or go ahead?

1. Clear communication at a lay level can really make a paleontologist's career. A knowledge of grammar et al. is essential, so you say "Okay, sure," and go with English.

2. You tell your English teacher, bless her, "Thanks but no thanks" and hold out for a place on the biology team, since geology isn't sending one (the English slot is guaranteed; the biology one is not).

3. You don't think you can both prepare for the exam and also keep up your geology grade, so you decide to pass on the scholarship test altogether.

Again, no "right" answer jumps out. But you deserve kudos because you are combining "stop and think" with serious consideration for the future. Which choice will best help you in the years to come? One more:

You are a girl whose parents don't have a lot of money. The best people at your school make it very clear that if you want to hang around with them, you're going to have to wear the right shoes and clothes and go along to the right places. In this case, "right" means $75 for the shoes, $150 for the . . .

Whoa!
Here are some choices that you may face.

1. You might pick up extra hours at your part-time job in order to finance the lifestyle you want to pursue.
2. You can ask your parents to help you out here. They may not be as strapped as it appears.
3. These are "the best people"? They don't want to be seen with you if you're wearing the wrong brand of running shoes, and they're best? They judge you harshly according to shallow, materialistic rules that change frequently, and they're best? Not quite. You can communicate to them by deed and perhaps by word that they can accept you or not as they choose, but you will be true to who you really are and forget the phony pretense. Five years from now you'll be working from a strong, solid, positive self-image, and they'll have paid a bundle for a closet full of worthless, out-of-date clothes.

I'll bet you know which choice I'd pick, but you have to make your own choice.

Stopping to think is a skill a lot of adults fail to master. If they really paused to consider the effects of their choices, the divorce rate would be extremely low, kids would grow up better cared for, there would be no such thing as drunk driving, the tobacco companies would be selling pencils on the street corners . . .

In the end, you see, when you choose happiness, that choice does not affect you alone. Your happiness and your choices produce a ripple effect that influences your family, your friends, and the other people with whom you regularly come in contact—teachers, bosses, the bus driver, the neighbors. You can be a blessing to them, to yourself, and most of all, to God.

What a great choice!

Happiness.

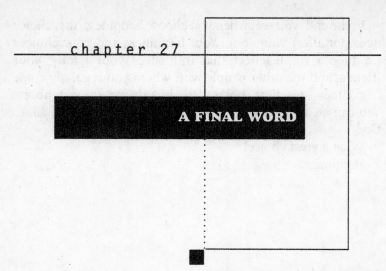

chapter 27

A FINAL WORD

We, Paul and Jan Meier, can provide advice deriving from our professional experience and our experience as parents. We trust it is sound advice. But our kids—sons, daughters, and nephews—are the ones who deal with, or have recently dealt with, teen living in today's culture. Their words from the trenches are the ones you really want to hear.

A lot of what they say has already been incorporated into the other chapters of this book. I'd like to end with some valuable bits and pieces they offer that did not fit clearly somewhere else in the text. They're too good to leave out.

Cheryl

Most of us these days are so caught up in *doing* something all the time. We're always trying to be entertained. When we're with our friends, we spend all our time going to movies or concerts or watching TV. And there's nothing wrong with any of these if discernment is used.

But sometimes I wonder, *Don't people ever talk anymore?* I don't mean a little in the car on the way to the movies or a quick word during commercials. I mean really talking, sharing our thoughts and ideas and feelings.

[My brothers, sister, and friends] talked about who we were and what we believed and what was important to us. And as we talked, we built trust and learned to love each other in a way that was genuine.

With this kind of love we could encourage each other, comfort each other, laugh with and enjoy each other's company. They saw me when I would be a little brat and have my temper tantrums, but they learned to look beyond that into who I was. They did not act like I was a perfect Christian but realized that I was, and am, a forgiven Christian.

Those really are the best times.[1]

Brent

A word to the wise: Watch debt! Debt is so easy to get into, so tough to get out of. Kind of like a greased mine shaft. Now credit card companies love to give credit to college kids. It was the easiest thing in the world for me to get a card. I received a generous allowance, so it was no problem. I made some really good purchases and some really bad ones—unwise.

But then, the next summer I decided to get a job and not go back to college. The allowance was contingent on college, so it ended, but of course, the debt didn't go away. I'm going to spend three years getting it paid off.

I learned a valuable lesson that will guide the rest of my life, but it's a hard, hard one. Incidentally, when Melanie and I married, one of the first things we did was draw up a financial plan. We're going to be very careful that we don't spend beyond our means. Ten percent to church, ten to savings. See? I'm learning.

Another thing I urge teens to do: Talk to older people whom you respect for their experience and wisdom. "How did you get where you are? What do you look for in an employee?" Pick their brains. For instance, I learned from others in the company where I work now that if you want to get far, college counts. It's not even the degree so much as the fact that you are showing that you finish what you start.

One other thing that I struggle with a lot. Everyone does. That is, apologize right away when you ought (maybe even times when you don't have to). Don't put it off. At times, I took unfair advantage of people. I regret things I've said and done. For example, how I treated my father. I rejected him when my mom died, and yet now I see how hard he tried to be my father. It was stupid of me. Ugly. And I really regret that. Do it while you can!

Elizabeth

I would caution against too much dwelling on fantasy. I went through school daydreaming and fantasizing. I don't think it was helpful at all. It taught me to escape from the present. Fantasy and a theoretical, intellectual world appealed to me better than the actual world did. If you're going to be truly compassionate, you have to be in *this* world. Spend your time being present with what's going on around you, and focus on surroundings.

Mark

Find a grown-up who believes in you. I'm a sports enthusiast, and I had the greatest basketball coach in the world during high school. He's the only reason I stayed in high school. My relationship with that coach helped me understand God. You didn't know fear until you had that guy as a coach, and yet, he always wanted what was best for me. He taught me what friendship is, what teamwork is, and the value of being logical.

I really think being logical—approaching a thing intellectually—helped me avoid depression. I learned to put feelings aside long enough to move back from the self and see the situation more clearly. That's not stuffing feelings; it's more like recognizing them by looking at them from arm's length.

Incidentally, I remember exactly when I found out life isn't fair. When I was eight years old, I fell into a four-foot-deep mud hole. I thought I was going to die, in choking mud almost up to my neck. Some guy came along and pulled me out. When I told Dad, he thought I was lying and punished me for getting muddy. It's a depressing thought when you're eight years old, finding out that life's not always fair.

And what about the guy who saved me? Throughout my life, many times I felt that God was too nice to me. Spiritually, He'll pull me out of sadness. Many times, I've seen the hand of God intervening in the circumstances of my life.

Example: I married Katie, my high school sweetheart, two years ago. After the honeymoon we went into a restaurant and I realized I'd locked the key in our car. Our only key. I really felt bad, because now we were going to have to call a locksmith or a tow truck. Those aren't cheap. A coat hanger, which is cheap, wouldn't work. As I turned around to walk back inside to the phone, a locksmith parked next to us, helped us, and didn't charge. Things like that happen a whole lot. I don't know why God is so good. But I have realized that He loves me, even though I don't deserve it. That helps cheer me like nothing else.

Paul and Jan Meier

Happiness is both a choice and a process. By now you realize that there aren't "ten easy steps" that will bring you nothing but bliss for the rest of your journey here on planet Earth. But there are dozens of helpful suggestions in this book. We hope you will personally benefit from them, and we'd like to leave you with a final thought:

You are going to live forever. Choosing your friends and your future mate are very important choices, but the choices you will make about your personal friendship with God can bring you a joyful life not only right now but for eternity. He loves you. He's knocking at your heart's door. Please open the door and let Him in. Nothing in the universe can bring you more eternal joy.

The
Happiness Is a Choice for Teens

ACTION PLAN

■ Figuring out how to deal with problems and emotions is never easy. Especially when you are a teenager. You probably think you have more important things to do like get to soccer practice, wash your hair, or watch the latest music video awards show. But you know, if you are feeling a little out of sorts, or sad—maybe you can explain why, maybe not—you need to deal with your feelings eventually. And the longer you put off doing the work necessary to feel better, the bigger and harder your problems and emotions become.

Remember that depression is 100 percent curable. And that's why we've created this action plan to go along with our book. Working through this plan will help you determine whether or not you are depressed or just having typical teenage blues. Some of the questions will probe deep into your family history and your own behavior patterns to see if your depression is caused by something physical—an illness, substance abuse, or genes; or maybe it's behavioral—bad patterns of relating with friends and family that have been passed on through generations. Though you may not have complete answers to the whys and hows of your battle with the blues, you will have a better sense of how serious your depression is and whether or not you should seek the help of a professional counselor or psychiatrist.

We'll end the action plan with our guidelines for happiness. Even if you're not truly depressed—in the clinical sense—these guidelines will help you bring balance into your life and find a more fulfilling, happy way of living.

If at any time the questions are making you really sad or uncomfortable, stop for a minute and give yourself a break. This is serious work here. But by all means, try and continue. You don't have to answer the questions all in one day, or even in one week. But once you start on this action plan you may start dealing with some heavy issues. And you don't want to focus on just the bad stuff and forget that your goal here is to be happy! Also, a crisis hotline or counselor is always just a phone call away. Please don't ever be afraid to ask for help. Sometimes the trick is just knowing the right person to ask. Most schools have counselors now, and so do many churches. Both places could hook you up with someone who can work through these issues with you.

Again, *depression is curable.* You are not doomed to a life of misery. There may be some easy solutions to your blahs, or the solutions may be more complicated, including doctors and counselors. But don't fear. As God's creation He desires His best for you. That means He wants you to be happy. So go ahead. Begin this action plan. Choose to find out what's going on in your life. Choose to be strong and purposeful. Choose to be happy!

chapter 1

INNER
REFLECTIONS

1. What prompted you to read this book?

2. What "raw deals" (see Chapter 1) that you can identify from your past have been barriers to your happiness?

Remember: Three things determine your personality and how you turn out: Genes, environment, and the choices you make. With proper guidance and heavenly help, your choices can, over a period of time, make up for the raw deals you may have gotten from genes or environment.

chapter 2

**WHO ME?
DEPRESSED? NAAA!**

Please take this next exercise seriously. You've started reading this book because something has been bothering you. Your answers to these questions will help you get a handle on how serious this problem is and, should you seek help from a professional counselor, will help them understand the scope of the depression.

1. Are you depressed? Check all that apply.

____ Moodiness, particularly sadness

____ Can't sleep

____ Change in appetite (either eat more or less)

____ Headaches

____ Heart flutters

____ Change in bowel patterns

____ Irregular menstrual cycle

____ Increased anxiety

____ Painful thinking

____ Constantly thinking about one's problems

____ Can't think of anything positive about oneself

____ Delusional thinking (hear voices or see images no one else does)

____ Anything out of the ordinary of one's daily patterns of behavior or feeling

If you checked more than four of the above items, you may have a problem with depression. If you checked less than four you may still be depressed, or you may just be having typical teenage blues. Your hormones are going crazy now and there's no telling how that will make you feel. In any event, if you think you need to, please read on. We're now going to look at some of the causes of depression. Once you've got a better sense of what is at the root of your depression you can make an informed choice about how to approach getting better.

Note: If you think you are fine and don't need to continue with the action plan, keep the book handy anyway. You never know when you might change your mind or get into a sad mood you just can't get out of. Also, we recommend reading the Guidelines for Happiness in the last sections of the action plan for everyone—depressed or not. These are simply good guidelines for living.

Remember: Depression is 100 percent curable!

chapter 3

BRAIN JUICE!

1. Seratonin, a chemical in the brain, controls so many aspects of behavior and personality including happiness. Do you think your levels may be low? Check the areas where you could improve your seratonin production.

____ Better diet ("Brain foods" include bananas, turkey and other meats, and dairy products. Eating any of these will help build up your seratonin levels.)

____ More sleep

____ Stop using alcohol and drugs

____ Let go of grudges and stress

____ Manage anger

____ Evaluate prescription medications

____ Get over illness (Like mono)

____ Exercise

2. Choose three positive things you can do to improve your seratonin flow and list exact steps you can take to achieve that goal.

A.

B.

C.

3. Is there a conflict or grudge that you have been holding onto that might be blocking your seratonin production and causing your depression?

4. How did this conflict or grudge start? How does it influence you now?

3. Is there someone you can talk to about this conflict or grudge? (Close friend, counselor, parent?) If so, do it.

4. Write a prayer to God here about the conflict, and ask Him to help you let go of your negative feelings and change your outlook on the situation.

chapter 4

GOOD GRIEF
CHARLIE BROWN

1. Has something happened in the last year or two that has caused you much grief and sadness? (Death of a loved one, getting dumped, parents divorced, didn't make a sports team?)

2. Do you think you could be stuck in one of the stages of grief? Check beside all of the stages you have worked through. If you reach one you can't check, review that section in Chapter 4 and then list some ways you might be able to work toward passing through that stage.

____ I. Denial (not believing the event has really happened).

____ II. Anger Turned Outward (blame others or God for what happened).

____ III. Anger Turned Inward (depression and guilt).

____ IV. Genuine Grief (sadness, weeping, true mourning).

____ V. Resolution (accepting reality and going on with life).

chapter 5

THE PROBLEM
OF PROJECTION

1. Who projects onto you? (Projection, remember, is being anxious around or rejecting people with faults similar to your own.)

2. List what you see as that person's faults. Is there any clear relationship between that person's shortcomings and the topics that person complains about in you?

3. Do you think explaining the projection problem to that person will help overcome your difficulty or just make it worse?

4. Do you think counseling (for both of you) would help?

5. Are you willing to confront and forgive the projectionist?

6. Can you protect yourself from future verbal abuse by the projectionist? Are you willing to?

Remember: The pressures of projection can impact you physiologically and can influence depression. The above steps are necessary and responsible actions for making a choice toward happiness.

chapter 6

THE ROOTS
OF THE PROBLEM

Genetic factors can greatly influence how likely you are to have depression. Consider the following questions.

1. Has anyone in your family been diagnosed with depression? Attention Deficit Disorder (ADD)? Bipolar Disorder or Alcoholism? Schizophrenia? Nervous breakdown? Drug addiction?

2. Might anyone, particularly in your close family, be subject to undiagnosed depression? Review the major symptoms from Chapter 2 and see if the description fits.

3. Has anyone committed suicide? Go back a couple generations if you can.

Remember: These tendencies never indicate that you will fall prey to the same thing. It means only that you may be more vulnerable than most. With this knowledge you can make wise choices that will help you determine the path of your future.

4. List the environmental factors, as described in Chapter 6, that have negatively impacted your outlook on life. Describe how they have affected you.

A. Culture

B. School

C. Home

D. Siblings

■A SPECIAL CASE

<u>chapter 7</u>

WHY NOT END IT ALL?

1. Review the list of risk factors for potentially suicidal folks on pages 69 and 70. If you identify with one or more of these factors, talk about it with someone you trust *immediately*. The rest of this action plan will wait.

Remember: Depression is 100 percent curable! No matter how rotten and black you feel, it won't stay this way forever. You can get out of the dump you're in. Suicide is not the answer.

Other Problems That Can Influence Depression

Yeah, okay, everyone has problems. And for many people, their problems, if taken to an extreme, would end up as a serious psychological disorder. Most of our problems don't ever get to that point. But when people read chapters about serious psychological problems, like the ones in this book, they tend to see themselves in every disorder and think they're going nuts! Well they aren't.

We are including the material on these problems for two reasons: 1) If you have one of these problems you may be more likely to get depressed, and 2) All of these problems come in different degrees. Even if you don't have the full-blown disorder, you may have some of the traits that still might make you more likely to be depressed.

We are not including the material to give you a complex or make you even more depressed. Use the information wisely. If you really identify with one of the following profiles, then again, find some trusted person to talk to.

_____ chapter 8 _____

OBSESSED

1. Are there any activities in your life that may be an obsession—a single-minded focus that consumes all your other activities?

2. Use the following three questions as a measure of obsessiveness.

A. How much time is it consuming?

1   3   5   7   9
Not much   I'm thinking about
                            it most of or all
                            the time.

B. Is the activity interfering with normal daily living?

1   3   5   7   9
No, I can still keep up with   Yeah, I'm falling
my daily responsibilities   behind in many of
                                      my activities

C. Is it damaging or potentially dangerous?

1   3   5   7   9
No more dangerous   Yes, it could be.
than stamp collecting

If your answers range in the sevens and nines, you may have a problem. Obsessiveness, if left unchecked, can take over your life and lead to serious behavior problems and depression. Again, you may need to seek our help from a trusted counselor or friend.

Remember: Happiness is a choice, and the first step toward breaking the cycle of obsessiveness and it's control over your life is to choose to seek help.

chapter 9

CONTROL

1. Is there someone who uses an unreasonable amount of control over your life? (Again, take this seriously, many parental rules are not unreasonable!)

2. List the power struggles that take place between you and the controller.

3. Knowing that the easiest way to deal with a controller is to back down from the power struggle, list the ways you can break your usual relationship patterns and get out of these ongoing battles.

4. Are you a controller? List the people who you tend to control and identify whether or not your control is legitimate. If it's not, list ways you can stop being controlling in these relationships.

chapter 10

HISTRIONICS

1. Check the following that apply to you.

____ My parents didn't let me make decisions for myself. They made decisions for me.

____ If I cried and threw a fit, my parents would let me have whatever I wanted.

____ Growing up, nothing was ever my fault. My parents always blamed someone else even when I did do something wrong.

____ My parents would always give in.

____ All my parents cared about was how good I looked.

____ I was treated like a queen any time I was sick (or pretended to be).

____ I have always been taught not to trust the opposite sex.

If you checked more than four of these you may have a tendency toward histrionics. The problem with this is that it is almost impossible for this person to recognize. It is important to remember that having grown up with these attitudes and behaviors is a sure recipe for depression. Even if you don't think it's a problem now, it may be in the future. But there is hope because your adult personality is not yet determined and is your choice to make.

chapter 11

PARANOIA AND OTHER TRAITS

1. Do you have difficulty trusting anyone and believe that everyone is out to get you?

2. Do you believe that people like to hurt you and that you're not worth much?

3. What other "lies" (see Chapter 11) about yourself have you come to believe?

4. Can you identify anyone who seems to show some amount of care for you—someone who could be safe?

Remember: God has created you in his image and wants you to be safe and happy. Falling into the cycle of negative thinking and fear is possible to break with His help.

chapter 12

STRESSORS AND STRESSEES

1. Do you have trouble concentrating, no matter how hard you try to apply yourself?

2. Are you often impulsive—acting without thinking—and reckless?

3. Do you have trouble doing more than one thing at a time?

Maybe you have already been diagnosed with ADD but are still having problems with depression. Let your doctors know what you are feeling. Chances are they will be able to adjust your medication or suggest some therapy that will help you feel better.

Still More Factors Related to Depression

Beyond named psychological disorders, many more ordinary problems can lead to depression. Use the following questions as an opportunity to identify what other factors could be causing your depression.

chapter 13

OTHER STRESSOR–DEPRESSORS

1. How is your self-image? Rate yourself in the following areas:

A. Relationship with parents. Do they trust and understand you? Do they support and nurture you. Do you truly believe that they care about you and want what's best for you—even if you sometimes disagree?

1	3	5	7	9

Nothing above fits
my family.

Yeah, my parents
are great.

B. Myself. I feel good about myself and am pretty realistic about my abilities and weaknesses. While I don't know what the future holds, I do think I can make the most of my life. I look forward to the future.

1	3	5	7	9

No way I'm that together.

Yes, the above
describes me.

C. School. My teachers and friends would describe me as friendly, sensible, and good hearted.

1	3	5	7	9

Not a chance.

I think they would.

If your ratings are in the ones and threes you may not have a very good self-image. Spend some extra time reviewing the Guidelines for Happiness at the end of this action plan. It will give you some good tips for improving your sense of self-worth and overall happiness.

chapter 14

GUILT AND SHAME

1. Are you suffering from false guilt—grief you're giving yourself or someone else is dumping on you that has no basis in truth? Be honest here. Describe the situation below.

2. Write a note to yourself or your friend identifying why you believe you're being dumped on with false guilt and why you don't deserve it. Now forgive yourself and tear up the letter.

3. Review the descriptions of true guilt in Chapter 14. Are there any things for which you were truly guilty but still need to ask forgiveness from another person or from God? Describe that situation here.

4. Again, write a letter asking for forgiveness. This time you may want to actually give the letter to the person you hurt.

Remember: God's forgiveness is free! All you have to do is ask.

chapter 15

PREGNANCY

1. Read through Chapter 15. Do you see any ways that you might be at risk for acting out sexually and getting pregnant? List them here.

2. Write out a commitment to yourself, noting the rules you will follow about sex and the lines you will not cross.

GUIDELINE ONE: MAKE TIME FOR WORK AND PLAY

1. Make a blank calendar for a typical week, use the sample here to help you. Now fill in all of your appointments and scheduled events. Now put a **W** next to all of those items that are related to chores or work, put an **S** next to all of those items related to schoolwork, and put a **P** next to items that are just play.

MONDAY

6:00	3:00
7:00	4:00 shift at McDonald's /W
8:00 school /S	5:00
9:00	6:00
10:00	7:00
11:00 lunch /P	8:00 homework /S
12:00 school /S	9:00
1:00	10:00 watch TV /P
2:00 softball practice /S	11:00 bed

TUESDAY

6:00	3:00
7:00	4:00 homework /S
8:00 school /S	5:00 dinner
9:00	6:00 party at Cindy's /P
10:00	7:00
11:00 lunch (yearbook meeting) /W	8:00
12:00 school /S	9:00 homework /S
1:00	10:00 watch TV /P
2:00 softball practice /S	11:00 bed

Do you have tons more work and school items than play items? Or do you spend all of your time hanging out and not getting down to business. The first step toward happiness is to make sure you are living in a way that is most likely to make you happy and fulfilled; you need to get a proper balance between work, school, and play.

2. In what area are you weakest?

3. List three ways you can improve the balance.

A.

B.

C.

chapter 17

GUIDELINE TWO: DEVELOP FAMILY RELATIONSHIPS

1. Take inventory of your family. Who are the members with whom you can most likely develop a close relationship? With what members will you need to invest the most work?

2. Choose one or two people with whom you want to improve your relationship. List the specific steps you can take to better your relationship.

chapter 18

GUIDELINE THREE: BUILD FRIENDSHIPS

1. List the friendships you now have that are truly close.

2. If you are low on close friendships, list some folks who you would like to be friends with.

3. What are some steps you can take to build friendships with the people listed above.

4. If you need to start from scratch in building relationships, where are some places you could meet people with similar interests to yours?

chapter 19

GUIDELINE FOUR: DO SOMETHING NICE FREQUENTLY

1. List something kind that someone did for you in the last few years. Were you able to return the favor?

2. When was the last time you did a good deed for someone else? How did it make you feel?

3. List some good deeds you can do for your neighbors, family, friends, or community.

chapter 20

**GUIDELINE FIVE: COMMIT
YOURSELF DAILY TO
GLORIFYING CHRIST**

1. What are your own fears about making a commitment to Christ?

2. What words of Christ can give you the strength and courage to follow Him every day?

3. Write out your own daily commitment to glorifying Christ using the guidelines on page 210.

chapter 21

GUIDELINE SIX: SPEND TIME DAILY IN THE WORD

1. What are the things that you do every day without fail?

2. Are there any barriers that would distract you from daily devotions? Suggest some ways to get around those distractions here.

3. Develop a plan for daily devotions. You can use the guidelines on page 214 or develop some of your own.

chapter 22

GUIDELINE SEVEN: GET RID OF GRUDGES DAILY

We talked about grudges a little bit in Chapter 3, but we will look at them again here for one simple reason: Grudges are a daily battle. If you let them take over, you could probably find something to be angry about or hold a grudge about every hour of every day! But if you did this you would be a miserable person indeed.

1. Choose one grudge you have held recently and write it down here.

2. Using the above mentioned grudge as practice, go through the steps for getting rid of grudges (see Chapter 2) and write out how you would do this.

A. Step one: Admit you're angry!

B. Step two: Decide if your anger is inappropriate.

C. Step three: Give appropriate anger the special treatment it requires.

D. Step four: Good-bye grudges!

<u>chapter 23</u>

HIGH ANXIETY

Often, anxiety goes hand in hand with depression. Anxiety is a fear that occurs when you don't know what you're afraid of.

1. Have you had any feelings of anxiety lately? Describe what it was like?

2. Can you identify anything that might have contributed to your feeling anxious?

3. Make a plan for countering your anxieties using the suggestions on pages 236-40.

chapter 24

WHAT ABOUT MEDICATION AND HOSPITALIZATION?

1. After reading Chapter 24, do you still have any concerns about medication or other methods of treating depression? If so, list them here.

If you are at the point where a doctor or counselor has recommended medication or hospitalization, it is very important that you tell them about your fears or concerns. This way they can help you by modifying your treatment plan, giving you more information about treatment, or provide you with additional support to work through your problems and find happiness.

chapter 25

STUFF TO BANK ON

1. Okay, you are on the road to happiness. Now it is time to develop a plan for staying healthy! Get a notebook or journal and make your own plan using what you've learned from this book and from your own self-discovery. Following is a checklist of the parts you need to include in your plan. Mark each one off once you have made it a part of your daily or weekly routine. This may take a while, but don't worry. Every wonderful thing takes time to create.

____ I have a weekly schedule that has a balance between work, school, and recreation.

____ I am getting enough sleep. At least eight hours for most teenagers!

____ I'm doing best to keep my seratonin levels up by eating a balanced diet (including bananas and other seratonin producing foods), exercising, and letting go of anger.

____ I've been trying new things to find new friends and explore areas that might really be interesting to me.

____ I'm really working on my friendships. Sometimes it is slow going, but I look for every opportunity to meet new people or build the friendships that I have.

____ My family has become more important to me lately. Even though they are not perfect, I've been trying to forgive them and love them for who they are. (It may take you years to check this one off. Don't worry, keep trying; but know that if you are doing your best, you've done enough.)

_____ I've tapped in to God. Prayer and Bible reading are a regular part of my life. Also, I'm doing better at giving up my worries and fears to God and trusting Him for help.

_____ Yeah, I'm staying away from wrongdoing. As simple as it sounds, it's not so easy. But I'm doing my best to live an honest, healthy life.

_____ The seven Guidelines to Happiness are now a part of my daily life.

_____ I'm laughing tons. I must be happy!

chapter 26

TRIUMPHING IN A HAYWIRE WORLD

1. In what ways has popular culture impacted your life? List both the good and the bad.

2. Are there any difficult areas—friends, parties—that you have trouble resisting?

3. List three ways you can resist cultural temptations and stay on the path of health and happiness you have chosen.

   A.

   B.

   C.

chapter 27

A FINAL WORD

We want to say again, happiness is a choice, but it is not just "ten easy steps." It often takes hard work and soul searching. But, Wow, is it worth it. Choosing a personal friendship with God can be key to improving your happiness not just now, but for eternity. We hope that as the last step in your action plan you will consider opening your heart to God and letting Him in your life forever.

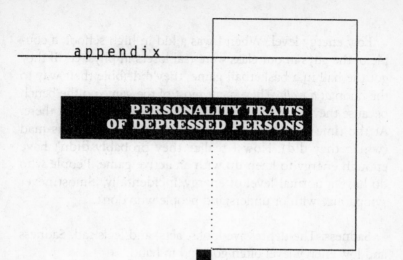

PERSONALITY TRAITS OF DEPRESSED PERSONS

Because teens are neither kids nor adults, they may show either childlike traits or grown-up traits. Often both.

Worry. Everyone worries. Some worry is good; it warns you of danger ahead. But the depressive rides worry to death. The depressive thinks and expresses false worries (things that aren't likely to happen), inappropriate worries (things the depressive couldn't change anyway), excessive worries (mountains out of molehills).

Gloom and pessimism. Pessimism is thinking the worst possible. "Oh no! Uncle John is calling at 10 P.M. He *never* calls this late! Someone must have died! That's got to be it!" (Actually, Uncle John called because he accidentally locked his keys in the car and he wants you to fetch his spare set.) Pessimism is also seeing only the dark side of everything. Example: "Congratulations! You just won a ton of gold!" "Yeah, but it's tarnished and now I have to polish it all." Grumble, grumble, grumble. To the pessimist, every silver lining has a cloud.

Low energy level. When I was a kid in high school, a couple of the guys in our class were real losers in phys. ed. If they got the ball in a basketball game, they'd dribble their way to the hoop *at a walk*. They spent most of the game on the bench because they played like molasses, and they preferred it there. At the time I thought they were just trying to get us mad (which they did). Now I realize they probably didn't have enough energy to keep up with an active game. People who do have a normal level of energy, incidentally, almost never sympathize with or understand people who don't.

Sadness. The depressive looks, acts, and feels sad. Sadness and low energy level often go hand in hand.

Anger and bitterness. In spades.

Sense of futility. "What's the use? Nothing's ever going to change." (And then pessimism speaks up: "At least, certainly not for the better.") Why work for grades? It's no use. Why try to please others? They aren't going to be pleased no matter what you do. Strive to excel? Why bother?

Sense of worthlessness. This is the partner of futility, futility turned inward. "I'm not worth any time, effort, money, or affection that you would care to expend on me. I'm taking up space others deserve more."

A fixation with the past. The depressive dwells excessively upon the past. Broods upon it. Regrets it. Never does the depressive recall the glad events. Sometimes the depressive can't even remember a joyous occasion; it's slipped away completely. Always recalled are the sour ones, the ones the depressive wishes could be fixed. "If only I had . . ." The depressive also obsesses on things that happened that most people have forgotten. "The way she looked at me in algebra. What did she

316

mean by that? I know it wasn't good." The depressive also enlarges insignificant things from the past, almost always negative things, dwelling upon little slights and fancies. Too, the future looks so bleak that the depressive takes refuge in the past.

Guilt. We've already treated that at length. Remember simply that depressives feed on *false* guilt the way piranhas devour cows. They feel a lot of remorse as well, usually unjustified.

Agitation and anxiety. Adults and some teens express this in the expected, recognizable way. They're nervous, fidgety, fearful, excitable, and sometimes emotionally explosive. Kids and some teens express agitation and anxiety by what we in the trade call "acting out."

Acting out. The depressive gets mad instantly, often over nothing significant. He or she acts snappy and cross, disobeys, shoots up or drinks, lashes out at anyone and sometimes even tries to hurt. The acting-out depressive often gets sexually involved, perhaps with more than one partner. The depressive seems bent on breaking rules and then whines when consequences result.

Lack of confidence. Call it a feeling of inadequacy. Depressives are certain they cannot do whatever it is that has to be done. They pretty much defeat themselves before they're even started on a thing.

Brain slowdown. The depressive can't think clearly, can't concentrate. Teachers, parents—all of them—complain, "Why can't you listen? Everything I tell you goes in one ear and out the other!" This is a major reason grades go down.

Hypochondria, even a fear of dying. That is, imagined or overblown physical illness. The depressive knows something is drastically wrong. Physical illness elicits sympathy; depression does not. If only this misery can be blamed on physical disease, the depressive need not bear the stigma that comes with emotional problems. Even better, the depressive can blame an outside agent—germs or whatever—and need not accept any responsibility. On the other hand, depressives are subject to:

Increased frequency of headaches and infections. Depressives catch more colds, develop more allergies, fall victim to more diseases than do most people. They get more headaches. Muscular aches and pains may also be a part of the picture.

Self-absorption. Every little thing that happens in the universe bears importance only as it relates to the depressive. Most people are egocentric to some extent; that is, they relate the world around them to themselves (Do I like this? Does this affect me?) Depressives carry that to extreme. Also, the depressive's attention turns not to the needs, interests, or opinions of others but only to the self. Me. My feelings.

Weight change. Usually, depressives lose weight, in part because they lose interest in eating. Sometimes, they gain weight, mostly because of lower activity levels. Ballooning and wasting away are both bad signs.

Eophobia. That's not a real word. It's a term I coined, meaning "fear or dread of dawn." It describes the depressive's belief that morning is the pits, absolutely the worst time of day. The depressive doesn't want to get up, not because he or she is still tired, but because he or she now has to face another day of gloom.

Somewhat reduced circulation. Cold hands and feet.
Sleep problems. These may be the inability to sleep, too much sleep, awakening in the night and unable to go back to

sleep or waking up too early—any kind of abnormal pattern or major change in sleep patterns.

Constipation. Occasionally, the opposite—irritable bowel syndrome. That is, spates of urgent diarrhea interlaced with constipation.

Menstrual problems. Girls' periods become irregular or cease altogether. Depression makes PMS—pre-menstrual syndrome—much worse also.

Frequent weeping, or at least the urge to cry. Guys often stifle this, but the feeling is still there. The depressive can dissolve in tears at the drop of a hat. He or she can't stand a real tearjerker movie—a dying puppy story or such—and will probably leave in the middle.

Reduced interest in appearance. Guys quit shaving. Girls quit using makeup. Dress and habits turn slovenly. Body odor may become a problem (for everyone around the depressive; the depressive neither notices nor cares). The depressive just doesn't care anymore.

No sparkle, no spontaneity. The sense of humor is the first thing to go. In fact, that's one of the first things I look at when evaluating a depressive. Teens normally have a lively, ironic, even cynical sense of humor, very quick and well developed. A lack of that gift indicates problems. Too, the depressive displays little initiative; that is, does not start anything or step forward to participate. The person's a lump.

Reduced social contact. The depressive takes little interest or pleasure in normal social contacts, hanging out with friends, even dating. At the same time, friends and potential dates are turned off by the depressive's dismal attitude. Also, the depressive in his or her negative mood comes to expect rejection.

Combine this expectation of rejection with the depressive's inflated self-absorption, and the poor person becomes all mixed up. Others can't follow the person's thinking, and they often simply give up on the depressive.

Paranoia. Combine rejection, self-absorption, and projection and you get paranoia. Depressives project their negativity and hostility onto others and then falsely believe those others are out to get them or don't like them.

Masochism. Masochism is inflicting pain on oneself. Depressives dwell on painful thoughts and may actually seek out painful experiences (usually not consciously, but effectively, all the same). They sabotage themselves. A caring friend or other outside observer asks, "Why in the world do you always shoot yourself in the foot? You would have done fine if you hadn't [done that] [said that]."

Whining and clinging. The depressive picks a person (lucky person!) and attaches like velcro. Goes everywhere with the person, has to do everything with the person. "Well, if you're not going to the game, then I'm not either." Usually, the depressive then complains the whole time he or she is in that person's company. This clinging gets the depressive into double trouble. When depressives try to attach too tightly to persons, the intensity of that attachment (plus the negative attitude) is likely to make those persons back off and reject the unhealthy closeness. Worse, that desire to attach too tightly acts as a huge, tall antenna that attracts people, unhealthy in their own way, who take advantage of that kind of relationship. Add the depressive's tendency to masochism into the mix and you get unwholesome relationships rife with abuse and dysfunction.

Negative response by family members. Depressives are very good at making close family members angry, disgusted, exasperated, frustrated. A depressed thirteen year old can be the most irritating, infuriating thing in the world. When evaluating depression, we look closely at family relationships, watching for this anger and exasperation.

Religious extremism. The depressive really digs into extreme church legalism, where every T has to be crossed, every I dotted, or you're not a Christian. Or the depressive goes the opposite way, towards a church where feelings and emotional titillation are all that matter and doctrine is zip.

On a more positive note, all of these negative personality traits of a depressed person are correctable through the process of "cognitive restructuring." With quality counseling, the "computer brain" of a depressive can learn to exchange all of the above lies and misconceptions with the truth about biblically correct facts, feelings, motives, and behaviors. And when a depressive person learns and applies the truth, the truth sets him free from depression. It may take a year of counseling for some depressed teens or adults to learn and consistently apply the truth, but when they do, *happiness becomes a choice.*

notes

Chapter One

1. Frank Minirth and Paul Meier, *Happiness Is a Choice* (Grand Rapids, MI: Baker Book House, 1978).

2. See, for example, Harold Bronheim, M.D., "Faith and Healing," *Directions in Psychiatry,* vol. 13 no. 21, Oct. 13, 1993.

3. Dr. Paul Tournier in his foreword to Frank Minirth and Paul Meier's *Happiness Is a Choice* (Grand Rapids, MI: Baker Book House, 1978), p. 11.

4. Ibid., p. 12.

5. Cheryl Meier, *I Know Just How You Feel* (Nashville, TN: Thomas Nelson Publishers, 1994).

6. Matt. 7:13-14.

Chapter Three

1. For a book on the importance of dreams and how to understand them, read *Windows of the Soul*, which Robert Wise, Ph.D., and I wrote (Thomas Nelson Publishers, 1995).

2. John 2:13-17.

3. Lev. 19:17-18, (CEV).

4. Eph. 4:26-27, (CEV).

5. Rom. 12:1-2, (CEV).

6. Rom. 12:14-21, (CEV).

7. Matt. 10:16.

8. Ps. 139. Read the entire psalm; it's pretty short.

Chapter Four

1. John 11:35. When you have to memorize a verse in a hurry, pick this one. Two words.

2. Gen. 45:2 and 50:1. A powerful story! And notice in 50:4 that they took time for the fourth stage of grieving.

Chapter Five

1. Matt. 7:3-5 (NIV).

Chapter Six

1. I read this in a May issue of the *Dallas Morning News*.

Chapter Seven

1. These and other points come from an article by Dr. Herbert Hendin, the executive director of the American Suicide Foundation. "The Psychodynamics of Suicide with Particular Reference to the Young," *Directions in Psychiatry*, vol. 12 no. 16, August 7, 1992.

2. Ibid.

3. Rom. 12:9 (RSV).

4. Rom. 12:15 (RSV).

5. See Dr. Sue Chance's article, "Helping Suicide Survivors," in *Directions in Psychiatry*, vol. 14 no. 6, March 23, 1994.

Chapter Eight

1. 1 Tim. 5:8. Also check out 1 Tim. 3:2-6 and Titus 1:6.

Chapter Nine

1. John 20:1-18.

Chapter Ten

1. Rom. 8:29.

Chapter Twelve

1. You probably memorized 2 Peter 5:7 when you were little. It's still true, you know.

Chapter Thirteen

1. Drug use: Gal. 5:20, Rev. 9:21, Rev. 18:23; drug dealer: Rev. 21:8; drug user: Rev. 22:15.

2. Ex. 2. Then study Heb. 11:24-26.

3. The book of Daniel, especially chapter 1.

4. 1 Kings 11:1-3.

5. 1 Kings 4:22 provides the complete menu.

6. 1 Kings 4:24-28.

7. 1 Kings 4:29-34.

8. 1 Kings 11:4-13.

9. 1 Peter 5:8, 9.

10. Ex. 18:13-26.

11. Acts 6:1-7.

12. Luke 5:15, 16.

13. As in Lev. 16:31. Even the land needs rest, Lev. 25:4.

14. Matt. 8:24.

15. 1 Tim. 5:8.

Chapter Fourteen

1. 2 Sam. 11 and 12.

2. Rev. 12:10.

Chapter Fifteen

1. Minirth, Meier, Hemfelt, and Hawkins, *Love Is a Choice* (Nashville, TN: Thomas Nelson Publishers, 1989).

2. Heb. 4:12.

3. Ex. 34:7.

4. Taken from testimony before the House Subcommittee on Human Resources of the Ways and Means Committee, by Dr. J. S. McIlhaney, Jr., President, Medical Institute for Sexual Health, March 12, 1996.

Chapter Sixteen

1. Matt. 11:30.

Chapter Seventeen

1. Paul Meier, M.D., *Don't Let Jerks Get the Best of You* (Nashville, TN: Thomas Nelson Publishers, 1993).
2. Ex. 20:5 and Deut. 5:9, for instance.
3. The books of 1 and 2 Kings and Chronicles.

Chapter Eighteen

1. Prov. 13:20.
2. Prov. 27:17.
3. Prov. 17:22.
4. Luke 15:11-32.
5. Prov. 18:24 (NIV).

Chapter Nineteen

1. Acts 2:41 and the story preceding.
2. Acts 6:1-6.
3. Gen. 1:26.

Chapter Twenty

1. Matt. 5:10.
2. Matt. 5:11.

Chapter Twenty-One

1. W. Penfield, "Memory Mechanisms," *A.M.A. Archives of Neurology and Psychiatry,* vol. 67, 1952, 178-198.
2. Jer. 17:9.

Chapter Twenty-Two

1. Is. 63:3.
2. Mark 11:15-17.
3. Ex. 32:19.
4. 2 Sam. 12:5.
5. Matt. 5:45.
6. Matt. 18:15.
7. Rom. 12:19.

Chapter Twenty-Three

1. Acts 15:37-40. One of the wonderful virtues of Scripture is that it never whitewashes its heroes. These are real people!
2. See 2 Cor. 11:24-26.

Chapter Twenty-Four

1. John J. Haggerty Jr., M.D., "What Is the Significance of the Thyroid in Depression?" *Harvard Mental Health Letter,* 1993.
2. Pamela R. Hartley, R.N., M.A.; Charles B. Nemeroff, M.D., Ph.D.; Michael J. Owens, Ph.D., "The Corticotropin-Releasing Factor in Depression," *Directions in Psychiatry,* vol. 13 no. 8, April 14, 1993.
3. Louis Jolyon West, M.D., "Principles in the Psychotherapy of Depression," *Directions in Psychiatry* vol. 14 no. 5, March 9, 1994, p 4.

Chapter Twenty-Five

1. Diane Plumberg, "Finding Hero Label Hard, Police Officer . . .," *Daily Oklahoman*, May 12, 1996, p. 9.
2. Gen. 4:5b-7.
3. Gen. 4:8.

Chapter Twenty-Six

1. For an excellent explanation of this problem, see Mary Pipher, Ph.D., *Reviving Ophelia* (New York: Ballantine Books, 1994).

Chapter Twenty-Seven

1. Meier, *I Know Just How You Feel.* I highly recommend this devotional, and not just because my daughter wrote it. It's by a teen for teens.

PAUL MEIER, M.D., is cofounder of the Minirth Meier New Life Clinics, one of the largest mental health care providers in the United States, with headquarters in Dallas, Texas, and more than seventy branch clinics in cities across the nation. Dr. Meier is the author or coauthor of more than forty books, including *Windows of the Soul, Don't Let the Jerks Get the Best of You, Love Hunger*, and the best-selling novels *The Third Millennium* and *The Fourth Millennium*.

JAN MEIER is a marriage and family therapist with a master's degree in early childhood development. She has also begun doctoral level studies in mariage and family counseling. Together, Paul and Jan have raised six children—four of their own and two nephews.

CHERYL MEIER has a master's degree in psychology from Rosemead Graduate School of Psychology and is currently working on her PsyD. at Rosemead. She is the author of *I Know Just How You Feel*, a devotional book for teens.

MARK MEIER is completing his studies in computer graphics in Phoenix, Arizona, where he lives with his wife, Katie. She is working toward a teaching degree that will allow her to teach fine arts on a university level. Together, they are writing a devotional book dedicated to "GenXers" like themselves.

ELIZABETH MEIER is the youngest of the Meier children. She lives in Arizona, where she is pursuing a college education in arts.

DAN MEIER is the oldest Meier child. He is a graduate of Biola University with majors in theology and philosophy and is currently preparing for a ministry in Colorado.

BRIAN VERKLER is the oldest of two nephews who lived with the Meiers until he left for college. He and his wife, Danielle, are both pursuing graduate studies in physical therapy.

BRENT VERKLER is the other Meier nephew. He works as a computer trouble-shooter. His wife, Melanie, works in a bank.